GAIJIN KAISHA

RUNNING A FOREIGN BUSINESS IN JAPAN

JACKSON N. HUDDLESTON, JR. worked in Japan for many years, first for Chemical Bank and later to introduce the American Express Card as General Manager of American Express Travel Related Services. He now teaches occasionally at the University of Washington and consults for foreign corporations selling products and services in Japan.

An East Gate Book

Jackson N. Huddleston, Jr.

GAIJIN KAISHA

RUNNING A FOREIGN BUSINESS IN JAPAN

M. E. SHARPE, INC.
ARMONK, NEW YORK
LONDON, ENGLAND

An East Gate Book

Copyright © 1990 by M. E. Sharpe, Inc.

All rights reserved. No part of this book may be reproduced in any form without written permission from the publisher, M. E. Sharpe, Inc., 80 Business Park Drive, Armonk, New York 10504.

Available in the United Kingdom and Europe from M. E. Sharpe, Publishers, 3 Henrietta Street, London WC2E 8LU.

Library of Congress Cataloging-in-Publication Data
Huddleston, Jackson N., 1938–
    Gaijin kaisha: running a foreign business in Japan /
Jackson N. Huddleston, Jr.
        p. cm.
    Includes index.
    ISBN 0-87332-720-9
    1. Industrial management—Japan. 2. Corporations, Foreign—
Japan—Management. 3. International business enterprises—
Japan—Management.
    I. Title.

HD70.J3H83 1990
658'.049'0952—dc20   90-37354
                                                          CIP

Printed in the United States of America.

MV 10 9 8 7 6 5 4 3 2

Contents

Preface

THIS IS A STORY that has evolved over the past thirty-three years of studying, teaching about, and working in Japan. It is the story of the general manager of a foreign corporation in Japan, his and his head office's expectations, and his network of support at home and abroad. In many ways the story is my own, for I carry my experience, knowledge, and prejudices acquired over the years. It is tempered, however, by the experiences of the many people I have interviewed and met along the way.

There is no one way to do business in Japan, any more than there is one way to do business in the United States or Germany. Aside from personnel issues, which are critical to a successful operation anywhere, there was little repetition among those I interviewed, for the products and the head offices varied markedly. There was also very little complaining during the interviews, though a great deal socially.

Nothing assures success for a foreign or domestic operation in the ferociously competitive market of Japan. Nonetheless, it is the largest retail market in the world, and first or second in many industrial products. It can only grow more important. This book is for those who appreciate Japan's competitiveness, creativity, and market potential, and who personally are willing to make the professional commitment and sacrifice required to achieve even the possibility of success.

Chapter titles are for ease of reference, but no chapter stands alone. For the general manager on any given day, it is difficult to give a heading to any one or combination of management issues.

They are always interrelated. This book should be read not as a "how to" for any of these subjects, but for an awareness of what is needed from an organizational and management perspective to run a foreign business in Japan in the last decade of the twentieth century. The global marketplace makes these lessons appropriate for any overseas general manager and his head office, regardless of the country in which they are operating.

When I went to Japan from Princeton University in 1958, it was a fun experience that whetted my appetite to know more about a part of the world that my countrymen discussed only in terms of war. Subsequently, when I began to study Japanese, the work began. It has been work and more work ever since. Through this work I have come to respect the tremendous economic and social accomplishments of Japan and its neighbors. I have also come to appreciate how little effort Americans and others have made to understand what is happening and the impact it will have on them and on future generations. I feel they often have avoided involvement out of fear, and out of a hope that the competition will self-destruct. Of two things I am confident, however: Japan will continue to change and progress socially and economically to the benefit of its citizens, and competitively it will wait for no one.

No matter how much one thinks one knows about Japan at any particular time, that knowledge is at best a snapshot. The changes over the past thirty-three years have been enormous, and they will be easily as great over the next thirty years. Those of us who have worked in Japan have found that one can quickly become obsolete. The shelf life of a Japan expert is short. As one general manager said after eight years in Japan, "I am a dinosaur."

My thanks to all those who granted me interviews. In addition, during the academic year 1987–88, when I was Kermit O. Hanson Professor of Business Administration at the University of Washington, a number of individuals participated in student and faculty seminars on running foreign corporations in Japan and Japanese global finance. Since I promised anonymity to all my sources, I have simply listed in the appendix those people who participated as speakers in the seminars, and those who were interviewed formally. Attribution is generally not given to specific quotations or thoughts.

Douglas Merwin at M. E. Sharpe believed in the book from the beginning, and Anita O'Brien, my editor, was simply superb. To both my sincerest gratitude.

I would also like to thank a few specific individuals who have traveled this road with me: Professor Robert Butow, with whom my journey began; Professors Dan Henderson, Ken Pyle, Tom Roehl, and John Haley, who have encouraged me not only to do but to think about what I do; Sandra Faux, who persuaded me to write about it; Griffith Way, who never let me off the hook; Dean Nancy Jacob, who gave me the support; Professor Mary Sullivan Taylor, Professor Shumpei Kumon, Clyde Prestowitz, and William Valenti, who made constructive comments on the manuscript; the late Clifford J. Thompson, banker, friend, and boss in the best sense of the word; and Keiko Nakajima, my wife, at times business partner, and severest critic.

It has been said that for a foreigner to run a business in a culture as alien to the West as Japan, it takes a general manager with the wisdom of the founder, the tolerance of a naval chaplain, and the toughness of a field general. One might also add the zeal of a missionary. To these past, present, and future general managers, this book is dedicated.

GAIJIN KAISHA

RUNNING A FOREIGN BUSINESS IN JAPAN

Introduction
Foreign Firms and
Their General Managers

THIS BOOK is about the *gaijin kaisha*, the foreign firm in Japan. James C. Abegglen and George Stalk, Jr., introduced the business corporations of Japan—the *kaisha*—to the foreign reading public in their superb book, *Kaisha, The Japanese Corporation*. *Gaijin* is the appellation the Japanese give to all foreigners, or aliens, with an emphasis on the alien concept. Thus, gaijin kaisha means an alien company on Japanese soil. More specifically, it represents a Western company in Japan, since to date few companies from Asia, South America, the Middle East, or Africa have established more than token corporate representation there. The term gaijin kaisha in this book refers to a Western corporation in Japan that is either a wholly owned subsidiary, a branch, or a joint venture with proactive foreign management. A foreign/Japanese joint venture without proactive foreign management is in reality a Japanese company. The term also does not refer to a corporation of convenience, such as a one-man office for tax purposes.

In 1989 there were approximately 1,300 foreign wholly owned subsidiaries, 1,400 foreign branches, and 1,600 foreign/Japanese joint ventures. Thus there were at least 2,700 general managers or presidents of foreign-run or heavily foreign-influenced companies in Japan. The additional 1,600 joint ventures had some foreign management. Foreign capital–affiliated companies employed 300,000 to 350,000 Japanese in their operations. The general managers of the subsidiaries and branches have been sent to Japan as aliens, or the parent companies have hired local Japanese to run their operations in Japan. Most of the alien general managers are linguistically illiterate, and Japan is more often than not an entirely new culture and experience for them.

Why and how do corporations expect their management to function responsibly in an alien culture without historical, cultural, and linguistic knowledge of the environment in which they are placed? Jim Firestone of American Express Japan asked me in 1980 if a foreign corporation can succeed in Japan. As we begin another decade, I would ask Jim the same question: If foreign companies continue to disregard the history of Japan and of their company in Japan, the vast cultural differences, and the language of the country in which they are trying to function, can they even hope to succeed?

Too many foreign corporations take the attitude, "We're not paying you to go over there and learn a language. We're paying you to do a job." Why do they not realize that language is part of a job? Would any foreign CEO in the United States go to work without reading the *Wall Street Journal*? I doubt it. Every day in Japan, 99 percent of the foreign general managers go to work without knowing what is in the current *Nihon Keizai Shimbun*, the principal economic newspaper in Japan. Nor can they understand the television news, advertisements, or social commentary. Who would run a business in the United States without knowing English, or a business in Paris without knowing French, and without being able to communicate with employees in their native language? Is it out of ignorance or arrogance that we think we can run businesses successfully as illiterates in the second most important economy in the world?

Few people want to live in Japan over a sustained period without knowing the language, for they realize they can only navigate the streets by using landmarks. In effect, that is how they have to manage their businesses. They are in and out in three years, with a few landmarks as memories. Nevertheless, we try to get along without the language. Some businesses, like Coca-Cola, find it possible, but most cannot replicate that company's success in Japan.

In my conversations with general managers, many expressed their frustration with the situation:

I don't know how you bring the foreigner into this market, get him involved. We ignore a lot of the criteria for success anywhere: knowledge, product, and distribution.

We have been here for 120 years. What I find interesting, demotivating, depressing—all at the same time—is that I am having the same problems we've had for years. What are we doing here? Why are we making all this effort with resources: human, financial, and otherwise?

It was my secretary who said, "You've been here six years. Your Japanese must be an embarrassment for you." She called up the school, and I am still studying after sixteen years. Perhaps I was the problem, since it is very difficult to find highly qualified Japanese who speak English. That is when the operation began to turn and the whole group became knitted together. Unlike with 99 percent of the foreigners, the Japanese staff knows I am staying. Japan is not just a country to work in. Japan is a way of life.

In the pages that follow, I explain just what a foreign firm's head office and its general manager must do for their company to have the potential to be successful in Japan.

1

The General Manager

"THE COMPLEXITIES and difficulties of doing business in Japan are the primary barriers to greater investment by foreign companies," concluded Booz, Allen & Hamilton, Inc., in a 1987 study prepared for the American Chamber of Commerce in Japan and the Council of the European Business Community. The head office and its Japan general manager must come to understand the complexities and difficulties of doing business in Japan if their present and future investments there are to be successful. They must start with the concept that they have to be in Japan as part of their global business strategy. The chairman of the board has to be committed to the idea that Japan is critical to the company's long-term business success. There is nothing in American or European business that precludes giving this type of visibility to Japan.

To say merely that the company will have a long-range financial commitment to Japan begs the question, for it means that the country is being considered as an investment *option*—instead of a five-year pay-back, ten years, but if it does not come in ten years, then the company will look elsewhere. What is required instead is the commitment that the company's Japanese business either succeeds or fails in Japan: The company will be in Japan. Perhaps Westerners should look to their forebears, the Vikings, who, when they invaded a new territory, burned their boats. There was no retreat. A successful company does the same:

Come hell or high water we are going to be in Japan. Japan is not a discretionary investment program. It is a country you believe you must be in. There is no retreat out of Japan. If you fail, find another approach. The

Japanese competition just waits to see how deep are your pockets. Nine times out of ten the foreign company doesn't have the staying power.

The Japanese competition is not saying that it will shut down and concentrate on another area if it does not gain a position in the United States or Europe or Asia in such and such a time. The whole world is its marketplace.

With only 3 percent of U.S. global foreign investment in Japan, Japan has clearly not been a top priority, or even a secondary priority, for most American or European corporations. American companies invested approximately $1.9 billion in Japan in 1987, $2.5 billion in 1988, and an anticipated $2 billion plus in 1989. The total U.S. investment there today is approximately $19 billion. Each year American investment has been equivalent to the price of ten to fifteen Boeing 747 aircraft—not much when one appreciates that Japan had invested $48.5 billion in the United States by 1988, almost three times more than the cumulative U.S. investment at that time in Japan. Japan did not really start to invest in the United States until the early 1980s, but in the early 1990s it could easily be investing annually as much as the U.S. cumulative investment in Japan.[1]

Today Japan has 14 percent of the world's gross national product and is a country market second only to the United States. Japan is not only the economic giant of Asia but the role model for all Asian countries. South Korea, Taiwan, Hong Kong, Singapore, and Thailand all have followed Japan's lead. Their economies, as well as those of Indonesia and parts of eastern China, are being integrated into the Japanese economy. Their plants, equipment, and resources are becoming an integral part of a Japanese-dominated Asian economy with interests that range far beyond Asia. There is also no dominant country in Europe like Japan is in Asia, even though there are not the geographical distances within Europe that there are in Asia. Although this situation has been building for a quarter of a century, the enormousness of it has not been appreciated, certainly not in the head offices of most Western companies. As Western businessmen contemplate their future in Japan, in Asia, and in global markets, they cannot ignore this reality if they wish to continue to sell their products and services

---

[1]ACCJ Review & Update of U.S. Direct Investment in Japan, September 1989.

successfully at home as well as abroad. The other countries in Asia respect Japan's economic success and anticipate success themselves. As it was for Japan for so long, success is survival, and that puts competition on a level that the current generation of Westerners, particularly Americans, have not experienced.

How much money a foreign company can make or lose in Japan is determined by the market for the company's product and the effort expended in selling to that market. The overall Japan market is the second largest in the world, with enormous consumer and corporate spendable incomes.

How does one go about doing it? What does it take? Once the head office has this conception, it gets more serious about what it is doing. As in track, the number of hurdles you knock down does not matter, only the time in which you finish the race. Japan is no longer an optional investment; it is like your arm or leg. The key is having the right individuals in both the head office and Japan. Institutionalizing coordination does not accomplish much if the right individuals are not there to support the institutionalization.

Head-Office Support

The general manager in Japan is usually placed in the schizophrenic position of having to be at the same time both the head-office man in Japan and the Japan man in head office. The individual in the head office responsible for Japan, however, should be as important to the success of the operation as the general manager in Japan. How that person contributes added value is crucial. In the idiom of American football, there is a two-platoon system: one platoon plays in Japan while the other plays at home. The object is for both to contribute to a winning team effort—a difficult process at best because there is always friction. Many general managers do not want a strong person at home. The Japan operation, though, is too important to be run independently. What is needed is a healthy, creative dialogue that will have plenty of tension. We are all big fellows. We have to work in a world of tension, arguments, pulls, and counterpulls. We just have to do it *respectfully*. The higher the person in head office, the better for timely and meaningful responses, unless he has too many people reporting to him. Then he will likely anoint a staff person who shuffles papers, and everyone will escape responsibility. That is the worst combination. Japan is so far away that the person in head office can never run the business in Japan; only the general manager there can do that.

The role of the sovereign is to appoint the general. The role of the general is to wage the war.

As important as the focal contact person is in head office for the Japan general manager, the latter also has to keep many more people than just one individual informed and comfortable if he is not to be put in the position of constantly defending his Japanese stance in head office and his head office's stance to his Japanese staff, leaving little time for building the business. Yet there is a tremendous momentum toward making decisions on an institutional basis, especially when the head-office individual responsible for Japan is also in charge of international.

There is just a drive to make everything consistent, which goes against everything else you are trying to do.

The chief executive officer of the corporation must be the person ultimately responsible, because without his support the people and money necessary for success in Japan will not be available. To build a substantial business in Japan is expensive for any corporation, big or small, and therefore the board of directors must feel confident that their chairman knows why the financial resources are being committed and is on top of what is happening.

You have to have the shortest line to God!

Everyone in the organization must understand that the chairman wants the best people in Japan, and that a stationing in Japan is therefore an important career builder. Where and how the general manager and his foreign and Japanese staff progress is crucial to building an ongoing, substantial presence in Japan.

In many foreign companies, the Japan operation still reports to a regional head in Singapore or Hong Kong. This will not work, however, because neither is anything like Japan, neither can ever have the potential of a Japanese marketplace, and local staff in both have a great deal of difficulty understanding Japan. Such a procedure puts one more layer of misunderstanding in the communication link with head office and lowers the profile of the

Japan office tremendously. Japanese staff certainly do not appreciate reporting to what they consider minor city-states.

Hong Kong has a bureaucracy that is unbelievable. It's a fairyland down there; it's another world. It is bad for our Japanese organization. Sometimes you have an American in head office talking to a Chinese in Hong Kong who then talks to a Japanese in Japan. God, right there you have trouble! It is always a source of low-level conflict, and your time is taken away from your preeminent job.

Should the regional office be in Japan, with the Japan general manager reporting to a regional head there? Should he wear both hats himself? The former is acceptable if the regional head is a very senior member of the corporation; the dual-hat trick is a monster.

I feel sorry for the guy who comes in with a regional responsibility and is expected to build a business in Japan. The countries are completely different from each other and the area is enormous. One of the dumbest decisions.

Selecting a General Manager

The general manager himself should come from within the company and should be well known in head office. Only an individual who has absolute credibility with the chairman and his board and the ranking staff can possibly succeed in Japan. If that quality of individual—someone who knows his company and its products or services intimately—is not available, then the Japanese operation is not important enough to warrant the time and money required in head office. Hiring a foreigner knowledgeable about Japan but not knowledgeable about the company has little chance of success in the Japanese marketplace. An outside foreign hire with no intimate head-office product or service knowledge is looked upon as a job hopper by the Japanese inside and outside the company. Little loyalty is therefore extended. (Twenty or thirty years ago, when Japan was not a global competitor, it might have worked.) Hiring a Japanese who knows neither the company nor its products and services has almost no chance of success. In both cases the existing or potential Japanese competition realizes immediately that the company is not bringing product or service knowledge to the market. If the product or service is a good one, the Japanese will follow the investment strategy and tactics carefully and then go at it with a full-court press on their home court. Without a seasoned team that has leadership on the floor and can call credibly for home-office reinforcements, the foreign firm will soon be exhausted and whipped. Far too many foreign corporations, particularly from the United States, have believed their own multinational propaganda, succumbing to the idea that to be multinational is to go native in whichever country they are doing business.

A foreign company must send stars, winners, to Japan. They are, of course, the hardest to convince to go there. All the questions of contemporary America, although not necessarily Europe, occur. "What about my spouse's career?" "I said international, London or Paris, not Tokyo or Calcutta." It is as if there are two different worlds out there. With second-rate people, a company permanently suffers in three ways. First, the performance is second rate. Second, the individual's reputation undermines his ability to accomplish anything with head office. The response will always be to say, "That is your opinion, but if I was over there, I would find another way." Lastly, if the Japanese do not respect them, they will simply suffer them, knowing they will go away. Once a company gets beyond a certain critical mass in the size of its Japanese staff, and when the Japanese have gained self-confidence, then they will just kill a guy. "It is not just that they can, they will."

Every foreigner has to be an expert in his business. You don't send anybody here to just learn. This is not a development office. The only way we can succeed here is to bring experienced people and to bring this experience to bear on our business. Everyone likes to go where there is a success. We have no problem getting good people to work here.

Probably 45 percent of my job is to see that my company gives what it promises to the subsidiary we have here—technology, management expertise, production and distribution know-how. All our other operating companies are too busy doing what they are doing. This isn't a volunteer endeavor. I need to know where to go in the company to get that type of expertise, whether expatriates or advisers.

To build a substantial business in a foreign environment, a company also must be able to draw from a pool of excellent local talent. In most countries it is difficult for a foreign company to hire first-class management talent, but perhaps in no country is it more difficult than in Japan. A male Japanese who works for a foreign company is generally a social cripple in Japan. Although educational performance, a divorce, or previous employment could be the reason, at times it is simply a self-fulfilling prophecy: he is working for a foreign company, and therefore he is outside Japanese society. Once he works for a foreign company, he can never enter or return to a substantive Japanese company.

A Japanese who upon retirement goes to a foreign company goes there because his original company cannot find for him a second career within its family of companies. His title or position in the society is considered to be the highest rank obtained at his Japanese company, not at his new foreign home. He is therefore restricted to that level in his business contacts in the future. At first that can be acceptable as he calls in his chips among friends and former associates for assistance, but later it becomes difficult for him to expand his horizons and thus his new company's business. To receive help from friends and former associates, by necessity he must give. If a product or service is new to Japan and confidentiality is lost, it is quickly subject to being preempted by Japanese competition.

When starting a new operating company or expanding and building on existing business in Japan, it is necessary to hire a disparate group of these social cripples. Employment in a foreign company is surely not their first choice. The general manager must mold them into a team that functions effectively, building and rebuilding a new machine with used parts. The office or plant must function well internally. The sales force must define and work its existing and potential clients with confidence; the regulatory and financial community must be guided and not vice versa; new employees must be recruited initially and on an ongoing basis; confidentiality must be maintained; and the head office must be kept apprised of what is going on and must feel confident that the office in Japan is being managed effectively. This is all heady stuff for a foreigner or a Japanese who does not know the business. If he does not understand the business plan and what the company is trying to accomplish, then he will never be able to carry it out. Also, a Japanese manager who is good at working with people surely would have been retained by his former company, for the Japanese respect and need this talent in a rapidly changing environment.

A Japanese general manager of a foreign company would be squeezed by all the Japanese relationships. Because of his upbringing, he would not be willing to speak up to the parent CEO when the CEO is wrong. I don't think he would tell headquarters, "No, goddamn it, you can't do it that way, and this is why, and if you don't understand that, then you've just got to believe me." There comes a time when you've just got to do that. No Japanese will ever do it. He's not conditioned to do it. You've got to be willing to put your job on the line.

Japanese general managers who have not grown up in the company tend to fail not in the market execution aspect but in explaining to headquarters what they did and why. This is followed by a deterioration in communications, loss of trust, and then abrupt and unexplainable flip flops by headquarters.

The Japanese general manager of a foreign company has a very difficult time when his company does something the Japanese community does not like. Every time IBM has a problem in Japan, Mr. Shiina (President of IBM Japan) gets it in the neck from the Japanese press. When he had to be an apologist for the Hitachi scandal, he really had a tough time.[2] People say: "How can you work for an American company when they do these kinds of things," and then he has to be extremely careful as an apologist, perhaps going overboard to show he is still a Japanese while being a manager of a foreign company that operates and sells in a Japanese market.

According to Edward Nanas, it is apparently not necessary for IBM's non-Japanese employees to speak Japanese and therefore take the heat off Mr. Shiina. At the time of the Hitachi incident, Mr. Nanas was Group Director, Communications, IBM World Trade Asia Corporation, stationed in Tokyo. In a letter to the *New York Times* on March 3, 1989, he stated: "The effort required to use Japanese effortlessly in business is, in my opinion, a colossal waste of time, energy and money." Even though he had a supervisory responsibility for communications in Japan, where IBM's market share had been eroding, Mr. Nanas had to depend on what the IBM Japanese staff wished to give him in translation. He certainly could not understand what he was seeing or hearing in Japanese newspapers, magazines, radio, and television.

I am reminded of when the Japanese newspapers ran front-page stories on the foreign banks lending to the sarakins (usurious

---

[2]Marie Anchordoguy, *Computer Inc.: Japan's Challenge to IBM* (Cambridge: Harvard University Press, 1989), describes Hitachi's stealing of IBM technology.

money lenders) to improve profitability. The high interest rate on these loans reflected the risk and the fact that the Ministry of Finance was curbing the lending of indigenous Japanese banks to these institutions after much social criticism. I mentioned to Keith Kaneko, general manager of Manufacturers Hanover Trust Co.'s Tokyo branch, how happy he must be that his company's name was not on the front page, since they did not lend to sarakins. He responded that he was doubly happy because he had translated the articles immediately and sent them to his head office to show the correctness of the decision not to lend. Phone calls to other foreign banks, who were lending, revealed that they did not even know that their names were in the paper, apparently because the Japanese account officers did not wish the foreign management to know. When the president of one New York bank eventually learned, he exploded and demanded that these loans be paid down immediately—certainly the right decision, but not the way to run a business. Few will have ability in the language like Keith Kaneko, but they do need all the other personal attributes necessary to run a foreign business in Japan, as well as an experienced Japanese staff.

The person chosen for general manager should be a recognized, capable, fast-track employee of the company with excellent operational skills and outstanding personnel ability. He can mold and lead the management team and impart confidence to the staff and community: corporate clients; university and technical high schools for recruiting; the financial community for funding, reasonable rates, and intelligence; and the regulatory community, including ministries and tax authorities. He can have the courage of his convictions, knowing that head office will support him throughout it all. He is also immune to social pressures from the Japanese community, whether they be suppliers, customers, banks, or tax authorities. Most importantly, he can reach much higher levels in the Japanese business and government community as a foreigner with the title of president/general manager than can a Japanese who has been hired from the outside to work for a foreign company.

Managing a foreign business in Japan is hardball, and it takes a Casey Stengel: wise, experienced, and tough—someone who can communicate at all levels, including with the people at home. There is no turning back. In the United States you can reverse yourself or come back, saying money is money, profit is profit, and slap each other on the back and get on with it. But the Japanese do not touch each other, and to them, a loser is a loser.

By starting with and continuing with a known employee as general manager, the chances of successfully exploiting the market are much greater. The capability and capacity of staff initially hired or in place can be carefully evaluated. Wrong personnel choices are avoided up front and at critical growth stages. It is very important not to have a poor clutch that jerks this new or used car around. It is essential for the general manager to know the business and to exert leadership with confidence in an alien environment.

The Japanese look upon the foreign general manager as if he existed on paper rather than as a person. He is scrutinized in a way that they never scrutinize themselves. Whether it is people, projects, or assignments, they are seen as exclusive entities rather than as part of a flow of events.

It is up to the general manager to make certain that they are put in context and humanized. In doing this he sees his role in two contexts: managing the local company within the context of the local market, and managing that business in its totality within the context of the company.

The president has to be very, very tough—inwardly tough and outwardly a soft and patient creature. A Japanese organization is not all harmony; tremendous infighting, ambitions, envy. You have to hold a firm grip on a company; you have to know exactly how things move; and you have to know whom to believe. You can manage better if you don't show how much you know. You have to speak Japanese when you have a drink with your managers to learn about the smoldering fire. But above all, you have to be very, very firm. Otherwise, as a foreigner, when confronted by another world, you are lost.

I spend 70 percent of my time within the Japanese market and 30 percent within or versus my head office. Head office does not like to recognize this division, but it is a fact of life. The degree of reporting required in an American company is very extensive when you do not have the tacit understandings that exist when you are operating in the same country. I take most of the reporting on myself to allow my Japanese staff to operate without incremental burdens. People in head office say, "Why is he interpreting, involved again?" The constant difficulty is always being aware of what it is you are trying to get out of this correspondence. Have I given him enough, too much? Have I positioned my views in a manner that he is capable of understanding and agreeing to? If you are not successful with this 30 percent of your time, your other 70 percent will be drastically affected, as will the organization underneath you.

The general manager must create and maintain an environment in which the local entity can function, getting goals accomplished but at the same time allowing for mistakes without always a cause and effect. If head office will not allow mistakes and requires a sacrificial lamb, it will soon stultify the operation. The U.S. attitude is often chemical: it fails or it works. This is perceived to be professional. Extraneous elements are viewed as ill-conceived, ill–thought out, fuzzy, soft plans. In real life anywhere it is more likely a sequence of events: mistakes are made, recovered, not recovered, but there is an intertwining.

I have seen general managers take a perverse pride in saying they are not political animals. But a degree of political acumen is essential, not necessarily in promoting your own career but in terms of promoting issues and the environment.

The natural reaction to underachievement is to control, to tighten up, rather than to loosen up, especially if it is seven thousand miles removed. If that becomes the rule, the local organization stops taking risks, becomes paralyzed and worse, "Head Office says" becomes the rule. It becomes a crutch more than anything else. Running amok of the palace guard, which functions by reason of their proximity to line authority without line accountability, can be disastrous. To counter this possibility, we have encouraged and requested visitors, but unfortunately they have very short memory spans. The difference between a good and bad staff man is residual value. Often the process is time consuming and discouraging.

We always downgrade politics, but politics permeates everything. Politics is like oxygen; it is everywhere. Politics is the art of getting along with other people; knowing what you've got to do; where you have to compromise; who is most important in assisting you to accomplish your objectives. The guy out here has to have it. You have to prioritize your time and that is politics.

Representative Director

The foreign general manager will immediately learn the term Representative Director. The Representative Director of a branch or a subsidiary may in effect legally sign for the company. It is an additional title that a general manager will want for himself. There may be more than one Representative Director, but because of the authority empowered legally in the position it is not given or taken away lightly. For many it carries as a title the most prestige of all. Legal counsel can explain all the enormous ramifications of the title.

A Japanese Chairman

But a gaijin general manager/president can only do so much, for he is operating in an alien environment. From the beginning he should be making every effort to identify a first-class senior Japanese to be or act like the chairman of the company. The chairman in Japan is an honorary position, much like the retired chairman in the United States who acts as the chairman of the Executive Committee of the board. This individual would be responsible for enhancing external government, customer, supplier, and university relationships. If, despite every precaution, he does not work out, he can be gracefully retired. That is not the case with a Japanese general manager/president and is therefore another reason to have someone from head office in that capacity until such time that a Japanese replacement can be developed and seasoned. There are a few seasoned Japanese general managers in foreign companies in Japan today, and the successful ones are with firms that are well established in Japan. In short, these managers grew up in the business in Japan and have also had extensive exposure to head office.

I've only met fifteen or twenty Japanese in thirty years of working in Japan that I would ever consider to be my number two and eventually the head of our business in Japan, because of the inherent conflict with Japan, Inc., and the divided loyalties that engenders in any Japanese—the family, tax authorities, bank, MITI, and Ministry of Finance. However, I do not see the American way developing the people required for Japan and elsewhere in the future. We need to develop a cadre of international talent and experience in business like the foreign service.

As president you have to be willing to do anything to get the job done, because you don't have all the support you have in head office. Your objective should be to get the job done. One should not come with any reservations about doing anything. I will do whatever I have to to get the job done, while at the same time I have to be able to step back and provide the focus and leadership over the midterm for the entire company. I have to see that the opportunities here are understood and evaluated and decisions are being made to allocate the necessary resources to develop those opportunities. It is a fine line between shunning and being bogged down in detail.

To be successful in Japan, the general manager will spend approximately 50 percent of his time on personnel, foreign and Japanese. Unless the operation is quite small, he is going to need excellent expatriate staff to assist him in building and driving the business. He is also going to need the best Japanese staff he can lay his hands on.

The issue I find the most disturbing is staff development. I really wonder about our ability to pull it all together. If I had known how difficult it is to recruit and develop staff, I probably would not have come. You have to have access to your leading-edge people in head office, and that means they have to be committed to the time. It is tough because often they do not quite appreciate the time required.

Personnel is an all-consuming task for everyone in management involved in the Japan operation.

2

Personnel

THE MOST IMPORTANT personnel decision has been made. One of the best managers in the organization has been assigned to Japan. He is experienced. He has run an operation in the United States or overseas, or preferably both, with full personnel, financial, marketing, sales, and control responsibilities. He knows what it is to run one of the company's lines of business and to interact with its staff. He has the seniority it takes to get in the door of Japanese companies that can provide a product or service needed by a foreign company. He is therefore by all odds over forty and closer to fifty, and no more than one or two levels removed from being president of the parent company. This might seem like overkill, but without such measures a company can expect to fail in the Japanese market and be left to face an even more dangerous competitor at home or in a third country. If a foreign firm refuses to place the emphasis on the Japanese market that the Japanese place on the United States or European Community market, it should stay home. There is no sense in spending a lot of money to be a loser. The Japanese have little use for losers. There are few individual or corporate Horatio Alger stories in Japan; the Horatio Alger story there is Japan itself. Being a loser preempts a company from entering the market again later. A loser is a failure, and so is everyone associated with a loser, because they were fools to be associated with one. Comebacks are generally impossible. Ask Pepsico Japan, Reader's Digest Japan, 7-Up Japan, Heinz Japan. The list is long.

Often the first question a foreign company asks when it contemplates coming to Japan is, "How long will it take to establish ourselves in Japan?" One can answer very specifically the time it will take to find or build a plant or decorate an office. These times are comparable to any other major industrial country. The real question is, "How long will it take me to have an effective staff in place that can build a substantial business for us in Japan?" The answer has to be a minimum of ten to fifteen years. This also applies to any company that is substantially realigning its organization in Japan.

> You constantly fight the battle on staffing. Every once in a while things break your way and you get a good player for your team. It is like taking a beach, a lot of what you take at first does not stay with you, and that is what happens with much of recruiting. For the first ten to fifteen years you have a holding action; you are trying to make do.

Foreign Staff

Accompanying the general manager as part of his management team in the beginning, and for a long time after, should be head-office personnel in the roles of principal departmental heads: Control and Finance, Marketing, Sales, and Production. At the outset, the general manager should double as head of Personnel.

It is essential to be comfortable with financial reporting. It is extremely difficult to recruit Japanese who know financial planning and reporting as practiced in the West. They must be developed in house or hired from another foreign firm. Therefore, in the beginning the head of Finance should be a gaijin with exceptional training skills.

Many foreign companies say, "I accept that the general manager and the financial planner should be gaijin, but the market is Japan, and Japanese understand Japan better than foreigners. My general manager needs the input of a Japanese marketing manager and a Japanese sales force manager." This is logical but not necessarily correct. It depends on the company's product or service. Are there Japanese who are at the cutting edge of the industry? Perhaps yes, but it is unlikely they will be available to the foreign firm. Again, to market and sell a product or service it is necessary to have people who know these products and exude confidence in them. The general manager cannot perform these functions because 50 percent of his time will be occupied with personnel, and a substantial amount in dealing with the head office, seeing that it or other company offices are delivering what Japan needs to fulfill its promises to the market. The Japanese market is deep and wide, and to penetrate it takes extraordinary marketing and sales skills. Proven skills developed overseas often work in Japan after being tested and adapted to what the marketplace tells you. Only an experienced marketer familiar with the company's product can do this.

Selling is different in Japan. It is unlikely that success will be achieved by duplicating what the competition is already doing. The sales force manager must direct that sales force, maximizing the usage of personnel time and talent in a cost-effective manner that sells. A staff must be trained. The Japanese personnel generally are not good enough to work for a good or even average Japanese company. They have probably moved from one foreign company to another—for salary or because their previous employer failed. They often go in selling with their head down; they are looked upon as foreign and feel unreliable in making fulfillment promises. A critical member of the management team is a foreign employee who can train and sell side-by-side with his Japanese sales staff. Next to the general manager, this is the preeminent leadership assignment.

Technologists from head office will obviously have to be involved in any start-up or enhancements, particularly if there are global interface requirements. Because of the constant need to improve product and service attributes, a wide range of specialists will be involved over the years. Besides technical skills, they should also have excellent teaching skills so that they can impart their knowledge as effectively as possible to the Japanese staff. There is no room for the black-box mentality that permits the trainer to return again and again, giving out information in bits and pieces. Training assignments should be on a defined-time basis, with the option of the general manager to extend upon consultation.

At Chemical Bank and American Express there were some individuals who made a living by traveling around the world, imparting just enough information to insure that they would have to be invited back, all the time living off expense accounts. Because they never stayed long enough to understand the Japanese marketplace, the systems they installed were often worthless. This caused a tremendous credibility gap for the foreign management with the Japanese staff. One operational accountant from Chemical announced to our senior Japanese operational officer: "Either you do it my way or I am going home tonight." Not only was this not the way to behave anywhere, but, even worse his way was totally incorrect. My only choice was to take the visitor out for a drink promptly at 5:00 P.M. and ask him, "What time are you leaving tonight?" With his financial existence threatened, such an individual will back off. But if there is weak international management in head office, he will do everything possible to sabotage you personally at home, and you are not there to defend yourself. The person in head office responsible for Japan is clearly as important to the Japanese operation as the Japan general manager. Each must respect and support the other if they are to work together effectively to the benefit of the company. Quality and integrity are also as essential for the visitors as they are for the people assigned overseas. If a person is not appropriate for an overseas assignment, he or she should not be sent as a staff visitor to get them out of management's hair at home.

A senior foreign consultant after five years in Japan:

> If you look at those who should be successful but are not or are struggling, sales is a huge part of the problem. They have said, "We'll leave it to the Japanese. We'll do it their way. We'll let them control that side of the business." That is a mistake. Each key position in the organization has to have a top foreigner until you are absolutely certain you have developed somebody locally. If it is a business where technological application is essential, then some of your best technologists have to be part of the team several layers down. The big problem: "Not in my career plans." You see it too often. It should be going away. I spend more time trying to convince corporations that either they have to send top-level American management or they are wasting their money and time and are losing an opportunity, than I ever spend discussing some of the clever ideas we have about ways to build business.

To run a successful international operation, including Japan, the people assigned overseas and those who travel overseas as support must have integrity and knowledge of product and service.

How long should an assignment be? As one general manager said, until you work yourself out of the job and into a better job.

Since there should not be many better management jobs in the company, and because of the time and money required to penetrate a market as deep and wide as Japan, an assignment should not be less than five years. The decision to leave Japan should be carefully thought out: perhaps it will be taken in order to make a run for the top tier of the parent, or because other knowledge skills are required in a changing market. Perhaps the decision will be to stay until retirement to provide corporate stability in Japan. All three choices require careful management-succession planning, which is something American companies, in particular, talk a great deal about, but, as with most personnel issues, handle miserably.

Once an assignment is terminated, there should be a succession overlap of a minimum of six months, preferably a year, with a return to Japan six months after departure to discuss with the successor why certain things were done or not done in the past. Historical continuity through understanding prevents many misunderstandings and saves enormous personnel and financial costs.

Thus, on the corporation's organizational chart, all expatriate gaijin employees should have red circles around them for five years; that is, they should not be touched by anyone without the parent CEO's permission, but their career advancement should be as fast as anyone's in the organization. If performance does not warrant such advancement, they should be replaced immediately.

How do you put a red line around these people and say they are not to be touched for five years? I don't know any other way than to say, "This is just goddamn important." You are so confident he is on the way up, and he is so confident of it, and you have such a strong commitment to Japan that you and he are willing to commit five years of his career to doing what is necessary.

Managing a foreign business in a competitive Japanese environment while interacting with a head office requires energy that the Japanese competition does not have to expend in their own backyard. They can concentrate on the market at hand. Thus, the foreign management team, hand-picked by the parent CEO and his immediate staff, not only should be given superb support as needed but should be freed from any unnecessary travel or reporting to head office. Only what is essential to running the parent company should be required, once the goals and strategies have been mutually established. Tactics are really none of head office's concern. Goals should be reviewed once a year, unless there is need for substantial modification, and the general manager left to manage in Japan.

Foreign Visitors

As can be seen from the above, visitors are a subject often discussed by foreign management in Japan. Working visitors, who come at the request of Japan management, are always welcome, as are audits. They are part of running a business. People who create reasons to come to Japan, with their spouses, are not. Frequent flier programs have been the bane of many a general manager and his wife. There are two ways to solve this problem, neither generally appreciated by those whose trip is not permitted. The CEO's office approves all travel requests to Japan, or all requests can only be initiated through Japan. Whom they do not see is also as important as whom they do see. As Jack Loughran of Morgan Guaranty noted, "Someone has to work out a way to manage visitors."

A respected Japanese general manager of a major foreign corporation comments on the Japanese view of visitors:

> When you position yourself as an occasional visitor to Japan, you are not conceived of as an insider. You are a guest of honor. You can come here fairly frequently, but you are still a visitor, a guest of honor. I do not really listen sincerely or seriously to what you have to say.

A foreign general manager of one of the world's largest corporations notes:

> Far too much of my time is spent on creating agendas, ordering cars, going to the airport, doing all kinds of logistical support for an extraordinary number of visitors. If I don't pay attention to what they are doing here, nobody else will. This is at the top of my list of worries. They don't understand why I have to make the government appointments. "Can't your Japanese staff do that for you?" Although if they wanted to make an appointment with a government official in the U.S., they wouldn't use their secretary. They still have the little-Japan mentality.

As a rule of thumb, if there is not sufficient reason for a follow-up visit then there probably was no need for the original visit, unless it was agreed upon from the beginning that it was a one-of-a-kind need. The Japanese staff must be informed that just because someone asks if you want them, you do not have to say yes. The visitor should also write a report on what he has accomplished during his visit and the follow-up required, and then discuss it with the general manager or his designate before departure. Too much is forgotten or altered once one leaves Japan. As a result, the head office will be ill informed and staff in Japan disappointed.

I kid the Japanese staff, saying: "You guys think success is taking a new product manager from the States on a week-long binge in Tokyo and a couple of love calls. Then he's an expert on Japan. You ship him back on a plane and you go back to what you were doing." That is a dereliction of responsibility.

Overseas personnel must be very careful in their contact with the Japanese staff, either when visiting Japan or when the Japanese staff visits them. People overseas generally do not know how to treat a person from Japan according to his stature in Japanese society and in the company. People naturally want to be nice, but they often resent being advised on how to deal with others. They may even tell the Japanese what you advised, causing real problems. Collegiality unfortunately does not mix well with status, and one must guard against good Japanese staff being ruined by visitors or by being sent overseas without proper preparation on all sides.

A chairman or president cannot be told not to come or what to do during a visit. Every effort can be made, however, to use the occasion of such a visit to enhance the status of the Japan operation both at home and in Japan.

You have to educate the senior executives on visits. They do not know what they are looking for. You have to hold their hands and say, "Look at this, look at this." You've got to keep the communication channels open so that Japan has a high priority within the corporation. Because when there is trouble, those channels get locked. It is just critically important. The payoff is big.

The following "Letter from Japan" was published in New York in October 1982 by the Japan Society in its newsletter. It is just as valid, if not more so, for the chairman or president of a foreign corporation visiting Japan today. These visits can be extremely beneficial to the Japan operation, as well as the global operation, if looked upon as serious, hard, and often trying work. Otherwise they can be a complete waste of time; even worse, without proper preparation and implementation, they can do serious harm.

Letter from Japan

Mr. John Q. Chairman/President
U.S. Multinational Corporation
Somewhere, U.S.A.

Dear Sir:

I have just learned from your Tokyo representative that you are planning a twelve-day business trip to Asia/Australasia in April to coincide with the cherry blossom season in Japan. I was delighted to learn that you will be spending two days in Tokyo before proceeding to Peking, Hong Kong, Singapore and Sydney to visit your other facilities in the area. (This would be the unlikely equivalent of a Japanese chairman visiting his Western operations by spending two days in Chicago and spreading the next ten days among Mexico City, Caracas, Sao Paulo and London before returning to Tokyo.)

Without being presumptuous, I might suggest that you give consideration to what you plan to accomplish on your trip in the spring. I will confine myself to Japan, for that is what I know best, but would anticipate that on the trip as planned you will see as much of customs, immigration and airport counters, to say nothing of the interior of an aircraft, as you will of your management and employees. To put it all into perspective: it takes as long to fly from Tokyo to Singapore as it does from New York to Athens, and there is no Atlantic Ocean along the way; only land, people and varied cultures.

Over 500 People in Two Days

I have been told that you wish to visit your general manager for Japan, the president of one of your joint venture companies, the president of your principal bank, a major securities firm, a plant site of a competitor, your attorneys and auditors, your advertising agency, have an interview with the *Nihon Keizai Shimbun* (Japan Economic Journal), call on the vice-minister at MITI and hold a reception for approximately 500 people in the Heian Room at the Hotel Okura. Your two days will be full from breakfast onward.

I have had extensive conversations with your general manager, an old friend of mine as well as a business acquaintance, to understand what you hope to accomplish during your two days in Tokyo. He will, of course, meet you at Narita when your plane arrives from Chicago and take you to your hotel. As you know, it usually takes three hours from the time your plane arrives in mid-afternoon until you clear customs and immigration procedures and arrive in town, so nothing is planned for that evening. I am sure you will be a bit tired, but as time is short, he will brief you fully during the ride into town. In any case, you will have been given an extensive trip book on current political, economic and business aspects of Japan, your company in Japan, and the people you will be meeting. I think, though, the only person you will have met prior to this is the president of the joint venture company when he visited you two years ago.

Receiving Lines or Small Dinners

It has been arranged for Mrs. Chairman/President to visit Kyoto or Nikko for one day and to have a luncheon in town on the other day, see the cherry blossoms and one of those magnificent Japanese department stores. As you requested, since your wife always acts as hostess for your entertainment, a dinner will be given by Mr. and Mrs. with some close foreign friends.

Tell Mrs. not to be upset if not many Japanese wives come to the scheduled reception. They just do not see it as one of their business responsibilities. Nevertheless, we will be sure to see that some of our foreign friends from the American Club bring their wives so she will have someone to talk to when the receiving line breaks up. (I'm sure we can get a picture of the receiving line in the social column of one of the local English-language papers.)

Perhaps you would consider, instead, a series of dinners with you and your wife arranged by your general manager at his home. Japanese wives would be more likely to attend and you would have a better opportunity to get to know your guests. Many of your counterparts here have had or can expect two or three overseas assignments; couples will welcome the opportunity to visit a foreign home and to become better acquainted with you and your wife.

Establishing Company Relationships in Japan

Mr. Chairman/President, may I suggest an alternative approach to the entire spring trip? Why not make Japan your sole destination? Japan is a part of your Asian/Australasian network only because of geography. It has little in common with Peking or Hong Kong or Sydney; in fact, different languages are spoken in each of these places and their cultures, ideologies, etc. are as different from each other as Russia, Bahrain and England. More important, Japan is the second most powerful economic power in the world. Why don't you visit the Osaka area, your suppliers there, and your joint venture in Kobe instead of asking the president to come to Tokyo? You could spend a relaxed weekend in Kyoto before or after your visit, walking the streets, observing the Japanese at work and play. You might want to go to Fukuoka/Kita-Kyushu where you are considering establishing a major supplier relationship for your Tokyo plant. Each of your visits with your attorneys, accountants, advertising agency, etc. could have a specific purpose; and they would have a first-hand opportunity to learn about you and your company's present and future plans.

You would have time to sit down and really talk to your general manager about operating a business in Japan; whether there are primary and secondary business barriers, and if so, what might be done about them on a nonemotional political and business basis.

The Brightest and the Best

All of your Japanese employees do not come from the universities of Tokyo, Kyoto and Hitotsubashi. Foreign firms do not normally have access to these elite graduates like the leading Japanese corporations, much heralded for lifetime employment. (Staffing your operation here is something like trying to build a new car while only the Japanese companies have access to gleaming new parts.) Therefore you will learn that your personnel issues are different from those of Mitsubishi Bank, Mitsui & Company or JAL; much as their concerns in the United States are different from yours.

You and your head-office associates' support of your employees in Japan is extremely important. What better way to support them than to sit and talk and listen?

Executive Involvement Equals Success

I realize that you are coming here to "show the flag" and that as the Chairman/President you already have corporate planning, personnel, marketing and finance departments. However, it has become patently obvious that those foreign firms that have succeeded or will succeed in Japan, 100 percent parent-company owned or joint venture, whether a Texas Instruments or a CBS/Sony, have done so because their American chief executives were totally involved in getting the Japanese venture off the ground and remained fully involved thereafter.

You are playing a deadly serious game on someone else's court, and the rules are different than in America. To not keep your interest in Japan at the board room level is, in effect, to ignore or merely to dabble in the second largest economy and consumer market in the world, to give to Japan no competition at all in its own backyard. You cannot copy Japan in the United States or Europe because it is a different culture, but you can surely share in its technological developments.

Representing Your Best Interest

Listen to your general manager in Japan, your attorneys, accountants and consultants. Be certain to choose people to whom you are committed and have confidence in, for you must have long-term continuity to succeed and continue succeeding. If you have not been pleased with your and your associates' choices, replace them with the right people.

Remember that your general manager represents your interest. To your joint venture partner here and to Japanese firms in the same field, you often represent the competition. The advice you seek and receive from them on running a business in Japan will, therefore, not necessarily be in your best interest.

Spend some time here; bring to the table your background and experience in business and with people. I hope that on your departure you will set the date for your next visit. I know your general manager, employees and the Japanese community—from your joint venture president to the press—will be most impressed, and much more likely to take very seriously what your company does in Japan. And please make yourself available to these same people when they visit your offices as well. Soon you will find you have an ongoing dialogue on Japan and your operations here. Your bottom line will reflect your support and involvement and that of your associates.

Yours sincerely,
Jackson N. Huddleston, Jr.

Tokyo is the most expensive city in the world for foreigners to live in, and costs alone preclude the luxury of assigning more than a few foreigners to Japan. According to Organization Research Counselors, Inc., consultants in human resource management and competition, an American on a three-year assignment in Tokyo with an annual salary of less than $100,000 could cost an employer more than three million dollars, including moving costs, overseas incentive compensation at the time of assignment and/or upon return, housing, differentials for the cost of goods and services, the cost of an automobile and possibly a driver, allowances for children's education, annual home-leave expenses, and income tax equalization.[1] These figures underline the importance of carefully selecting a competent Japanese staff.

Japanese Staff

It is essential to understand what job mobility means in Japan. The job mobility rate there is 13 percent, not a small number when one considers the size of the work force but a significant decline from 20 percent in 1970. The mobility is mainly in the companies with fewer than three hundred employees—the bottom two-thirds of the structure that supports the upper one-third. Often the mobility is forced upon the employee because the company gets squeezed out of existence, not because the employee did not like where he was working and wanted to quit.

In short, those Japanese who will work for a foreign company normally do so because there is not employment available for them in good Japanese companies or because they are mavericks.

---

[1]*The Wall Street Journal*, February 10, 1988.

It is always nice to have a certain number of mavericks on staff anywhere, but few managers want to run a company full of mavericks in an alien environment.

For Japanese, working for a foreign company is considered much less desirable than working for a domestic firm. The goal of Japanese parents, who put their children in the escalator system from kindergarten through university, is to get them into a prestigious company. This makes all their efforts worthwhile. Morgan Stanley might not be a name that the parents want to hear. IBM is the only foreign firm among the top ten companies in Japan favored by both engineering and liberal arts graduates.

A foreign general manager with over thirty years of experience in Japan observes:

> The attractions of a foreign company as an employer are probably no different today than they were thirty years ago. However, some foreign companies are not the strange entity they were thirty years ago. They have grown, have demonstrated commitment, have perhaps built an application laboratory, and have their own employees who can do university recruiting and dispel some of the concerns and uncertainties. But the best will still not be available. It is no different today for a new entry. What incentive is there for a Japanese to join an unknown future in a foreign language and in a place where people put their feet on the desk? A person who does join is odd and most likely a dropout.

How does one build a Japanese staff to participate in the management and functioning of an operation? Slowly! The most dangerous time is the fast-growth period. It is important not to be rushed into hiring. Once someone is hired, it is likely he will be around for life. It is like getting married in Japan. Japan's divorce rate is low, if for no other reason than a father rarely sees his children after a divorce. The Japanese talk about the changes in hiring practices as if they were dramatic, but by American standards they are like molasses. They are not changing nearly as fast as the industrial and consumer markets. The effects of lifetime employment will continue for the foreseeable future. The annual raise marches on. Foreign banks and airlines have been particularly hard hit over the years as the volume of their business has fluctuated, and surely in the future the same will happen to foreign securities firms.

Rodney Clark, the author of *The Japanese Company*, states in his book that "The Japanese labor market is best understood in terms of employees and firms, rather than jobs and skills."[2] In sum, when recruiting in Japan, the Japanese hire an individual based on his educational track record and then use him as they see fit in their organization. The man, not his skills, is hired. Any new-to-Japan or rapidly growing foreign company, however, will need to recruit skills to keep the business going, as does any new Japanese business that is not part of an existing group.

Finding a Japanese Chairman

It is probably undesirable, considering the downside risk, to hire the Japanese chairman in the beginning. In a start-up situation, it would be the best of all worlds, for he could then help recruit. Finding the right Japanese chairman is a critical recruiting process in itself, however. The Japanese government is a good place to start, but this is also where Japanese corporations themselves usually start when they have a management gap to fill. Japanese government employees—that is, those admitted to the thirteen ministries each year as Class A employees (usually twenty-six to twenty-eight per ministry each year)—are the crème de la crème of Japanese university graduates. They have competed nationally for these jobs, as they did for entrance to university, and most are graduates of the state-run national universities: Tokyo, Kyoto, Hitotsubashi. They are respected by their peers for the rest of their lives, for they won and they are few. Except for the Foreign Ministry, where each recruit is guaranteed an ambassadorship under the normal career progression, these ministry employees retire by age fifty-five. The General Affairs departments (read Personnel departments) of the ministries are as responsible for these employees' jobs upon retirement as they are for them while they are ministry employees. Some are better than others and therefore retire or "descend from heaven" later than others. The later the descent, the more prestigious and capable the potential hire. These have always been the best candidates for a chairmanship.

A natural choice is a candidate in the ministry that has a responsibility for the industry in which the business operates.

---

[2]Rodney Clark, *The Japanese Company* (New Haven: Yale University Press, 1979, reprinted by Charles E. Tuttle, 1987), p. 142.

These individuals have not worked for the competition, but since they are responsible for the particular business in the ministry, they know the competition's personnel, their own successors in the ministry, and often their counterparts and successors in other relevant ministries and government-sponsored industry associations. By hiring former government employees, a company immediately puts itself into the old-boy network. They don't know the details of the business, but they can be taught what they need to know. They would not have survived the competition without superb interpersonal skills and brain power. Above all, they are neutral in the corporate sense and dependent upon the company for their livelihood. Once they join a foreign company they cannot go elsewhere. Two experienced general managers commented on the need to hire former Japanese government employees:

> You will be at a tremendous disadvantage if you don't have the same contacts as your Japanese competitors, at least as long as government standards and regulations are as complicated as they are today.

> From a marketing point of view, we must appreciate that regulatory barriers are gradually breaking down and you don't have a lot of lead time. The administrative burden on the regulatory authorities is forcing them to change. You had better be wired to the authorities who administer the regulations in Japan and ready to implement a business plan when the opportunity comes. Otherwise it is too late.

It is important, however, that when a ministry contact is approached for the proper introduction to the General Affairs Department, everyone in the head office agrees with hiring a government official as chairman if the appropriate candidate is available. If this is not the case, you will find yourself writing a most unfortunate letter of apology, as I once did. Instead of enhancing your reputation with the ministry, such a reversal makes it difficult ever to show your face in its halls again.

The potential chairman should be interviewed by the Japan general manager and the head-office staff responsible for Japan, including the CEO. In this way, all the important players know why a particular candidate was chosen and what his role is to be from the very beginning. In making the selection, one looks for character, innate intelligence, and presentability for the Japan market, not for the head office or home country, since the chairman will be working only in Japan and will not be responsible for communications with head office or other corporate locations. Advice on these characteristics should be sought from one's closest advisers in Japan. The job offer should come from the Japan general manager since that is the person for whom the chairman will be working and to whom he will be reporting. A frequent mistake is to have the head-office CEO offer the job, implying some sort of direct reporting line to head office. But in Japan, as previously stated, the president/general manager, not the chairman, is the CEO, although that title is not used. It is extremely important not to confuse the reporting lines when the Japan chairman is hired, or during any subsequent replacement of the president/ general manager. If the Japan chairman looks to the head-office chairman or his designate as his direct superior and consciously or unconsciously circumvents the individual in Japan responsible for running the operation, the result will be chaos, particularly with the Japanese staff, who will gravitate naturally to the Japanese chairman rather than to the foreign president/general manager when there are the inevitable disagreements in the organization. The chairman has no inside operational responsibilities, only external government, customer, supplier, and university relationships.

General Affairs Manager

If the general manager spends the requisite 50 percent of his time on personnel, he will manage and set the tone through one of his most important departments and its head: the general affairs manager. General Affairs in Japan incorporates general administration, the rental and building of offices, the purchase of equipment, papers, and pencils, and, even more important, all personnel matters, from hiring to job placement on retirement. General Affairs is the nerve center of a Japanese company.

The general affairs manager is viewed by the staff as second only to the general manager. One's most trusted employee, preferably a senior Japanese, should have this responsibility. Any potential Japanese general manager should first have this assignment to test his personnel and administrative skills. Until a general manager is sure that he has the right person for this job, he should carry the responsibility himself. This is a work load, though, that cannot be carried for long in a growing business. Above all, a company should avoid establishing the type of personnel department often found in other countries: a department of has-beens, who could not make it in a line or operational staff position; chartists, if you will, who record or meddle rather than manage. General Affairs in Japan is a corporate function and management responsibility, well respected and extremely important. If there is not a strong head of General Affairs to act as a buffer as the Japanese are accustomed to, then the general manager is one-on-one with his staff on every personnel issue. A mistake here can be life threatening to the company's presence in Japan.

Personnel Investigations

The General Affairs Department is responsible for background investigations on all employees considered for employment. These background investigations take place before an employee is offered a job, even when there is an initial probationary period of employment. There are government guidelines on conducting personnel investigations; but Japanese corporations and parents of all potential brides and grooms do it, and so should the foreign corporation. Many do not, and applicants to foreign companies know this. Some do imaginative resumé writing in response. This is often the first and last chance to eliminate potential troublemakers. The General Affairs Department should look for gaps in education and employment. Everyone should be investigated, from the top to the bottom, with no exceptions. The Japanese do these background checks for good reason. A foreign firm has even more reason to do so, for not being a part of the fabric of the society, any mistake made will be amplified.

A foreign owner and president of a sizable service company in Japan recently hired a Japanese individual whom he had known through the Parent-Teacher Association of his children's school. Because they had worked together on school functions for a number of years, he did not inquire about the individual with his preceding employers, although all the rest of the employees were investigated. When the employee's erratic behavior caused the president to make inquiries, he was shocked by what he learned. Unfortunately, dismissal then involved an extremely costly lawsuit and a tremendous waste of management's time.

The one you catch justifies all the trouble of investigating the others. Two or three radicals or rotten apples can cause a lot of trouble.

General Manager's Secretary

An extremely important employee in the gaijin kaisha is the general manager's secretary. How she conducts herself on the telephone and her ability to interact internally with the staff can be crucial to the success of the foreign general manager. Many outsiders will judge the foreign general manager, who cannot speak in Japanese over the phone, by his secretary. In turn, the secretary will be judged by the way she speaks Japanese. Many a foreign general manager would be shocked by the opinion that the Japanese have about his secretary because of her Japanese. Japanese is a situational language and requires a good education and upbringing to be spoken properly, especially for women. When hiring a secretary it is essential to have a trusted senior Japanese employee interview her. He should be attentive to the impression she conveys in Japanese, not in English or another foreign language.

Seconded Employees

Japanese banks, suppliers, joint-venture partners, and customers will perhaps offer one of their employees when they learn a company is in the market for a chairman or other management employees. The immediate reaction is, "Isn't that nice! They appreciate the relationship we have had over the years or they really do wish to work with us." Again, caution! As previously mentioned, Japanese companies need good employees, and what they will give up is often just not that good. Also, as soon as a company takes someone from a singular industrial group (keiretsu), everything that goes on in the office is known to that group, and more than likely the other groups won't touch you. Neutrality is often a strength for a foreign company.

Seconded employees from banks and companies should be carefully scrutinized. Historically, Japanese companies have taken their bankers in as working board members and the only "outsiders" allowed in. This practice stems from when money was tight and credit information verbal. Today money is not tight and the sources for funding are numerous, including from foreign banks. Seconded employees usually do not have the growth potential to assist in building a dynamic and substantial presence in Japan.

One well-known large foreign corporation that has been in Japan for many years even today has an on-loan employee from a major Japanese bank who is in charge of corporate planning. This individual knows everything that goes on in the company he has been seconded to, as does his bank employer. In reality, the Japanese bank, through their employee, is running corporate planning for this extremely important foreign corporation in Japan. As a consultant, I watched the bank orchestrate which businesses the foreign company would enter and not enter. Sometimes this was in the foreign company's interest but often not, for it kept the company within its present scope and out of any new, growth industries. Incomprehensible but true! When I went with this employee to another major Japanese bank, seeking to work with it, this extremely intelligent individual was immediately asked how he happened to be working for a foreign company—in other words, people like you don't work for foreign companies. When he subsequently explained that he was on loan from, and shortly returning to, their competitor, polite conversation followed.

We don't look at our on-loan employees as career employees. They are not fast track to be cross-fertilized. They got us over a period of introductory growth very successfully. They are at best a near-term approach. The mistake is to look at them as anymore than a stopgap during an introductory phase.

The difficulty in finding skilled employees has led many foreign companies to choose the joint-venture route. Until the early 1970s, most foreign companies could only receive permission from the Japanese government to do business in Japan if they formed a joint venture with a Japanese partner. In the 1980s, one was free, with few exceptions, to have a wholly owned subsidiary or branch in Japan. While many former joint ventures have been bought out by one or the other partner or terminated, many foreign companies continue to prefer them for the acquisition of personnel and supposedly more rapid access to the market.

The problem with the personnel equation in this formula is that one rarely receives from the Japanese partner the type of employee that has made that partner great. Rather, the foreign partner receives those who have peaked out and need to be moved aside to make room for the high achievers to move up through the lifetime employment system. No one wishes to be assigned to a joint venture, for size determines prestige in Japan. In Japan, you are who your company is—no more, no less. The bodies are there, but these insecure individuals are always looking back to their Japanese parent for security.

A foreign company will be no more than a silent partner to its Japanese counterpart unless it has placed excellent head-office management in the joint venture and has a say concerning all who are hired. A new joint venture is much like a new wholly owned foreign company when it comes to university recruiting. The personnel problems in a joint venture are far more similar to a wholly owned venture than many foreign companies appreciate.[3]

Recruiting

The recruiting choices for experienced employees in a foreign firm are headhunters, newspapers, friends, and word-of-mouth. All major international headhunting firms are represented in Japan. They are generally run by foreigners and have the same problem recruiting staff as other foreign companies do. Their one advantage has been that they see a wide selection of candidates for their clients and at times have been able to recruit for themselves from this pool. The problem is that headhunting—the buying and selling of employees and the encouragement of job hopping—is anathema to most Japanese, unless it is from one foreign company to another. Being in a foreign company, they are really not part of the Japanese corporate world or Japan itself, so who cares what they do? The headhunting business is simply countercultural.

One experienced recruiter notes that the Japanese public he deals with is skeptical to the extreme:

---

[3]See James C. Abegglen and George Stalk, Jr., *Kaisha, The Japanese Corporation* (New York: Basic Books, 1985), chap. 9, for an excellent discussion of why the Japanese government generally required joint ventures between 1952 and 1973. As they point out, the era of the joint venture is drawing to a close.

People come to see me after an initial telephone call to see if they can obliterate their name or me, as the case may be. "Did my company give you my name?" If you get one person out of ten who may show a glimmer of interest, that is a tremendous percentage.

A respected foreign headhunter comments on his profession:

I see a lot of C-players being found and hired in this market, and it scares the hell out of me. I see it all the time. I shiver. A good recruiter manages the whole process and educates both the client and the candidate. Most Japanese recruiters aren't going to manage the process with the foreign company, telling them, "You are wrong. You have a nonstarter here." Our guys can't go nose to nose in a fair fight with some of our very aggressive foreign clients. Nor can the people we are placing compete against the competitive Japanese.

Most headhunters, as impressive as their foreign staff might be, have had to rely on C-class Japanese players to try to recruit for foreign clients. It is hard for a C-class player to recruit a B-player or even identify the A-players. The recruiting firms are doing everything possible to improve the quality of their employees, but one must face reality. Several Japanese recruiting firms stress that they are Japanese and have a large file of potential candidates. More often than not these are just lists. Finding a recruiter who understands the integrity of the process is essential. The time required to recruit a satisfactory individual for a job in Japan is at least three times that in the United States. If there is to be any chance of success, both sides must understand clearly the risk and potential. One must also appreciate that, if done properly, it will usually cost 50 or even 70 percent more than at home.

It will be necessary after a successful recruitment for the headhunter with integrity to stay involved to assist the company and the employee through the adjustment phase, which is bound to be traumatic. Thus, the original brief given to the headhunter on the attributes desired in the candidate and his capacity to advise you on what to expect realistically are extremely important.

For a candidate to be interested in a job, there has to be a negative propulsion force. There is not only interest in the position, but there must also be a reason why he is unhappy where he is. That reason has to be a stronger one than would propel a Westerner to the marketplace, and it is in everyone's interests to understand why the candidate is available. Thereafter, continuous face-to-face discussion is essential so that no one is outside the ongoing thought and educational processes. For most this seems only common sense and what they would do elsewhere. The difference is the intensity of differences at whatever level one is recruiting. The time spent up front is what gives one a slight chance of success; success being an employee who will be an ongoing contributor to the building of a business in Japan.

In recruiting a candidate one will be dealing indirectly with his present employer, his extended family on both his and his wife's side, and very likely his classmates, with whom he will consult. There are subtle pressures from colleagues: "Do you want to leave us? Do you really want to leave our group? You want to do that? Do you? Why do you want to do that? Please tell us! Is it just money? Are you really just grubbing around? Do you want more? Why do you want to do this?" His family, particularly his wife, will be opposed. All her prestige is based on where here husband works now. "Who's that foreign company? Whoever heard of them?" A tremendous strain is placed on the individual.

Ninety-five percent of the Japanese would not see moving to another company as an improvement on their present employment situation. With negative propulsion, in interviewing a potential employee, you have to determine if the problem is of his own making or completely beyond his control. Was his mentor passed over for the board of directors so he isn't going anywhere either? Has he been asked to go to India without his family? Or for that matter to Osaka, where he doesn't want to transfer his children to a new school that is not as good as the one they attend in Tokyo? Has the product, whose development he has been working on, been turned down by the board, and he is going to have to spend the next four years developing another product if he is to have any hope of getting back on the escalator? On the other hand, he could be a total bum, a loser, who has been protected all these years by the employment system. He knows he cannot be carried to the next level on the escalator and this is his chance to swim out. The reason will eventually come out, but if you don't ask, he will not tell you. You have to be inquisitive at the proper time, in the proper place and at the proper speed.

The headhunter is there to keep you from having to be out front all the time, to give you independent judgment on your choices, compensation, and, unlike in Europe or North America, to help the candidate through the process of leaving his present employer and becoming acclimated in the new company.

When he comes out of his tiered organization, where he might have fought like hell to get things done, he finds himself in a foreign company right next to the marketplace. He doesn't have anyone to tell to do this or that. He has to do it himself. He doesn't have his former company's name on his name card. He has to explain who his company is. Doors don't open automatically, and the individual wilts like a flower in July. He sort of just tilts over. He's finished. It takes tremendous internal drive to make the transition, especially when he is stuck in a room with a group of new people. He has perhaps at best met them only once and is now told he has to work with these people after being on an hierarchical escalator for the past forty years since he entered kindergarten. For the first time he is cut loose from his mother's apron string. By fiat he has new colleagues who were probably in their past corporate lives all archenemies. How is he going to work with these people? Very slowly! Only after a long period of time is he going to become comfortable. The foreign company that expects to put ex-enemies cheek-by-jowl and have them work together overnight as a team is in for a lot of disappointment. People have to be employed two or three years in advance to take over smoothly positions that are currently occupied. That requires a tremendous capability to project not only manpower but the needs of the business, which in turn requires the staying power to succeed in Japan. If you take the attitude, let's put him in a job and see if it works, it won't work at all.

There is always the conflict that while an individual was in a Japanese company he was being trained to be a generalist, whereas a foreign company generally needs specialists who can also manage. If by chance the individual has been trained as a specialist in a Japanese company, he has probably been looked upon as a clerk and has no management capability.

Even if you get a good guy, it is several years before you know what you have, because there is such an elaborate, painstakingly difficult entry for a Japanese into a Japanese organization beyond postgraduation entry level. It has nothing to do with being a foreign organization. He is isolated. I am incredulous at what these people go through coming into an organization. They are tougher than nails with each other. Really unbelievable! Head office doesn't understand. They want to go and give the person immediate responsibility. You have to do it slowly to see what you've got. If you don't, the Japanese staff will see that he fails before he starts. They are often far more understanding of foreigners than of a new-entry Japanese.

Another alternative for recruiting skilled employees is the newspapers. In the 1960s and 1970s they were unsatisfactory beyond the bilingual secretary level. Today on occasion an employee with a specific skill—accounting or computers, for example—is as likely to surface this way as any other way.

The best recruiting is through word of mouth and an introduction from a friend. A company's own employees often know people who for one reason or another might consider working for it. Employees should be apprised of what management is looking for in candidates. One must take care, however, that your employees are not building a faction within the company. This is a common occurrence. As one experienced foreigner noted, if you put five Japanese together you will end up with three factions. The social economist Shumpei Kumon points out that the Japanese are group oriented, but within the group there are many groups, each asking for special consideration. In that employees in a foreign company usually have little in common socially or educationally, or in terms of experience, the resultant insecurity often leads to faction building, creating one's own womb. Even Japanese companies watch this closely and rotate employees regularly, often laterally, to avoid it.

Once a Japanese leaves a Japanese company for a foreign corporation, no Japanese company will ever hire him again. He is soiled. This one-way door has created a class of Japanese who are even more career mobile than Americans in the United States. They job hop, float from job to job in foreign companies, and never make it anywhere, not unlike those men in Japan who cannot meet their financial obligations, leave home (often never to return), and float from one manual-labor or taxi-driver job to another. In short, those who job hop in Japan are by and large in lower-level jobs.

In joining a foreign firm a male has thus left the Japanese social structure. What will a foreign firm's name look like to his prospective bride's family, or, even worse, what will it look like to his children's prospective spouses or employers in twenty-five years? The first question after one's name and birthdate on an employment application is family history: one's father's name and employment. Foreign is fine for the mannequins in the department store display window but not for the resumé or family history.

Nevertheless, there are people in Japan willing to work for foreign corporations for economic, fast-track management opportunities, international travel, or personal reasons. For these people, satisfaction and security must come in other than the normal ways. Often, because they have stepped outside, their security requirements are great and their reaction to lack of security, whether real or perceived, can cause enormous problems for management and themselves.

Female Employees

For many foreign companies in the nonmanufacturing sector, women will comprise the majority of their employees. With the support of top management, women can be a valuable resource; probably a foreign company's only access to first-class education, which is what made Japan what it is today and what will be essential to stay ahead of the competition. A foreigner will be able to tap this resource much more easily and effectively than can a Japanese man, who throughout his career has ignored women as potential employees.

Japanese women can be extremely loyal, for you are giving them the earning capability and challenge that their own society restricts. Graduates of junior colleges and universities, many will remain with the company only three or four years, until they marry. A few will stay on for careers, and those who do can, with senior management support, become an effective part of management. Despite protestation on the part of Japanese men, they can also be effective in interacting with clients outside of the office. (It is a greater handicap to be with a foreign firm than to be a woman.) Legal working hour restrictions placed on women have now been greatly relaxed, and therefore a woman, if she chooses, may put in the same work hours as a man. That she can neither drink in the bars at night nor play golf with the boys on the weekend is just a fact of life. A company will have plenty of males who can and are more than willing to do so if the company picks up the tab.

Day care for working mothers in Japan is superb compared to the United States, and the same percentage of mothers are in the work force in both countries. In the past, these potential employees have not been given meaningful career opportunities in corporations, much as in the United States twenty years ago. Today, however, with a shortage of male recruits for technical jobs in a dynamic economy, women are being given the opportunity to climb the technical ladder in Japanese companies. This will eventually make recruiting even more difficult for foreign firms.

In the past two years we have hired ten female graduates. We have not found a male in this time up to the standards of the females. We don't attract the good males.

The women are absolutely outstanding. We are using them as chemists and in research and are beginning to break through some barriers in the building. Two are now in management. We are bringing them in slowly but surely.

Japanese parents are often willing to let their daughters work in foreign corporations as an internationalization experience, a chance to use the English they have studied for so many years and to work prior to getting married and settling down to raise a family. It is particularly attractive to girls from upper middle-class and wealthy backgrounds. These entry-level young women should be investigated like all other employees, and the basic Japanese criterion that they be living at home or with relatives should be maintained. These women can give stability to a work force, and care should be taken not to jeopardize this stability. Foreign personnel should in no way become personally involved with Japanese of the opposite sex in the office. If it is to be, then one or the other should leave the company's employment quietly and immediately. A broken engagement, pregnancy, or an affair will not remain secret, and the harm to morale will be enormous. Home-country sexual behavior or dating is not necessarily appropriate for Japan. Everything possible must be done to maintain a healthy environment in the office.

The work place is normally a place for Japanese to meet potential marriage partners. Unfortunately, the young women hired by a foreign firm are much more marriageable socially than most of the men hired. If they do not find a husband in two or three years, they will often move on. As an interesting aside, this also means that the general manager (but not his wife) will be called upon regularly to attend the weddings of his employees, giving a gift and making a principal wedding speech. The gift, monetary or otherwise, should be standard for weddings, funerals, births, and so forth for the company as a whole, based on the employee's rank. It should be paid for by the company as it is in reality a company gift, not an individual's gift. The general manager *is* the company, and that is why he is there. The monetary cost is far higher than what any individual should have to bear (usually $160 to $400 a gift), and this should not be an excuse not to participate. Employees' lives are the manager's corporate responsibility seven days a week.

On the other hand, a Japanese wife does not feel that attending a cocktail party for a visitor from head office is her responsibility. Office affairs are only her husband's responsibility.

Rarely will a resigning employee, especially a good one, indicate why he or she is resigning. This is often because, for Japanese, communication is based on the situation, not principles, while for Americans it is the opposite. A Japanese responds based on the situation, considering everything that has to be satisfied by his answers. Because of the nature of the society, there are many pressures that have to be taken into account in addition to the act at hand. A manager must have his antennae out in the company and the community to know why his employees are acting as they are. Young women from good families can be of great assistance in giving class to an organization and in maintaining the proper equilibrium. Like little birds, their chirping can often alert one to a problem.

University Recruiting

Eventually, any foreign corporation of substance is going to want to recruit university graduates directly out of universities. As a company grows and becomes known in Japan for a particular technology, product, or service, university recruiting becomes essential if it is not to receive only other companies' droppings. A serious recruiting program requires the participation of the general manager and the Japanese head of General Affairs.

Employees who are graduates of a particular university are an excellent introduction to the faculty for referrals. Unlike the United States, successful recruiting is not done through a placement office but through the faculty. One looks for every possible opportunity to receive an invitation to give an on-campus presentation, and in this way to enhance the visibility of the company with students and faculty. In the initial years a firm will have to send material to the university for distribution to the students. Most likely, in those early years it will receive only female applicants. At American Express in our third year of a serious campus program, there were only 3 men out of 225 applicants for jobs out of university. As a company builds its business and awareness, it consistently goes to the universities and always makes an effort to hire a few graduates every year. It is important not to turn the tap on and off, for then it is looked upon as an unreliable employer. For engineers and laboratory technicians, faculty recommendations are essential for successful recruiting.

Recruiting takes place in September at the beginning of the final semester prior to graduation in March. The students are invited to the office or to a public hall for an explanation of the company, including a serious question-and-answer period. Applications are then solicited, applicants are invited for interviews and testing, and jobs are offered by early October. The process is formalized, much as is the application for university admittance, and one must abide by the rules. Nevertheless, in a tight labor market, sign-up bonuses and other enticements do occur. In a tight labor market, moreover, employers have recently discovered a commitment is not a commitment until the employee actually starts work.

Deryck Maughan, who is in charge of Salomon Brothers in Japan, feels that in the 150 university graduates it has hired over the past five years, Salomon has an invaluable asset. Unlike foreigners from Salomon who must be Japanized or experienced Japanese who must be Salomonized, these employees from day one are Salomon and Japanese. Only one university recruit has left the company, and that was for a change of career.

MBAs

Japanese universities have only recently instituted MBA programs. To date Japanese companies have hired directly from undergraduate programs, preferring to train their staff themselves. Most of those in the few existing programs are company sponsored after working for a number of years in the company.

A difficult area is the hiring of Japanese who have had additional education overseas beyond their Japanese university degree. If they have only an overseas education, generally they were not good enough to get into a good Japanese university and should be carefully scrutinized before being hired, as should entry-level females who do not live with their parents or relatives. Many Japanese who cannot get into Japanese undergraduate universities go to American universities. They have not become part of the university alumni/alumnae network that is so important to relationship building in Japan. If they have a good Japanese university degree and have received additional university or equivalent education overseas through their own or their employer's initiative, this should be rewarded, but not to the extent it is in the United States and recently Europe. MBAs generally want to start at the top and are very hard to keep satisfied.

There is high turnover among Japanese who have obtained MBAs overseas and are recruited by foreign firms. Most Japanese MBAs overseas are company sponsored. The few who are not normally return and work in foreign companies, as they are not part of any Japanese organization. Recently, company-sponsored MBAs who returned to their companies upon graduation have been targeted by foreign headhunters as potential candidates for foreign corporations. These returnee MBAs are often frustrated by the lack of flexibility in their Japanese companies and are also aware of the astronomical salaries that their foreign classmates command right after graduation. It is almost impossible, though, for a foreign company that recruits them to satisfy their needs, if not their greed. They often make for much better employees on the rebound when they finally realize that they are going to have to stop and fit into some foreign corporation. Once they have gone to work for a foreign company, they can never return to a Japanese company.

Mid-Career Hires

Mid-career hires among Japanese employees also have a high turnover rate once they have made the first move. Moves escalate geometrically thereafter when they realize it is not life threatening and how easy and lucrative it can be. In any cross-cultural growth situation there is going to be constant strain. Tolerance and patience with urgent and unpleasant situations drops tremendously. In the long run few of these employees will remain satisfied, and they will move on to the next foreign company that is willing to buy them. Meanwhile, the original company has antagonized its other employees and heightened their latent insecurity.

Integration

The general manager and the general affairs manager must personally take responsibility for integrating MBAs and mid-career hires into the company and the departments to which they are assigned. Transplanted English-speaking Japanese staff are often rejected by their insecure colleagues. (Interestingly, transplants are not an acceptable medical procedure in Japan because society has not been willing to accept the transfer of a part of one person's body to another person's.) Even if hired for specific talents such as marketing or planning, such recruits might best be placed in General Affairs at first so that their integration can be carefully managed, as can the transfer to the next job. If this is not done, the individual will most probably find himself ostracized, if not jerked around unconscionably by colleagues who are jealous or feel threatened, to a point where he loses all perspective and is soon lost to the company.

Some foreign firms of considerable substance have found that they only have the energy and management capacity to bring two or three of these individuals aboard a year. If handled properly, however, these employees are one of the best hopes for building a management team ten to fifteen years hence. Often those hired fifteen years ago, who were outsiders themselves and generally second rate in educational qualifications, feel uncomfortable next to new employees with a good education and a working ability in both Japanese and a foreign language. The manager is constantly balancing age and talent in the organization. Unless longer-term employees can be convinced to support the company's recruiting and training endeavors, there will be malcontents at all levels.

A manager must hire MBA returnees, mid-career talent, and women for management, for if he does not, he will be like one general manager who said, "I am a dinosaur, and so is my general affairs manager." Nonetheless, such employees must be assisted in being incorporated effectively into the firm, for they are the aliens of aliens, entering an alien company. Senior Japanese must act as mentors, much the same way American schools have found that they have to have minority mentors for minority students.

Sink or Swim—They Will Sink

An excellent young Japanese was recruited from an American graduate school, which he had attended at his own expense. He had been actively involved in student organizations and was extremely well liked by his fellow American students. His English was excellent—a truly self-made young man. He entered the foreign company in Japan both enthusiastic and industrious, the type every American company is looking for at home. One evening after an office party, in my car in front of my secretary, he was swearing away in English in a conversation with me. The next morning I immediately called him into my office and explained that this was Japan, and that swearing in English was not going to do him any good at all. He then sadly related that when he entered the company his Japanese colleagues had isolated him, and that by swearing in English he was letting out his pent-up emotions. I knew that we had blown his entry and that there was little opportunity for recovery. I had personally done the recruiting in the United States, but I had not done the necessary follow-through when he joined us. We had soiled a potentially excellent employee, not only for our company but perhaps for the rest of his career.

The American "sink or swim" approach does not work in Japan. Employees must be taught to swim in unfamiliar waters and often with new strokes. This applies to middle- and senior-level entries as well as to young men and women. Giving responsibilities to a middle or senior manager in the first six months of employment is done at great risk. With over eight hundred employees in Travel Related Services in Japan, American Express has found that to bring in mid-level or senior foreigners or Japanese, it is necessary to have a six-month period of adjustment. Otherwise, assimilation does not take place, and the employee's effectiveness is minimal.

If you ask the new employee from Japan or head office to do a job while learning it, you are putting far too much of a burden on that employee. If you overwhelm them by expecting them to produce immediately, your success ratio is low. Overhire for positions. Put them in an easy task during the first year when they are learning the company. The second year is the real test of your personnel. I have twice as many managers as I would have for the size of the business when compared to the United States, Germany, or Great Britain. In effect, we carry both an expatriate and a Japanese management team.

As previously mentioned, foreigners and Japanese can be equally insecure in an environment that is truly alien to both.

A newly appointed foreign general manager of a long-established, large foreign company observed after one year:

> One of the great challenges to anyone in my position is adapting to the expectations of the younger generation of Japanese who don't necessarily accept the standards of the older people in our company. The young tigers say they joined a foreign company because they don't want to be stifled by a seniority system. "I want to be judged on my ability, my productivity and my achievement." Our older employees have sought the safety and security blanket of reverting back to the Japanese system. "Yes, we know it is a Western company, but we are doing business in Japan and we think the seniority system should play a major role." You have to look at it as constructive tension and manage it.

A foreign company that has gone native is often more Japanese than a Japanese company, in this way providing a sense of safety and freedom from anxiety for the Japanese and keeping any foreigners from head office at arm's length.

Young Foreigners

There is a good pool of foreigners twenty-five to forty years old who have learned Japanese, in some cases have Japanese wives, and are comfortable living in Japan. They can be found in non-business-oriented academic programs as well as in MBA programs and foundations. They know their way around. They have the potential to perform admirably. On the whole, the type of people who have put in the effort required to learn Japanese are pretty bright. After training them at home for two to three years, they can be sent to Japan with a specific product or service knowledge. They can then broaden themselves in Japan. They also have a Western perspective when looking at things Japanese. It is important that they have been trained in product skills and services and are not just looked upon as translators by head office. A foreign general manager who becomes actively involved in the recruiting process at home can be instrumental in hiring such employees. Along with the budget presentation, this is perhaps the most important trip home for the general manager. Since budgets are often presented in the late autumn, the timing is perfect for a dual effort. These individuals are the potential expatriate management for the future. To hope they will be developed through osmosis is ridiculous.

A major problem is foreign employees' promotions versus Japanese employees' promotions. There is no such thing as a truly multinational personnel policy, no matter how much lip service is paid by the chairman or vice-president of personnel in head office. If younger foreigners are respected by the Japanese, then there is an acknowledgment and understanding, if not an acceptance, that they are moving in two different worlds. That is surely the best that can be hoped for. A Japanese general manager of a major international firm, when asked about a foreign board member being younger than Japanese board members, responded: "No problem. What the hell, he's going to disappear in three years." He also said: "With a mixture of Japanese and foreigners in management, no one feels occupied."

Lastly, Japanese management, one or two deep, eventually have to have as good an understanding of the corporate culture as do the traveling expatriates. That means true overseas working assignments with management responsibility. This is a difficult goal to reach but one for which to strive.

Unless we think we do everything perfectly at home, reflect on what an American general manager experienced:

> The hardest personnel issue was selling New York on my Japanese operational manager when New York couldn't even communicate with London operational people because the cultural gap was so huge. I have to admit I couldn't understand those guys from Brooklyn myself.

Managing in an Alien Environment

Constant rumors about inconsequential matters are one of the most difficult issues for foreign general managers in Japan. The Japanese in a foreign company have an idealized view about what a Japanese company should be, often precisely because they are outsiders in their own society and do not know what a comparable Japanese company is like. With the factionalism that exists one sometimes wonders how Japanese companies get anything done.

They appreciate the problems of factionalism within their organizations, however, and religiously guard against it or break it up through horizontal transfers. Every transfer is not necessarily a promotion, and foreign companies must understand this concept. If left unattended, factionalism increases and there is constant infighting. Employees will single out an individual, Japanese or foreign, find a weak point, and go at him or her like sharks. "They look for it. That is what is amazing." One way or the other, the problem must be sifted through and controlled or the organization becomes dysfunctional. When and if the manager gets to the core of the problem, he must act firmly and relentlessly to clean up the mess and let it be known that a continuance will not be tolerated under any circumstances, no matter who the perpetrators are. It is particularly important that outside visitors are not used as direct conduits to head office for complaints. If visitors approach the Japanese staff or are approached directly and respond, they will confuse loyalties. Any dialogue must be in the presence of the general manager or his clearly identified designate.

When it is difficult to tell who is working on whom, it might be appropriate to go out for a little lubrication. Generally, those who make the most noise drinking are the worst employees, so the manager has to know when, where, and how to take them out without getting everyone involved. He also has to learn how to isolate them. Americans often do not know how to separate people. Foreign staff should be selective about when they go drinking with the employees. They should be friendly on these occasions but also remember their rank in the company and behave accordingly. The Japanese often say that one is not accountable for what one says when drunk. This can, of course, be true with peers and close friends. Otherwise, it is absolutely not true. Such behavior would do a great deal of harm to a career in a respectable Japanese company. Japanese in foreign companies will use this as an excuse, however, to tell you everything wrong with the company and even with you, knowing full well what they are doing. The first time it starts, the individual or individuals must be politely cut off and told privately the next day that they represent themselves and the company wherever and whatever they are doing, no exceptions, and you know they understand.

The word will spread quickly throughout the office.

Sometimes it suits me when they play rough with each other. We're not the Salvation Army. If they know you know, they are no fools. There are ways to pass messages when things go too far.

Foreign visitors again should be cautioned not to get drawn in, and above all not to become an ear for perceived or real grievances at such sessions. Any problems should be referred to the general manager immediately for resolution.

Foreigners operating in this atmosphere can feel pretty insecure as well. Their Japanese staff will often refer to the Japanese way if it appears advantageous to them personally; the head office, meanwhile, will refer to the company way if it appears advantageous, or will try to encourage the foreign management to be more Japanese than the Japanese. Perhaps the personnel manager in head office has just attended a seminar on Japanese personnel management in a Japanese company or read a book on Matsushita, both of which have little to do with life in a foreign company in Japan. A foreign company is neither at home nor truly in Japan, and it can never be sure which way is best or which should dominate. It is a separate breed. It is neither a white dog nor a brown dog, but the offspring of the two—a spotted dog. Every spotted dog is its own breed, and it is this new breed that is to be cultivated and nourished by the management and employees of a foreign firm in Japan.

So how does one nourish the spotted dog? One lets the dog know who his parents are. Managers are not changed every two or three years. Management and staff get to know each other and their families, their education and desires, as well as the company's history, its present and future plans. The company creates as secure an environment as possible, because at times it is an island among 123 million people.

Making your company "their company" over the years is the most difficult management job. You can't make that happen. You have to create the circumstances through what the Japanese refer to as a warm, wet atmosphere that permits it to occur.

Friends of a Japanese usually are his classmates or officemates, not someone he meets in the normal course of business, as is often the case in other countries. Peer group classmates and officemates become lifelong friends. This bonding must be encouraged in a foreign company. Older and younger workers have relationships similar to that between teacher and student, respectful and confidential. The older workers help the younger. It is a principal part of their jobs. Age is very important in the social structure. One middle-aged foreigner said about age, "I hope to achieve it." Foreigners, particularly Americans, are prone to calling a business acquaintance, no matter what the age difference, a friend, and they make the mistake in Japan of thinking they have a friend in or out of the office when all they have is a business relationship. Perhaps in ten or twenty years it does become a friendship. A good adage to remember is that an American can never become a Japanese while a Japanese can always become an American. Nevertheless, unity must be encouraged in the office.

People who come over from our company want to call everybody by their first name. Call me Jim, call me Joe. Everybody is on the same level. That means we know each other. It does not mean that at all if he is your boss. Japanese don't call each other by their first or last name unless they are in the same entering class in the company. They call each other by their titles. I wince every time my boss tells our Japanese staff to call him Don. A Japanese would never call his boss Don or Taro or Jiro. If a Japanese employee calls my boss Don in a meeting, the people who hear him are going to think he is somewhat unusual or he has become too American or he is no longer as Japanese as he should be and is learning foreign manners.

Openness permits group participation. As in a family, there are no secrets in a company operating in Japan, whether Japanese or foreign. Working in Japan is like living in a gigantic boarding house. To cultivate an energetic, healthy, and solid organization, the foreign firm operating in Japan must instill affection, continuity, and security, while clearly making known the purpose for its existence and what it hopes to accomplish. It must keep its goals in mind at all times and communicate them to everyone in the company, at home and in Japan.

Job Descriptions

Job descriptions can provide stability for a foreign corporation in Japan, although they are totally unnecessary in a Japanese corporation because everyone knows each other's responsibilities and where they rank vis-à-vis each other. In a foreign corporation, management generally changes far too often, leaving unclear lines of authority and responsibility. The job description gives one the comfort of knowing one's responsibilities and those of others around one. It also lets the rotating foreign management know what their and their employees' roles are. Lastly, it curtails the men playing games with the women's job responsibilities.

There are no maps for the foreign corporation in Japan, for the foreign general manager or for the Japanese employees. This translates into a lack of consistency. Everything is helter-skelter. When there are no maps in Japan, everything goes haywire since there is not a defined community. The familiar signs are not on the main street.

In a foreign company, the Rules of Employment are the only map.

Rules of Employment

Much of the above is formalized through the Rules of Employment. Formal, written Rules of Employment are required under the Labor Standards Law once a company has ten employees. Article 89 of the Labor Standards Law stipulates that Rules of Employment should cover virtually all practices, policies, and benefits affecting employees. The rules must be submitted to the Labor Standards Office along with a statement of opinion from a "majority representative" of the employees. There can be disagreement on this statement of opinion, but the Labor Standards Office must accept the rules unless they contain illegal clauses or clauses that provide benefits inferior to those in the Labor Standards Law.[4]

In that the rules offer an opportunity within the law to establish a corporate philosophy in writing, they are important not only as a legal document but as a proactive management tool. These rules are specific, binding, and extremely important to the general manager in managing his business. Many foreign general managers, unless they assisted in writing the rules when the operation was established in Japan, are hardly aware of their existence.

---

[4] Thomas J. Nevins, *Labor Pains and the Gaijin Boss* (Tokyo: The Japan Times, 1984), p. 20. This is the only book in English on the subject but should only be read for questions to ask an attorney.

Worse yet, sometimes they do things that set regrettable precedents that do not conform with the rules themselves. Often this requires amending the rules at the least opportune time, during a labor problem. One general manager stated, "I wish somebody had explained them to me right up-front. They are a living document."

As soon as a general manager learns that he is being assigned to Japan, he should request a copy of the existing rules, or he should initiate upon arrival in a start-up situation a meeting with his attorneys to establish rules. He should emphasize to the attorneys that their responsibility is to protect him under the law, but that he wishes to have his corporate philosophy and personality permeate the rules. Care should be taken not to make the rules so onerous that negativism permeates. It has not been unusual for advisers on rules to overemphasize tightening down the hatches in fair weather in anticipation of foul weather rather than putting up the sails when the sun is out and the wind behind you.

Since the employees generally affected are Japanese, the proper spirit means that the Japanese-language version should be binding, not the English-language version used by the foreign general managers or head office. Careful translation is therefore essential. As a word of caution, these rules can be binding on and also protective of foreign employees, particularly if dismissal becomes an issue. They are not binding upon corporate directors unless so specified in a separate contract. Japan is not a legalistic society, but it is a society of rules. Those managing a company had better understand how these employee rules apply to the business. To put it simply, law is the codification of rules, so never underestimate the importance of the rules in Japan. But one still has to know how people relate to each other, effectively or ineffectively, what makes the company tick, and how to get things done. One European company closed its office on Christmas day for many years. Since all its suppliers and customers remained open, the company went to its employees and said, "Let's work on Christmas day and take another Japanese holiday." The response: "Absolutely not, that is the only day the golf courses are free!"

Of course, the Rules of Employment and the company organizational chart will not tell you everything. That is why the effective general manager will spend 50 percent of his time on personnel.

Personnel Problems

Two areas of business can bring a company to a standstill: credit/accounting and personnel problems. Personnel problems in Japan can drag out for years if they involve the courts, and few foreign companies have been winners. The problem can be avoided by doing the rules right in the first place and then using them as an effective management tool. Since the manager is trying to mold together a group of social outsiders and mavericks, however, problems will at times arise. A foreign company is not part of the social fabric of the society, so it is often not in a position to apply social or extralegal pressures as a Japanese company can. Therefore, the original employee investigation and recommendation letters are the best recourse for keeping troublemakers in line until such time as they can be turned around or managed out of the company. If at any time a manager thinks he has a serious personnel problem with an individual or group of individuals, he should discuss the situation with his attorneys and their labor advisers immediately. This is especially true when dismissal, with or without cause, is necessary. Don't wait for something to happen. Don't rely on what worked elsewhere, and don't follow procedures mandated by head office.

Foreign attorneys at law firms that work for foreign corporations in Japan have had to spend an inordinate amount of time on personnel issues, especially when they have been placed by a foreign company's management in a reactive rather than a proactive role. Japanese Rules of Employment are governed by Japanese law and courts, not by any other jurisdiction. It is not unusual for a foreign company to have to pay years of salary to an employee whom the courts determine has been wrongfully dismissed and then to have to reinstate that same employee in a lifetime job. As previously stated, personnel problems can bring an operation to a standstill and can do incalculable harm to future plans.

If I were to repeat my career, I would do one thing differently. I would be very careful in dealing with unions and probably would not have terminated the three leftist employees. I would be much more understanding of labor's wishes than what our headquarters' employee relations people tried to advise us. I think they tried to apply their experience to the Japanese situation. That was one area where we erred very badly. The headquarters' people deal with unions in typical American fashion. It is gain or lose. It is always, if we give something, we ought to receive something back from the union to balance out. That was their philosophy. That was wrong. We did that, and it caused serious problems.

Unions

One area often discussed and debated by the gaijin kaisha is whether or not it should have a union. In Japanese companies, unions are organized along company lines rather than trade or industrial lines. The employer must bargain with every union that demands this of management. This is because Article 28 of the Constitution guarantees the right to organize and bargain collectively. Even a union with two members is entitled to bargain. Some foreign companies feel it is best to establish their own enterprise union in the company, making every effort to have their employees feel comfortable and therefore controllable. Others prefer a strong, effective General Affairs Department that keeps its fingers on the pulse daily and avoids a union.

In Japan I use my personnel committee on compensation and promotion. Head office goes crazy every time I say I am giving something to the committee to discuss. They look upon it as a threat. I look upon it as a tool, not a threat. They are not going to ram something through that the general manager is upset about, nor do they expect the general manager to ram something through that they are obviously upset about. Basically anything that is discussed, that is fair, that is reasonable, and that is laid out in the open is accepted. It would be nice if it were done in the U.S. That personnel committee is a jewel, a superb safety valve, and it keeps the union out.

A foreign general manager considering introducing or permitting the growth of a union or unions should once again remember that his company is not Japanese, and that an organization that he probably has little ability to control might become a real headache one day, especially if it brings outside elements into the company through affiliation with external organizations, as happened with the original foreign banks in Japan. If a union is a fact of life, then the general manager should be well informed about its activities. The best young employees should be encouraged to be active in the union so that the General Affairs Department through them can be proactive in its participation with the union's membership. These young people, after achieving union management responsibilities, should be promoted up and out in their mid-thirties to corporate management responsibility, much as Japanese companies do. Nevertheless, with all the complexities and differences of running a foreign corporation in Japan, one less organization to deal with is certainly preferable. As in school, other forms of letting off steam and bonding can be provided: sports teams, classes, outings and weekend recreational facilities.

Language Study

One class that is essential is English, and perhaps also a second language for non-English-speaking head offices. Japanese children begin studying English at the latest in junior high or middle school. The students often become quite proficient in reading and even writing, but with a lack of native-language informants, the spoken language has been historically weak, considering the number of years studied. For a Japanese to enter the management ranks of a foreign corporation, English or another appropriate foreign language is essential. This is not to say that one hires for language ability (one is very careful *not* to hire for language ability alone), but its subsequent learning should be mandatory. It is the company's responsibility to provide first-class language instruction. There are many fly-by-night language schools and inexperienced foreign part-time teachers. These will not suffice. Experienced English-as-a-second-language teachers should motivate, encourage, and grade employees, to enable the company to learn if those employees wish to be part of management.

Language study is not an extracurricular activity. Employees must know they will be graded fairly, separately on ability and effort, and that their performance will be recognized in promotions and annual salary reviews. If the Japanese staff wish to move to the top, they have to have excellent English and broad cultural adaptability. Give them every opportunity to develop these skills. If they do not, they should be told that their future is limited, but they should not be fired. With most foreigners illiterate in Japanese and likely to remain so, the ability of the staff to speak, read, and write English or the language of headquarters becomes critical to the introduction of technology, ideas, and culture. It is also a necessity for any Japanese staff who wish to be assigned overseas and to acquire knowledge that they can apply in managing an overseas post themselves, or in subsequent management in Japan. This whole language process is difficult at best and requires minute attention to the teaching and learning process if it is to be successful.

Foreigners should enter a compulsory Japanese-language program and be tested as the Japanese studying English. Attitude for both is most important, for teamwork is the goal. The Japanese will appreciate the interest in and the effort made to learn their language. Foreign staff in turn will appreciate the effort being made by the Japanese to learn their language. Japanese is so different from any Western language that the effort expended by either party to learn the other's language is enormous.

Language is the discipline of the culture. You should at least try, because it is the most sincere interest you can take in a country and its people. Language opens insights to the minds of the people and their culture. Most foreign businessmen start out studying the language and then they reach a business crisis or a language problem and drop their study. They apologize for stopping and are then on the defensive in the society, which is doubly unfortunate because they don't know what they don't know. It is a real struggle. You just have to keep at it.

Defined Responsibilities and Compensation

Matrix management is a phrase that is not in the vocabulary of a successful general manager in Japan. Japanese do not understand dual reporting and the dual loyalty required. They are accustomed to nice, neat vertical structures. They implicitly do not like matrix, lateral management. Since Japan is a hierarchical society, they do not think of cooperation in a matrix sense. They only think of cooperation within a group or with groups. The general manager is responsible for communicating with head office, and he and his foreign department heads should keep this burden off the

Japanese staff until such time as they have become familiar with head office staff, politics, and culture. They are not American, German, or British, and nothing will break them faster than to be thrown into the head-office ring without lengthy preparation. They will not know how to interpret what is being said or written, and they will soon find themselves innocently misinterpreting or, worse yet, caught up in office politics. They should be kept out of it for their own sake, and visitors should not be allowed, in their own narrow interests, to suck them into it. If they are, everyone will be the loser, especially the Japanese employees, and the general manager won't have a clue as to what is going on in his office.

Employees know their own responsibilities, and they know management's. They know how they fit on a general organization chart, but this should not be so well defined that their group becomes more important than the whole. They also know that their responsibilities will change in the future, and that they are as likely to be moved laterally as vertically. Employees will not be demoted unless they fail to make an honest effort or they do something in violation of the Rules of Employment. We never demote our own children, and there is no reason to demote our own employees as long as they are part of the company.

Job Titles

How are people rewarded as they help build a substantial business in Japan? Job titles—who you are on a name card—are extremely important to Japanese. Titles are an intangible benefit of great magnitude to the individual in a hierarchical society. They have to be Japanese for a Japanese subsidiary, but for a branch they can be the titles of the parent.

It is legally impossible for an individual to be president of a branch, though one can play games with titles, making a branch head a "president," as American Express's branch in Japan does. Foreigners from head office will play along with this for their own prestige, as they know where they really rank in head office. The Japanese know that if they have a fictitious title it can be eliminated tomorrow, which is one reason they clearly prefer working for a subsidiary rather than a branch. Most also know that there is no place for them in the head-office hierarchy and are therefore much more interested in the title they can obtain in a Japanese incorporated company. There is a great deal of title inflation in foreign companies to make up for either real or perceived inadequacies.

Most Western managers do not anticipate the seriousness with which Japanese take titles. In fact, they are second only to job content and above money. Titles represent status in an extremely status-conscious society and must be handled with great care. A person with a senior title, even though he has been moved aside, can run amok since no one will put him down or tell him what to do. Titles should be given in accordance with age, job content, and the company's relative status in the corporate society. At senior levels they should also be understandable in head office. This can require dual Japanese and head-office titles.

Corporate titles are standard for all Japanese companies, from *kaicho* (chairman) and *shacho* (president) to *kakaricho* (chief clerk). They are therefore readily understandable inside and outside the company. Playing with such titles by adding lengthy job descriptions can cause confusion outside and, more important, internal political jockeying. To inflate titles is in the long run to make a mockery of the company and will often make it difficult to bring along capable younger people. The entrenched mediocre will not permit their ascent. To be stingy, however, destroys morale, creating a we-they attitude.

All title changes should be reviewed by senior management. They should be consistent and understandable throughout the company and in the community, and they should be something the company can live with as long as the employee is with the company.

> One problem in Japan is when you give a Japanese the title of vice-president, he immediately assumes he is no longer a worker. He is a thinker and withdraws. His productivity goes straight down, and that is frightening. He is no longer an employee; he is management; he is looking at the big picture. You don't have that in Western culture. As a result, we have become very careful about whom we give titles to and what those titles are.

Name cards should be routinely called in once a year to confirm that games are not being played between English and Japanese.

All titles should reflect the level of responsibility and the job content.

Salaries

Salaries are always difficult to deal with when you are a foreign company in an alien environment. Historically the situation in Japan was much easier. The strong dollar meant that yen-translated salaries were generally reasonable. Moreover, Japanese salary ranges have been and remain considerably less than in America and usually less than in Europe. CEO salaries in Japan today for major Japanese corporations average approximately $330,000 including salary, bonus, and incentives, as opposed to $983,000 in the United States and $403,000 in Germany.[5] The perks of a Japanese CEO are minimal compared with the wealth an American executive can accumulate, and they are only in effect as long as the individual remains associated with the company. The U.S. CEO's pay is many times higher than an entry-level professional's, while in Japan it is much closer. One reason is that the Japanese board is almost entirely in-house workers, which keeps the superstar syndrome in its proper place. The best university graduates receive no more than $25,000 when entering a company in Japan, and thereafter their salary moves in accordance with the wage increase ranges agreed to by the in-house board and the in-house union. There is little room for the superstar disparities and much less of the feeling of, "If he can have it, why can't I?"

When recruiting, foreign companies have historically offered higher salaries at all levels than their Japanese competitors. Now that the yen has appreciated markedly against the dollar, it is difficult for American and many European firms to continue to follow this practice. Foreign firms have attempted to entice employees by offering shorter workdays and weeks, particularly no work on Saturdays—often because the expatriates don't want to work on Saturdays nor do the visitors from head office. This means that they have tried to be competitive with lesser-quality employees working fewer hours. This is a tough way to compete.

---

[5]*Fortune*, June 6, 1988, p. 78.

It is ludicrous to limit the workday and week to less than the Labor Standards Law permits, especially when overtime is involved. But foreign company after foreign company does just that, resulting in less work at greater cost than their Japanese competition.

American companies (and to a lesser extent European companies) have been prone to sell the American concept of promotion and compensation according to performance, emphasizing the individual's worth and reward over the group's. In that the Japanese company generally emphasizes the group, this leads to the foreign company recruiting the maverick, the individual, if you will, as opposed to the team player. The major American banks and airlines did this in Japan in the 1950s and later paid an enormous price in labor unrest, court cases, and industry unionization as opposed to enterprise unions. For several decades American companies showed they had learned from this experience. But with the entry of the investment banker and his European/American recruiting and pay practices, everything learned in the past flew out the window in the mid-1980s. The cost of hiring young Japanese has been inflated, especially for those with overseas work or educational experience, not only in finance but across the board, for the same headhunters are recruiting for all foreign companies. As the market has become considerably larger, so has the demand. Salaries are often astronomical by Japanese standards, turning the heads of even the most sensible and making for probably the most unhealthy hiring environment for foreign firms since the mid-1960s.

In 1988, one American bank, which has had considerable problems at home, recruited a thirty-eight-year-old foreign exchange trader at $500,000 per annum from a middling Japanese bank. This individual then blabbered to the foreign press about his salary and the lack of opportunity at his previous employment. How do the other Japanese employees at his new bank feel? The Japanese community surely feels he is nothing but a money grabber who is chasing dollars, and they will treat him accordingly in his business dealings. He is single and therefore does not have to worry about a wife, in-laws, or children's futures. Did his new employer have any idea what they were doing in Japan or was New York/London their only reference? One suspects the latter.

What happens to all the foreign investment firms with their overcompensated, overrated staff when the music stops at the same time? One can only expect the type of labor problems faced by the early banking and airline entries and a further spillover into the credibility gap of working for a foreign firm in Japan. Salary imbalance within an organization in Japan can only lead to morale, labor, and management problems. One wonders how many foreign general managers would participate in this salary inflation if they knew they were going to be responsible for Japan ten years hence.

Housing and Recreational Facilities

Because of land costs it is too late for the foreign corporations who have not already done so to compensate their employees by buying real estate for company housing or recreational facilities, which Japanese companies provide. Employees must therefore be compensated in other ways, such as loans for housing at a certain level of management. Most foreign head offices do not make housing available to their home-office employees and are therefore unsympathetic to any housing arrangements. In Japan they had better adjust their thinking if they wish to retain good employees. A housing loan is much more binding than a raise. Recreational and team facilities, such as tea ceremony, baseball, and ski weekends, should also be provided. These are good ways to bond employees to the company and to each other. It is also beneficial if the foreign employees participate, if only as an umpire or line judge.

Company Outing

An institution peculiar to Japan is the annual autumn company outing in which all the employees participate. Arranged by the General Affairs Department with the employees' social committee, this is quite an event. It is not inexpensive, since participants normally go by bus for three or four hours to a mountain or seaside resort. All costs in a foreign company are generally borne by the company, though this is not necessarily the case in Japanese companies. In effect, the cost is one more way for the foreign company to compensate its employees in lieu of alternatives. Drinks and food are broken out as soon as the bus pulls away from the curb, and with song and scheduled pit stops they continue until the group arrives at the precisely ordained moment at the resort's front door. The men sleep in assigned rooms together and the women the same. Hot baths are taken communally, albeit by separate sexes, and everyone proceeds on schedule to a mammoth room for dinner, entertainment, and more sake. By now the adult fraternity/sorority party is getting very merry. By the time the dinner is over and the groups break up to continue on their own, everything is pretty much out of control until everyone stumbles on the bus at the prescribed time in the morning and sleeps most of the way home.

Some do not appreciate these events at all, but the peer pressure to participate is great. As with the Christmas parties or *bonenkai* (forget the year) parties, the foreign staff should participate but mind their behavior, because the potential for problems are real. It is best to ignore what you can't control by going to sleep after the dinner.

Salary Reviews and Administration

One of the most sensible aspects of Japanese salary administration is that everyone is reviewed and raises are given at the same time. This permits management to compare all peer groups simultaneously and to plan transfers and raises accordingly. It also permits salary scales to be related on a comparable basis to others in the industry.

Salary reviews take place annually in March and are effective in April, since April is the beginning of the school year and the time when school graduates therefore join a company. Any new or mid-year hires should join with the understanding that after completing a satisfactory probationary period—preferably six months—they will be reviewed and salary increases made on a pro-rata annualized basis, whether at the time of the postprobationary review or the annual review. The probationary period is extremely important because during this period an employee can be dismissed without any repercussions, or he or she can be turned around if that appears worthwhile. It is a critical adjustment period that should be managed formally by the General Affairs Department from day one of a person's employment.

The Japanese are accustomed to and expect this system, and it is in a firm's interest to follow it whenever possible, deviating only on an exceptional basis—for example, a senior promotion. It is much more equitable and easier to administer than any other system. It does lend itself to promotion by time in rank and therefore seniority, but this can easily be balanced with lateral transfers that free up job slots for the next generation and therefore permit rewarding for performance. An emphasis on individual performance, beyond a merit increase of a few percentage points over the standard raise given all employees, will lead to more management problems than it is worth. Some will say that the only way to attract aggressive Japanese is by offering the foreign rewards of remuneration according to performance. The risk associated with the resulting salary imbalances are enormous and should be clearly understood. Foreign firms have to learn this if they are serious about building a stable employee environment in growth companies. As previously mentioned, there are no secrets in a Japanese company. Everyone knows everyone else's salary. This exchange of information cannot be stopped. In such a situation, it is better to distinguish performance through minor percentage differences in salaries while clearly recognizing performance through leadership positions, committee and study group participation, and overseas assignments.

This salary structure, including annual reviews for everyone at the same time, also allows much more flexibility in both lateral and vertical moves since the restrictions imposed by salary imbalances are eliminated. An individual can be moved easily, for example, from Sales to General Affairs.

One area where foreign firms can choose to differ from most Japanese companies is in giving women the same opportunities and the same pay as men. As previously mentioned, women can be some of a firm's best employees, and if they are, they should be compensated accordingly. Their performance and loyalty will more than make up for any backbiting by insecure male employees.

Bonuses in Japan are paid regularly every six months, in December and June. Today in foreign companies they reflect less the company's performance than part of the regular wage scale. Instead of the salary being paid in twelve equal installments, it is paid in twelve equal installments plus two other agreed-to monthly amounts, for example, a three-month salary equivalent in both June and December. A little history is important. When Japanese companies were strapped for cash after the war, they paid bonuses to delay their cash outlay and thus improve their cash flow. Pensions became tied to years of service and monthly salary, which excluded bonuses. In times of difficulty management's salaries and bonuses are cut first and then employees' bonuses and salaries. For foreign firms to be competitive in hiring, bonuses should remain fixed; they should be adjusted only in times of financial emergency. They should be paid in line with the overall salary structure of the industry. One must avoid the situation of setting and negotiating bonuses twice a year in addition to annual salary increases. Many foreign general managers have found themselves unknowingly paying their first retiree's lump-sum retirement payment based not only on base monthly salary but also on bonuses. Once done, it is hard to go back when the error is discovered and say to later retirees that it will not be done henceforth. This is one more reason to know the Rules of Employment and to have one's best Japanese employee running General Affairs.

It is best not to pay employees—even senior Japanese management—bonuses from head office or to give them stock ownership in a Japanese subsidiary or the parent unless one is willing to experience an inordinate number of legal and personnel problems. Pay them well according to Japanese standards, whether that is higher or lower than the scale in the head office. They will not understand if they exercise a stock option and later find, when they need to sell, that the price has declined. They will not understand why some participate and others do not. If a company is doing it to avoid taxable income in Japan, it is demonstrating that it is willing to break the rules. If it is done because ownership in the local subsidiary will give employees a feeling of ownership, that can be good, but it can be awful if someday they disagree with how the company is run. In any event, any head-office bonus, stock option or stock gift, or subsidiary ownership should be reviewed with the company's attorneys long before any discussion with employees. More likely than not a decision will be made to administer salaries in Japan as the Japanese do. It will not be cheap, but it will be fairer and more understandable to employees.

Commissions and Performance Bonuses

Two other areas of salary administration crop up with cross-cultural management. Salesmen elsewhere in the world are often paid on commission. In Japan, if an outside agency is used to perform the sales function, for whatever reason, this is perfectly acceptable. If the salesmen are a company's own employees, it is disastrous unless the intention is to make them totally separate for life from the rest of the employees. A separatist concept is normally not wise. Commissions also take salesmen out of the annual peer group review for all those of the same approximate age who graduated from school at the same time. It also makes it virtually impossible to transfer them into other corporate functions, such as General Affairs or Marketing, since very likely their salaries would have to be reduced. This is obviously not the way to build a team of management and staff. Salesmen are regular members of the staff, like all other departments; their outstanding performances can be announced at sales meetings and weekend outings. Leave it at announcements and golf balls.

Many readers will say, "Western-style performance bonuses have become de rigueur in Western financial institutions in Japan, particularly in securities houses and in the capital-markets groups of the banks." Nonetheless, this does not mean they are the way to manage Japanese staff. Commissions and bonuses are fatal to the group concept, as they separate the high performers from the group, who say, "We helped him achieve but we are excluded from the reward. That is not fair." In the end, they ostracize the high performers, which is exactly the opposite of what happens in the United States. The capital-markets manager of one U.S. bank's head office paid its Japanese capital-markets people a bonus directly from head office without telling the Tokyo general manager. When the general manager learned of it and told her this was self-destructive, she responded that the payment had been made through the bank's accounting firm and only the recipients would know. This is simply naive in light of the fact that there are no secrets in a Japanese office. Any such decisions must be made with the general manager's concurrence and approval.

You can get more out of your staff in Japan than in the United States, but you had better know how to do it. Otherwise, they will get more out of you than the staff will in America. When your Japanese staff tells you you can't do it and you know you should, you have got to be prepared to say: "Well I just did it; you understand why I did it; and if I have to, I will do it again."

Managing outside can be both transactional and by relationship. Managing on the inside is always by relationship. The general manager has to know whom to listen to, how long to listen, and when to tell them to go back to work. That is why he must never forget to spend the requisite time on personnel. Otherwise, he will be run by his employees, his suppliers, his customers, and above all by his competition.

3
Competition

COMPETITION should logically be the first chapter in any corporate decision on whether to and how to do business in Japan. Today, for many products and services, the Japanese set the competitive standards. A company should never decide to come to Japan or significantly enhance its presence there without thoroughly researching and understanding the existing and potential competition. Even before that analysis takes place, however, the strengths of the company at home must be analyzed. What are the resources that permit the company to be competitive in Japan? Many detailed questions must be asked and answered about the company itself in order to understand the costs of getting into the battle on Japanese soil. When management is sure that it knows itself, then it can try to understand Japan and its competitive environment in the context of the business.

Bill Hall, formerly of ASI Market Research (Japan), Inc., and currently President of Sterling-Winthrop, Inc. in Japan, is a frequent commentator on Japanese business practices at international marketing conferences:

When I say competitor analysis, I mean really in-depth knowledge of what your competition is doing. I remember giving a paper at a worldwide competitor analysis conference several years ago. The British approach at the conference could best be summarized as "What we mean, chaps, is we read the Chairman of the Board's statement in the Annual Report, check newspaper clippings, and somehow or other divine from that what our competitors are doing." The American approach was basically, "What we mean by competitor analysis is that we talk to our securities analyst."

My presentation on the Japanese approach to competitor analysis covered topics such as how many trucks leave the warehouse per hour; how many are leased versus owned; what is the confidential floor price below the standard wholesale floor price; what percentage of sales is given as remuneration to wholesalers for the sales and inventory reports they submit; what is the basic rebate, campaign rebate, etc. by major wholesalers? As my presentation unfolded you could see an increasing degree of astonishment on the faces of the audience, but having this level of knowledge about one's competition is standard Japanese business practice. They spend fortunes on finding out what is going on. When you go into negotiations, they know more about your position than you probably do. We do this type of work all the time to even up the odds for Western clients. We give them at least equal information when they go into negotiations. If they screw up, that is their problem, but at least they start off equal. Most secondary-published information is rubbish. Americans, unlike the Europeans, have always thought that looking at the garbage of their competition was not nice, was "un-American," until it was too late.

A foreign company operating in Japan must study not only the foreign competition in the marketplace, but, more important, the Japanese competition. Far too often, foreign companies, whether airlines, banks, securities houses, or cash register companies, have studied their foreign competition, only to find that the Japanese competition has surrounded and engulfed them. Historically, for the foreigner without language ability and without staff who could network as part of the corporate fabric of Japan, it has been difficult to learn what the Japanese are about. Today the facilities are available in the community to do competitive studies.

The line is thin between industrial espionage and competitor analysis, but trained professional investigators using a Japanese "human relations" approach in interviews with wholesalers, retailers, trade associations, and banks, and with competitors talking about other competitors as well as their own industries, can obtain detailed and reliable information. The approach is like the best investigative journalism—following up leads, cross-checking with various sources, and so forth. It is time consuming and costly, as studies take two to three months, but it is completely legal and aboveboard and should be pursued with vigor.

Confidentiality

One of the first questions asked is about how a company is perceived by the competition. Are they aware of its plans, and if so, where are the leaks in the organization or in the supply fulfillment network—bank, advertising agency, etc.? Although one accepts that there are no secrets in Japan, certain information is more important to protect than other information. One concentrates every effort on maintaining confidentiality in research, new product introduction, and strategy for advertising campaigns. Exclusivity arrangements in writing are made with the advertising agency, public relations firm, and market research firm. If they say that exclusivity arrangements do not exist in Japan, another firm can be found that understands the company's needs. This often will not be possible with legal or accounting firms because of the limited number that can handle foreign businesses, but they understand confidentiality and Chinese walls. Staff must be told from their first day of hire the importance of confidentiality, and that any questions about the company's business should be referred up the line to the departmental heads. At the same time they should keep their eyes and ears open and report to their managers any competitive information they receive.

Sumitomo Bank once told a client that I was a competitor of the bank. The client found this unusual and asked how. The response was, "Sumitomo Bank deals in knowledge and so does Mr. Huddleston." The Japanese understand perfectly the value of knowing corporate history, who is important and how you are going to work that knowledge. Bankers in Japan are accustomed to entering clients' offices freely, asking questions, and receiving answers. Except for information specifically germane to lending arrangements, this should be nipped in the bud, unless one wants the Japanese competition to know exactly what is going on in the office. If information is to be traded, do it at the very top, with full understanding of the ramifications under U.S. as well as Japanese law or any other jurisdiction involved.

Trade Associations

One of the most important arenas for learning about competitors is through membership in corporate trade associations. These associations exist for almost any line of business in Japan, from city banks to regional banks to credit cards to petrochemicals to imported writing pens. The associations are generally nonprofit, legal associations (*shadan hojin*) formed under the civil code and supposedly subject to Fair Trade Commission guidelines. One says supposedly, because the discussion that takes place, both formal and informal, within these groups is far more extensive and revealing than in the United States. A former member of the Fair Trade Commission once said to me that as a member of the commission he was placed in a very difficult position, because as a member of his industry trade association, which was excluding my company as a member, he was clearly violating the wishes of the Fair Trade Commission. That this was said in front of an independent translator says much about the enforcement desires or capabilities of the Fair Trade Commission. Nevertheless, the Japanese government requires the industry associations to be the watchdogs and spokesmen for each industry. This allows little room for an individual company to go its own way in its relationships with the government, particularly in heavily regulated industry sectors such as financial services, petroleum, and pharmaceuticals.

The foreign general manager faces two monumental problems with his company participating in these association meetings. Can he participate in Japanese, and if not, what is his designated employee discussing and agreeing to in these meetings? One foreign general manager asked his designate if prices were being fixed in the association meetings. He was assured they were not, only to find out his designate's level was not doing so, but salesmen in a subcommittee were. He just was not asking the right question of the right person. The American company, along with the others, was fined when this was revealed, and neither the head office nor the general manager was pleased when it appeared in the press. He summed up his feelings by saying, "It is difficult to get into the trade associations. Once you get in, you wish you hadn't"

These associations also often make political contributions, particularly to the party of long-standing power, the Liberal Democrats. For U.S. corporations this presents serious legal problems; it is important, therefore, to have in writing that the dues a company contributes will be segregated and not used for political purposes.

All of the above lead to a natural reluctance on the part of many

Japanese industry trade associations to have foreign corporate and individual participants. Reluctance might be too mild a word, for it is often outright refusal. There is a great fear that what takes place in the meetings might become public knowledge in a foreign jurisdiction and in turn in Japan. Then the Japanese participants themselves will be in trouble. Nevertheless, in any industry or service, this is where market sharing and prices are often agreed to and where, in newer industries, standards are set, such as VAN systems, point-of-sales terminals, and bulk-mail postal rate recommendations. Not to participate or to be excluded is unacceptable if one wants to compete in Japan. If a firm is excluded, it should seek home-government assistance with the ministry responsible for the industry to see that it can become a member, operating within the laws of Japan and not participating when it violates the laws of the home country if jurisdiction exists over its operation in Japan.

A clear example of the importance of belonging is the experience of one association's only foreign corporate member, whose foreign general manager speaks fluent Japanese, at the time of the sharp appreciation of the yen in 1986. MITI sent a letter to the association, saying they understood the association's members might be experiencing difficulties because of the sharp rise in the value of the yen. After the chairman of the association read the letter at an association meeting, corporate members each commented that they had made price allowances for an anticipated increase and there was no unexpected hardship. The response, nevertheless, to the MITI request elicited by the chairman was to say, "Yes, the association members are experiencing hardship." If the foreign company had not been represented, it would have wrongly thought its competitors were in a weak competitive situation and perhaps made disastrous strategic and tactical moves.

A foreign company joins these associations with its eyes open, realizing, though, that this is the one opportunity to develop good personal relationships with competitors, government ministries, and regulatory agencies. In turn, the company will probably receive valuable, timely information on the issues under review. Associations also give the Japanese a chance to get to know the foreigner. One general manager noted: "To have the opportunity (it takes Japanese language) to sit together at a table and work with them to solve problems that are not our specific, individual problems gives you a way of communicating with them that can be useful when you need to talk to them privately about something else that is even more important to you both. Without that contact, I would not know how to really keep in touch with my major competitors." Another Japanese general manager with long experience heading an American subsidiary noted there had been resistance from his American bosses, who felt that to become part of an industry association was to become part of collusion. He pointed out that they never officially discuss anything; it is just decided. Decisions are not transparent. They are reached through caucuses or informal golf outings. Clearly, though, there is price fixing.

An American Embassy official commented:

It is all very discouraging. You find that some American businessmen and their people here just do not have a map of their terrain. There are some major landmarks they use to drive back and forth to work and that is it. They don't know the other routes. The trade associations are very important. All the things people don't pay attention to: what do they do; who is in them; who is important; what can they do for you? If you've got a consumer product, you've got to be able to talk to the consumer product section of MITI or otherwise you're going to find yourself locked out one day.

Just wanting to join an association does not necessarily mean you will be accepted.

We were kicked out of the association when a second foreign company applied. The thing that surprised me more than anything else was that they were so open about it. They just did not want other foreign companies. There were no rules that said they aren't going to have foreign companies. They were just not going to have us.

We were told that you are an American firm and do not have factories inside Tokyo's city limits. Half our Japanese competition didn't. We were told politely we were not wanted, but we could join, though it would cost us considerably more than anyone else.

American Express has never been permitted to become a full member of the Card Association, which sets the standards for the industry, even after putting the subject on the U.S./Japan trade negotiation agenda in 1982. Citicorp's finance company subsidiary has never been permitted to join their industry association.

Another American general manager said:

> It isn't so much that the Japanese worry about having you here as a competitor; it is once you are here, how are they going to handle you? They no longer can have their clubby little associations. They can't throw you out of the club if you are not really in the club. All you do is interfere. You breach the daisy wheel. I can't say they do a very good job of controlling prices. What they do very well is control the business for the benefit of Japan and themselves, and then they go out and kill each other. That's a fair game. But Japan still has the business. "We Japanese don't need you foreigners. This is our business." You can't ignore associations. They are not going away!

In dealing with associations, one might consider following Esso Japan's policy. Each year Esso reminds all employees that they must abide by both U.S. and Japanese antimonopoly laws and has each person in a sensitive position sign that he or she will do so.

Lastly, a given association will take note of a member's feelings proportionate to the company's strength. If it is small and insignificant, they will laugh at it and ignore it totally.

A Competitive Mind-Set

Competition in Japan must be understood in the home country, not only by senior management, but by the rank and file. One German company brought representatives of its German union to Japan and explained why they had to work on Saturdays to meet deadlines or the business would be lost to Japanese competition. The German union also learned why production at home for Japanese consumption must be to rigid Japanese specifications, not what those at home thought was satisfactory for their market and therefore for Japan.

In the mid-1980s Kodak made the decision to increase its presence in Japan as a competitive response to Fuji. Albert L. Sieg, President, Eastman Kodak (Japan) Ltd., commented at an American Chamber seminar on Kodak's decision to go fully operative in Japan, after being for years no more than a twelve-man, all Japanese office: "We decided our strategy would best be served on a worldwide basis if we could influence the behavior of our major competitor, particularly in Japan where we were not influencing him at all, and in other world markets. We also felt we could eventually profit from the whole experience. To do that we needed to be here in force. We needed to use Japanese rules, and we had to have top management commitment." It has become Kodak's largest investment outside the United States. Some of the things they have done, though late in the game, apply to any foreign company that wishes to build a substantial business in Japan and integrate that business with their global business.

You must find partners to work with. No matter how large you are, you can no longer do everything yourself. You need R&D in Japan to be a power in Japan. Technical and management support must be on site. This is a world-class project that will be part of the world arsenal for the Kodak Corporation. [Kodak opened their Kohoku New Town Research Facility at a cost of approximately $80 million in 1989 with one hundred engineers and scientists.]

Because Japan is a technology center, and we intend to become a part of that, we will have complete control over marketing and distribution channels from all aspects, which is so very, very important. We are trying all the ways there are. So we would not continue to hear the phrase, "You Westerners just don't understand Japanese business," we found people to advise us who did: accountants, lawyers, and banks.

Japanese staff can also be very competitive and ambitious. If they see something done well elsewhere in the company, they will say, "We can do it as well or even better." Because they look to what is done elsewhere, they should be kept systematically informed so that they can compete. At American Express Card, when we set down measurable goals and provided other countries' performance records, we did exceedingly well competitively within the American Express organization. You compete on a goal, not the methodology.

Foreign competition cannot be forgotten in a changing environment. An exporter of large-ticket items to Japan observed:

The foreign-to-foreign competition is becoming more and more political in Japan. Sales used to be based on product, competing on American standards with American products. It wasn't that important if we weren't sensitive to cultural and political ramifications because our foreign competitors were all making the same mistakes. We have learned as the world and our competitors become more sophisticated that we have to become more political ourselves; understanding, for example, the political ramifications of balance of payments to offset some of these competitive pressures.

There is more risk of technology loss in the United States because of people switching companies than Japanese companies have in Japan with lifetime employment. The intelligence unfortunately tends to flow only one way, to Japan and rarely from Japan. This is particularly true with Japanese graduate students, researchers, and academics who study in foreign institutions and then return to Japan. Few foreigners choose to or are permitted to do significant research in Japanese institutions. Moreover, most basic research, as well as applied research, is done in Japanese corporations, who don't necessarily welcome outside researchers. This is also the case with the reverse brain drain occurring with native Taiwanese and South Koreans returning from U.S. universities and corporations to industries in their home countries.

A general manager in Japan who has done his job well will most likely discover that he and his staff are much more competitive minded than their head office. It is simply the net result of the competitive Japanese environment. The Japanese do not make a decision until they know how to implement it. Foreigners tend to be naive competitively when they say, "This is our decision, our objective, but we don't yet know how we are going to get there." Americans walk and talk at the same time. Japanese walk, sit, and then talk.

Thus, one of the joys of working in Japan is that, on the one hand, you can sometimes get together with the competition and have a good time. But when you are not with them, all is fair, and watch out! The lack of confidentiality in all areas—personnel, technology, strategy, and tactics—destroys much of your competitive advantage unless you sleep alone and have not talked to anyone, not even in your dreams. Meanwhile, you had better learn everything you possibly can about your competition because they are learning everything they can about you.

No government ever said it had to guaranty business from its own stupidity. You win or lose depending on your competitors. How much money do I make? As much money as my competitors will allow me to make. My competitors decide my profit margin. When you go up against Kao in Japan, you had better bring your lunch because it is going to be a long day, and that is what P&G found out.

A global approach is essential to competing in Japan. One is either going at the Japanese competition in Japan and elsewhere or is with them and knows why. That is how they look at competition.

4

Legal: Attorneys and Government

JAPAN IS A SOCIETY of status rather than contract. There is a homogeneity in the sameness of reactions to the same circumstances. Japanese do not need a detailed contract to tell them what to do with their fellow Japanese in Japan. From their somewhat identical backgrounds, they know how they should behave. In a society of status, an individual's particular role is determined by his or her position in the society or in a corporation, and that corporation's role in the society is determined by its status to a much greater extent than it would be in the West. The fundamental premise of Japan's legal structure is that all people do not have equal rights. One's status in the hierarchy of Japanese society determines one's rights. There is a much higher sense of responsibility than is found in an individualistic society like the United States.

An American can find it frustrating working in Japan because there is not the precision in the law found at home. U.S. law is considerably more precise than Japanese law, which reflects a civil-law country, not common law. In Japan, statutes and codes are supposed to cover the legal universe, with judge-made law filling in the blanks, whereas in common-law countries the basic law has been judge-made, with statutes filling in the blanks. When lawmakers try to cover every conceivable situation in a civil-law country, they have to be rather vague. The statutes and codes cannot be too precise, because the more precise the definitions, the more chance that something has been left out. General principles are stated in the codes, which are then applied to individual situations through deduction and cross reference to other sections of the code.

The second reason for the vagueness is the importance of the government and its bureaucracy. The bureaucracy is looked upon with great respect and feels it knows what is best for the country. Laws and regulations are deliberately vague so that the bureaucrats can interpret them in the way they feel is best for everyone. Individuals, unlike in the United States, do not go to court to challenge the government but rely on bureaucratic interpretation in practically all cases, using a little subtle negotiation if the bureaucrats are going against them, but never challenging the government head on. With administrative law the bureaucrats have a particular power of interpretation. Administrative law is, therefore, the law that covers the conduct of law, that is, who governs whom. This is frustrating for foreigners from common-law countries, again especially Americans, who want the answer in black and white in several books before they come to a conclusion or the answer to a problem.

In negotiations with the government, the cards are stacked in favor of big brother because he writes and interprets the laws. He is legislature and judge. Member bills are constitutionally possible but seldom used. Almost all laws are initiated by the bureaucrats through the cabinet—the government itself. The initiative and the interpretation come from the bureaucrats. Lawyers do not do any lobbying work. There are only thirteen thousand lawyers, of whom twelve thousand are litigators. Although there is not a lot of litigation in Japan, there is enough to keep twelve thousand lawyers busy. Since there are only one thousand business lawyers, they are too busy to do any lobbying. Furthermore, the Japanese group mentality means that the Japanese want to deal with principals, not with agents. If a company has a particular problem with or request of the government, the government wants to see someone from that company, not an agent or lobbyist. Lawyers only confirm or verify with the bureaucracy what a law says; that is, they only seek interpretation of what the government says it means. If a company wants the government to change its interpretation or if it wants an exception, it would be counterproductive to have its attorney represent it. The bureaucracy will think it is being slighted because the company has sent an outsider. Lawyers are not highly regarded in Japanese society, especially by the bureaucracy, which looks upon them as potential troublemakers since they might challenge the government, whereas a company never would on its own initiative (or certainly should not). A foreign company will have to work closely with both attorneys and government to satisfy its legal needs and, most important, to operate efficiently and effectively in Japan.[1]

Attorneys

Gaijin kaisha have been most fortunate in the postwar era in the quality of legal assistance available to them in Japan. Until 1955, foreign attorneys were permitted to join the Japanese bar, but from 1955 this was no longer permitted. Some brilliant individuals, many of whom learned Japanese in U.S. military language schools, have run their own firms in Japan, handling foreign corporate operations and Japanese international corporate business. The most notable of these have been James Adachi, Tom Blakemore, Michael Braun, John Christensen, and Richard Rabinowitz, each of whom headed his own firm. These firms and others superbly met the corporate needs of and provided counsel for foreigners doing business in Japan. Today these gentlemen are in or near retirement, and it is questionable whether their firms will survive them, or if the Japanese attorneys working in them will go their own ways. When these attorneys have all retired, we will lose a sense of perspective on business issues. It boils down to a sense of history, in knowing how hard to push or how far you may get pushed. We thus lose insight from a group that has developed a superb ability to communicate after years and years of trying to tell foreigners what it is all about.

There is not much they have not experienced. They have an ability to speak and write with conviction, which is often extremely helpful to the general manager in his communications with head office. It was always their Japanese lawyers, however, who worked with the bureaucracy to interpret the administrative law. The old foreign guard were not just guarding; they had their

---

[1] I am indebted to John Christensen and Thomas Blakemore for their discussions with me on the legal aspects of doing business in Japan.

Japanese field staff. They have no foreign successors in their firms, since only in 1987 were a new breed of foreign attorneys permitted, under the lawyer's law, to have a presence in Japan. A Japanese law firm may hire a foreign attorney licensed under the 1987 law as an employee who can opine only on his home-country jurisdiction and not on Japanese law. He also cannot become a partner of the Japanese firm.

Many of the major international legal firms are newly represented in Tokyo, though they must carry the individual practitioner's name on their door and can only advise clients in Japan on their home jurisdiction or international law, not on Japanese law. These firms also cannot employ Japanese nationals as lawyers unless these Japanese are admitted only in a foreign jurisdiction, not Japan. These Japanese, who are not admitted in Japan, can also not opine on Japanese law. These offshore firms therefore do not have a Japanese field staff. In sum, unless these new foreign entries overstep their permitted legal practice, they are of limited use to the foreign company in Japan in need of legal counsel. They can be very helpful to Japanese companies requiring legal assistance on the foreign company's home market.

Japanese attorneys, including the pre-1955 foreign attorneys, may employ foreign attorneys as law clerks, and this is becoming quite common. Some nonresident foreign firms have also made arrangements for their attorneys to work for Japanese lawyers as clerks, referring all their business to the designated firm. These foreign law clerks cannot put themselves up front as attorneys. This leads to many young, inexperienced foreign attorneys doing clerical work for Japanese attorneys. This was fine when the experienced American attorneys were involved, but as they become less and less so, the situation often becomes shaky at best. Some clerks, though, are accumulating considerable experience and a good track record.

A few Japanese firms have built up a substantial foreign clientele over the years and are familiar with their needs. They are also large enough in size and scope. Approximately 450 Japanese attorneys are admitted to the bar each year, but many of those wish to be prosecutors and litigators. Many of the remainder do not wish to work in large offices and go off to very small firms that cannot support a foreign business. The Japanese bar does not permit an attorney to be both a businessman and an attorney.

The relationship that a foreign corporation, its general manager, and staff have with their attorneys is quite different than that, for instance, with consultants. Consultants often do a specific job at a specific time, while attorneys are supposed to be there through thick and thin, counseling before a task is undertaken and throughout implementation. Attorneys will also have a relationship with the general counsel and management in head office, and with other outside legal advisers in the company's home jurisdiction. The depth of the relationship provides for a historical perspective as well as an ongoing appreciation of the business and its goals. Bastardized legal arrangements in Tokyo, where a firm bounces from one legal adviser to another, are not conducive to the cohesion required to manage a foreign business in Japan. Foreign operations in Japan need to contemplate and adjust to the realities of the Japanese legal landscape in the 1990s.

One adjustment that some foreign companies with substantive operations in Japan have already made is to send a competent attorney from head office or to bring aboard a foreign attorney who has apprenticed as a clerk in a Japanese firm. The latter often have language capability and, though not overly experienced in home-country law, are more familiar with Japan than anyone from head office. Whether they come from Japan or head office, they are invaluable in coordinating arrangements with the various types of attorneys practicing and servicing foreign needs in Japan. They also can be invaluable in coordinating communications with head office and in seeing that any legal questions head office needs answered are routed through the local office and not directly to the company's attorneys in Japan.

A costly habit of many foreign head offices has been to circumvent their Japan office and deal directly with their attorneys in Japan, often resulting in the same questions being answered over and over again at considerable financial cost, with little added value to the Japan operation. This can also be demoralizing for the Japan branch or subsidiary.

Legal advice can be very, very dangerous if you do not know the implications. A good law firm really makes you think through whatever you do, e.g., changing the company's legal status, names, rules of employment, collection policy, etc. In this market where there are so many hidden trappings, a general manager really has his head on the block if he does not have good legal counsel. There are things you should not mention or you will regret, whereas the natural American inclination, for example, is to play it wide open and pursue ad infinitum.

The attorneys can validate what the general manager is saying to head office. As one general manager commented, "When we go back with equivocal recommendations, they go crazy. 'Can you or can't you do it? Which is it? In one paragraph, please!' " Only one attorney to another can clear up these irritants.

Frequently, new-to-Japan foreign entries use hometown attorneys for their initial licensing agreements, without consulting with an attorney resident in Japan. One client of mine discovered in November that the previous February the company it was going to sign an agreement with on the following morning had bounced two promissory notes, which is the equivalent of going bankrupt in Japan. The client was new, and during an initial meeting something did not sound correct. I left the room, called my attorney and banker, and asked each to do an immediate credit check. An hour later we knew the situation when my attorney and banker each said: "You can't deal with that type of people." A public signing in front of a prefectural governor was immediately cancelled and later that evening serious, if not life-threatening, threats were received. In this case, the hometown attorney had bragged that this was his forty-fourth trip to Japan. If a St. Louis company does a deal in San Francisco, it will use Northern California counsel who know the local environment. If the company wants its entry to be smooth and its name not to be ruined before it even starts to do business there, the same applies when one does a deal in Japan.

The best way to use company attorneys in Japan is as a prophylactic, as a threshold adviser. John Christensen, who practiced in Tokyo for thirty years, commented:

> For all the knowledge about Japan overseas, there is no wisdom. And most important, there is within a company little knowledge of the history of the company in Japan that is used. There is often almost a determinism about its behavior in Japan, repeating the same mistakes over and over again. There are great mountains of books, some excellent, but they are read in the context of the reader's world. The reader immediately transfers everything to that context. You just cannot do that; you have to read these books and

transfer yourself mentally to Japan as you read them. You have to discuss them with knowledgeable people, and even the best book learning is not the whole answer. You have to get out and try it, or at least discuss with someone who has tried it, before you can put the book learning in a context that will be truly useful in Japan.

By using an experienced attorney as a prophylactic, a company is testing its ideas before it begins implementation. The attorney is then also aware of what the company would like to do, particularly if there are regulatory issues involved, and can keep abreast of changes. If one makes a mistake in Japan, the recuperation period, if you ever recuperate, is much longer than in the United States. The United States is so volatile and fluid that often a mistake is lost in the system. In Japan, everything is so rigid and hierarchical that if the wrong person is hired, the wrong partner chosen, or controls let go, it is difficult to come back. A general manager cannot work alone. He must use his legal and other advisers' experience to protect and further the business.

When a corporate change is made, it is not necessarily just legal, and this is also factored into any decision.

We changed to a *kabushiki kaisha* (Japanese corporation) several years ago. The whole atmosphere changed that day. I would rather be a branch any day. It is much easier with personnel. No longer does a Western way of doing things apply. Now you have traversed completely to the Japanese side. I could always before get away with the premise that what we were doing was the Western way. That is why we were doing it. I now have to remind people we are still an American company; where before, we were clearly an American company. Although good for morale and the trade, in managing your staff you are in an in-between status.

Regulatory Environment

A marked change has occurred in the regulatory environment in Japan. There is more freedom today for the Japanese and the foreign corporation; there is also freedom to fail. Before, when a foreign company did business with a Japanese company of substance, that company was not permitted to fail. In the "good old days" the Japanese government saw to it that when a foreign bank loan went bad, arrangements were made to have the bank paid back, whether legally called for or not. It will be paid back today only if the bank is legally protected and the resources are available from the company or the guarantor. A number of foreign banks discovered this to their dismay in the early 1980s when they tried to exercise their rights under an unenforceable comfort letter from Tokai Bank. There are failures now. One cannot rely on the comfort cushion. Before, one was a cocoon. It was not possible to move around very well, but it was so comfortable in the immobile position. Now, like a moth, one can move about, but in the light it is getting a little uncomfortable. Now one can fail. Japanese associates can fail. There is a clear breaking down of barriers. Deregulation is working for Japan. The weeding process is working effectively, making the economy efficient. For the foreign corporation the risks are greater than ever in this more efficient, competitive environment.

Regulatory Guidance

Professor John Haley of the University of Washington Law School, a specialist on Japanese law, often states that "although Japan is not a legalistic society in United States terms, it is a society of rules." These rules are open to interpretation and reinterpretation, depending on the situation at hand because the Japanese are situational and pragmatic. To find out how the rules are being interpreted, one cannot sit down and simply read a rule book. An attorney's task in Japan is to understand these rules and how they are being interpreted in the ministries at any given time in any given situation, and therefore what impact they have on the company's Japanese operation.

This does not take away from the general manager's responsibility to know the halls and occupants of the ministries. He must be in frequent contact with the government ministry responsible for interpreting those rules that impact upon the company's operations in Japan. The interpretation of the rules has become known as regulatory guidance. Management and attorneys have to develop personal contact with these bureaucrats, just as all Japanese businessmen do. Most of the bureaucrats were educated in the law faculty of the leading national state universities, and though not practicing attorneys, they are well versed in Japanese civil law. On a day-by-day basis they are the makers and interpreters of the law. Over 90 percent of the laws passed in the Diet (the legislature) are initiated by ministry bureaucrats. It is preferable that the courts play only a minor role, if any, in the foreign company's business, for they are notoriously slow at arriving at decisions. What is important is the interpretation of the law by bureaucrats.

Glen S. Fukushima, formerly of the Office of the U.S. Trade Representative, is an attorney with extensive experience in dealing with Japan. Any foreign businessman should pay careful attention to his observations:

> Differences between superficially similar statutes in the United States and Japan have often proved detrimental to American interests. Compared to analogous law in the United States, Japanese laws relating to antitrust, product liability, administrative guidance, trade, investment, and intellectual property, among others, frequently offer less protection to foreign interests than to domestic interests. . . . These differences in legal outcomes derive in part from the greater discretion held by the Japanese government in applying its laws compared to the U.S. government. For instance, no private antitrust actions can be filed in Japan until the JFTC has first issued a final decree. Thus the individual citizen or corporation in Japan has much less ability to use antitrust, product liability, intellectual property, or investment law against other parties (especially the government) than is the case in the United States. . . . Despite the common wisdom that Japan is a "nonlitigious" society compared to the United States, law is important for a foreign company in Japan. Indeed, many Japanese government bureaucrats and business leaders have been trained in law, think like lawyers, and base their decisions on laws, ordinances, and regulations. Thus a knowledge of the application—as opposed to the theory—of Japanese law is essential to understand the parameters of economic activity.[2]

The Bureaucracy

It is therefore extremely wise to keep one's attorneys aware of what one is doing and contemplating, to avoid running afoul of the wishes of the bureaucracy. The very concept of letting bureaucrats tell you what to do is an anathema to many foreigners, particularly Americans. Appreciate that they are the brightest of the bright and the interpreters and initiators of the national will. To cross them makes no sense at all. To participate in their work does, particularly if one can get them to respect and consider one's

---

[2]Glen S. Fukushima, *The Journal of Asian Studies* (November 1988), p. 898.

opinions. Working with the attorneys does not necessarily mean that they are up at the ministries representing one's interests on an adversarial basis. They often make inquiries on a no-name basis. The general manager and his designated staff represent the company's interests to the bureaucrats, being fully prepared when they do, that is, knowing whom they are talking to, what the authority of each is, and what ultimately both wish to accomplish. Patience and confidence building on both sides will allow one to become informed and will also permit one to seek more immediate answers on urgent matters. These bureaucrats are generally overworked, particularly when international issues are involved. If one can help educate or assist them and is straight with them about intentions, they will more than reciprocate. If you do not cooperate, it is best to pack your bags. This does not mean that one cannot disagree politely with them, or push them for innovative interpretations. Appreciate that, in general, anything one company is permitted to do now applies thereafter to all. It never hurts, though, to be first, even if the bureaucrats discuss with competitors what one plans to do. If what one wishes to do requires their permission, then they are just part of one's life and it is better to work with them, keeping one's corporate goals in mind all the time.

With Japanese government relations, like two porcupines, you've got to go about it very carefully. Eventually they mate. You've got to be respectfully obstinate, saying in some cases: "I'm sorry but I find it necessary to do what we are doing." At the end of the year, if you have a major revenue goal, nobody over at the Fair Trade Commission or the Foreign Ministry is going to raise a hand and say, "I'm sorry, we are going to have to share the fault with Mr. Huddleston because we didn't let him make his goal." You are the only one responsible, and you have to do whatever you think is necessary. It is the same way with head-office staff. At the end of the year, when the accounting is done, they fade away. That's human nature.

I have a real problem. The Ministry of Finance tells me it is not working just for my company. As far as I am concerned, however, it is just working for me.

If a bureaucracy is crossed, however, there is little point in going back to it for anything, especially until there is a staff turnover in the department one has been dealing with. If a law is intentionally violated, a corporation or an individual can probably never go back.

Apology

If one unintentionally or unknowingly makes a mistake, one apologizes, often in writing. This has been known to drive head-office legal counsel into apoplexy, especially in the United States, for they are not accustomed to apologizing to a government or government official except under extreme duress. In Japan it is a common occurrence. It is the simplest way to clean the slate and start over. It also avoids unnecessary confrontation, which is in everyone's interest. Just don't make the same mistake twice. A predecessor or another employee should never be blamed, for all represent the same institution. The apology is institutional and not personal. Not to apologize can bring ostracism.

Contracts

The Japanese are used to contracts now, even if they do not like them. Don't let the Japanese tell you a gentleman's agreement is a gentleman's agreement; because when push comes to shove, it will be important to have a contract for protection. Most significantly, the contract has to be with the right company. If it is not, and if it is ill conceived and badly worded, then nothing will work right. As a person who took over a company where it was not done right said: "I don't care how beautiful an organization or sales network you have, if that basic contract is flawed, you are going to pay for it someday."

Contracts are extremely important for a foreign company in Japan, and it is best to have specific terms and conditions, if only to reflect what has been originally agreed to and what both parties can live with.

Don't let anybody tell you Japanese don't like contracts. Don't let anybody tell you Japanese don't read contracts. When you negotiate a contract with a Japanese you had better be sure what you are doing because they will live by every word in that agreement. Japanese are very legal minded when they are dealing with Westerners.

It is not uncommon in Japan, though, to interpret the contract loosely in day-to-day operations. The attitude is, if you scratch my back on this one, I will scratch your back on the next one. If there is a loss on a project, you will be expected to share in that loss, and if there is a profit on the next one, they will make it up. Even with consensus we can make the wrong decisions. If the business is going the wrong way, the dialogue can gradually be reopened. The Japanese do not want to be on the wrong side of an issue any more than anyone else, so they will eventually come around to agreeing there is an issue, and one can proceed from there. If a situation is created whereby a problem becomes their problem, not "ours," they will find a solution. The key is to agree on a problem; don't come in with a solution first. The problem itself must be understood by all parties before any solutions are attempted. If not, you will never know why it did not work. Don't surprise your Japanese counterparts. Instead, try to give pre-advice, informally spelling out your desires. Give them a chance to think about what you want to discuss. A faster decision will be reached if they are allowed to chew on the idea. This is only common sense in a cross-cultural situation.

Tax

The general manager should also have at his fingertips people very knowledgeable on the tax laws in Japan. Both attorneys and accountants should be used to ensure having the best advice. This guidance is needed before rather than after a mistake is made. "Anybody that doesn't do it is a fool, an idiot." If head office does not agree, it should be made a matter of public record in a memo. That usually forces them to reconsider. As discussed in chapter 9, one must be careful.

Confidentiality

As mentioned, there is little confidentiality in Japan. One general manager who was burned on confidentiality related:

A disaster. It almost blew our deal. The stock registering bank found out about the deal and all of a sudden the market went wild. We had to pay a six-day moving average in accordance with our agreement with the government to buy a Japanese company. The price had not moved in the previous two years. The movement stopped when we spoke to the government, but the price should not have moved at all since we were not buying on the open market. There was no investigation whatsoever.

Review Legal Arrangements

Attorneys are therefore needed for more than contracts, collections (only an attorney or one's own employee can perform a collection in Japan), leases, and financial documentation. They should be one of the general manager's most important counselors. Whether the legal community will be able to continue to provide this service to the foreign business community in Japan in the 1990s and beyond remains to be seen. A foreign business in Japan needs to review now the ability of its legal advisers to meet its needs in the future.

Can the Japanese law firms that in the past were headed by a foreigner take care of future needs when these foreigners have retired? Can head-office counsel, who has recently opened an office in Japan to advise Japanese on home-country or home-state jurisdiction, act as a clearinghouse in introducing Japanese attorneys to take care of the corporation's needs in Japan? Do they have enough seasoning and actual experience in the Japanese market to give sensible introductions, or are they just providing references to an indigenous firm that they have made informal arrangements to tie up with? Is the pairing right for one of their non-Japanese clients but not for another? Is a home-country attorney needed on the corporate staff in Japan to facilitate communications during a period of great change in the legal architecture? Good in-house attorneys, though, will often drive local staff crazy with their persistent questioning. But they can substantially enhance a company's clout with suppliers and partners.

Because the ability and expertise of native Japanese attorneys have grown substantially over the past twenty years, alternatives exist among indigenous law firms that were not previously there for the foreign corporation in Japan. How does one access these firms and individuals, for example, a cross-border tax specialist? Unless there are further changes in the lawyer's law, soon one will be able to use only Japanese lawyers in purely Japanese law firms for advice on Japanese law and regulatory guidance, and for communicating with head office. A decision that was often simple before, using one of the outstanding firms headed by a foreign partner, has become more complex, as has the market. Regulatory guidance has also fluctuated. In many instances it is not as all-pervasive, though in other cases it remains so. The general manager now has the additional responsibility of identifying and managing on an ongoing basis those whom he should use as counsel in a changing legal and regulatory environment.

As in all aspects of doing business anywhere, there are always exceptions to the norm. The general manager and his head office at times will be successful only if they go against other companies' experiences. When Salomon Brothers Inc opened its representative office in Japan in 1980, it leased more office space than would normally be needed for such an office because an unusual amount of prime space was available with considerable room for expansion. Since its ultimate goal was a branch, it took advantage of the opportunity and leased the space. The bureaucrat with whom the company had been dealing at the Ministry of Finance learned about the additional space through a newspaper article and felt that Salomon Brothers had been presumptuous and had overstepped its permission for only a representative office. For eighteen months thereafter, although Salomon made every effort, with the advice of counsel, to do what was required, it got virtually nowhere. The ministry did not ask for information or comment on the information provided, nor would it respond to requests; it simply would not talk with Salomon. This was not because of a lack of effort on the company's part. Salomon finally realized that it would have to wait for the normal personnel rotation at the ministry. It also felt it was necessary to change its law firm, as the legal counsel was too closely associated with the problem and was getting nowhere with the ministry.

Salomon switched to a leading Japanese law firm where the Japanese senior partner personally took charge. With the eventual change of personnel at the ministry, the individual in question was assigned overseas. The change of counsel, specifically the use of the senior partner in the new firm, who enjoyed great stature within the Ministry of Finance, changed the situation dramatically.

George Hutchinson, then Managing Director responsible for Japan, recalls:

The reception accorded us in the company of our new legal counsel at the Ministry of Finance was night and day from our past experience. When we entered the Ministry of Finance building, it was apparent that this was a person of standing. Everyone deferred to this particular individual. We met with the director general of the Securities Bureau, who was a contemporary of our counsel, not some junior. Our counsel then continued to accompany us to the ministry and to handle our application. In very short order we were granted the necessary licenses to open a branch.

Clearly, senior Japanese counsel accomplished in this instance what senior foreign counsel and his Japanese associates had not been able to accomplish through circumspection. Perhaps with another company, another bureaucrat, and another time, it would have been the other way around.

The rules are there to protect as much as restrict a company. They are the one thing a foreigner can always fall back on if he has interpreted them as the bureaucracy would. Japan is a society of flexible, situational rules. They should be used with legal and bureaucratic guidance to one's advantage. Don't circumvent!

5

Government Relations

HOW DOES a foreign company work with the bureaucrats? Should a foreigner do it, or should it be assigned to a Japanese member of the staff?

There can be no question that a Japanese general manager of a foreign corporation, who has worked his way to the top of that corporation in Japan, has a much easier time walking the halls of the ministries than does a foreigner. One thinks of Mr. Yashiro, formerly of Esso and now of Citicorp, Mr. Sugihara of Mobil, Mr. Makino of Grace, and Mr. Kobayashi of Fuji Xerox as the perfect role models. The trouble is, there are not many others. Does that mean the foreign general manager cannot? No.

Japanese Ministries

If a product or service is regulated by a ministry in any way, then one of the first visits a manager makes upon arrival in Japan is a courtesy call on that ministry. He should find out from his predecessor or outside counsel in Japan whom he should call upon, particularly the right level for the position of the company in the global economy and in Japan. The person to call upon is most likely not the individual that he will continue to have contact with on a regular basis. Particular attention must be paid to who in the ministry arranged the appointment, who else is in attendance, and whom the senior turns to for background or factual information. They will most likely be the people to cultivate.

Unlike the U.S. government, but more like the French, the

people one gets to know and work with in the ministry will be in that ministry for at least thirty years. Though they transfer to various jobs within the ministry, they are always there for introductions to their successors or to other appropriate people. Rarely, though, will they introduce one to individuals in other ministries, for here rivalry is strong. Their careers will be made in the ministry they entered upon graduation. There are no mid-career entries. A principal check and balance within Japan is the rivalry and self-interest of one ministry versus another. One must be careful not to get caught in turf battles, though there will certainly be times when one uses a particular ministry to represent one's interest. Turf battles also occur within as well as among ministries—for example, the Security Bureau versus the Banking Bureau in the Ministry of Finance.

As will be discussed later in terms of one's home-country government, bureaucrats cannot be expected to do your firm's business for you. They are not businessmen. They are just the finest bureaucrats in the world, whose sole obligation is to further the interests of their country. To expect anything else from these initiators, reflectors, and administrators of the Japanese national will is ridiculous. If a foreign company or individual is ever going to become even a little bit of an insider in Japan, this is where to start in making the company a part of the fabric of Japan.

The mood has changed since the 1960s and 1970s. These bureaucrats often can see a foreign company's interest as part of their interest. This does not mean, however, that Japanese businessmen feel the same. They do not want you on their soil unless they can control you. Even then, they would most likely prefer to have any business on Japanese soil all to themselves. This is generally also true in South Korea and China.

Bureaucrats, as guardians of the national polity and self, often have a different agenda than businessmen, for they must satisfy educators, politicians, and press as well as businessmen. There are times when a company's interest will coincide with what the bureaucrats are trying to accomplish. The manager's job is to find out when and how and to act upon it in concert with them. His job is also to know when previously conceived plans are changing.

The bureaucrats are extremely busy, but they like to be kept informed, particularly about innovations in the market. Besides visiting them in their offices, lunch, cocktails, and dinner are appropriate ways to get to know them. Senior visitors are used as a reasonable excuse to get together: the bureaucrats can learn what is going on outside Japan, and one's access can be enhanced. In turn, if an official is in one's home country on a mission, an invitation from the head office to visit can be extremely beneficial in cementing confidence.

The general manager of a major European subsidiary remarked that every New Year he visits his appropriate ministry, takes a name card into an office after waiting in line, bows to an unattended desk, and leaves the name card on a tray. When he asked what would happen if his name card was not on the tray next year, his senior Japanese staff member suggested it would not be a good idea to find out.

Unless one gets the impression that these bureaucrats can be real ogres (though sometimes they can be), one must understand that they can provide protection from making some real business blunders if one is willing to be open and straight with them.

As one veteran of the halls and drafts of the ministries says:

> I get involved and go to the ministry. My staff does not like that because they are afraid I might rock the boat and upset any relationships they have. I like to carry the company flag and show my concern. I have to pick and choose my battle, but I go. The ministries do not like seeing me anymore than my employees want me to go. It raises the profile. It raises the concern. The bureaucrats have a lot of pressure on them from all the trade representatives: British, French, American, German. They are very sensitized to complaints. The time has never been better to go down to the ministries. They are a lot more responsive than they used to be. They value their foreign relationships for knowledge on what is going on outside. We are the window. When people see you at the window, it raises your profile elsewhere. It is also very personally and professionally rewarding.

This same individual feels "working here is a lot of fun. You are always learning. It is an absolute kick."

Another long-term trooper notes:

> I have used the Japanese government to my advantage by knowing who and where the bureaucrats are. Ex-bureaucrats keep me informed, so I know what I am doing when I meet face to face with the ministries. I let them know subtly early on that I know, and they are very careful about how they handle the situation. I know enough not to overplay the advantage because it is a

tremendous advantage for them to know that you know. Never be the bull in the china shop.

Negotiating with the Bureaucrats

When negotiating with the bureaucrats the approach suggested by the attorney John Christensen should be carefully considered.

We have a real problem here; that is, you and we have a problem. What can *we* do about it? Not adversarial. Say we, not you; bring the bureaucrats into our group and we into their group. Combine forces to solve a problem that you put outside either group, even if the problem arose because of the bureaucrats' interpretation. You are trying to get the subject to a group consensus, combining forces to solve the outside problem. Let's get together and solve this man-made problem, never mind which man created the problem. Let's just get together and solve the problem. Develop a conciliatory attitude because Japanese law is based on conciliation. Allow everyone to back off without anyone losing face. Set the ground for compromise, taking a low posture, humble attitude. Japanese like to decide matters in a circular fashion whereas Americans think linearly—A to B to C to the jugular. Don't go right for the jugular, because the jugular might be your own. Work for the exception; don't worry how they interpret for others.

When I was president in New York of Chemical Bank's Chemco International Leasing in 1978, we wished to open a wholly owned leasing company office in Tokyo, as we had in most of the major capitals of the world. At that time we were incorporated as a bank in the United States and were owned by a holding company. In Japan a bank can only own a maximum of 5 percent of another company. The law forbidding holding companies also presented difficulties, although foreign companies had been known to receive special exception to the law. Our attorneys in Japan in the spring of 1978 told us it would be impossible to receive Ministry of Finance approval. In fact, because of my Japan background, they were a bit shocked that I even asked about the possibility and politely but firmly told me so. In late August, while on vacation fishing on the Outer Banks of North Carolina, I received a telephone call from Chemical Bank's Tokyo Branch Office, asking me to come to Tokyo immediately, as it would now be possible to receive permission to have a leasing company in Japan. I was thoroughly surprised and skeptical. I was told that our Japan attorneys were certain. Feeling there must be some misunderstanding on the part of the Tokyo Branch, I asked them to check again with our attorneys. The next day another telephone call confirmed the original call, and shortly I was off to Tokyo.

In August 1978, following the second congressional report by Jim Jones on the restrictions to foreign entry in Japan, the Ministry of Finance bureaucrats made a conscious effort to begin the process of liberalizing Japanese financial markets for foreigners. It was only a beginning, but it was a beginning. They especially wanted the Americans to know that the process had begun.

Our attorneys had a young associate who had convinced his senior partners that Chemco could benefit from this liberalization. I remained concerned, though, about the 5 percent restriction and the prohibition to holding companies. For three days at the attorney's office we reviewed every possible way to structure an investment. We then made an appointment at the *kacho* level (late thirties in age) at the Ministry of Finance and, for the only time in my career, an attorney, albeit very young, accompanied me on a visit to a ministry, since he was the one who had initiated the dialogue. We sat down at one of the metal tables that are crowded into the corner of every ministry office, and I proceeded to explain who I was, with the attorney no more than a black, invisible stagehand as found in Japanese Bunraku puppet drama: there but not seen. After a lengthy explanation of our wish to have a leasing company in Japan, with a nod now and then from the two Japanese officials, the senior of the two looked up and said it would not be possible. The young Japanese attorney went bright red and almost passed out. Taking a yellow legal pad, I began to sketch out an investment vehicle that we had discussed in the attorney's office, whereby a company we had in Hong Kong, which was not classified as a bank, would be the nominal parent of the Japanese subsidiary. I knew that a similar type of arrangement for a finance company that was partially foreign owned had recently been approved. The ministry official took the legal pad, added a few lines as he asked questions, and wrote, "OK." I said, "Thank you very much," and we excused ourselves. Arriving at the front door of the ministry, I realized I had left my briefcase behind. The attorney was in such shock that he would not go back with me to retrieve it, fearing a change of mind on the officials' part.

Subsequently, the Ministry of Finance agreed to a delay in the announcement of the approval until the June 1979 summit meeting in Tokyo, as we wished to get our game plan together without showing our hand to our competitors. They were delighted that the announcement would coincide with the summit meeting, the first ever in Japan.

The telex from Chemco's attorney confirming Ministry of Finance approval and the suggested procedure for Chemco to thank the Ministry of Finance illustrate clearly what the relationship should be among client, attorney, and ministry.

Pleased to report that on April 18, 1979, Mr. A of the Ministry of Finance's International Finance Bureau, Foreign Investment Section, officially informed us Ministry of Finance will not repeat not announce Chemco validation on April 24, 1979, but will at that time announce all other validations issued during March 1979 and "one other." Ministry of Finance requests that when this Chemco subsidiary is established, Chemco so inform Foreign Investment Section of the Ministry of Finance (in addition to filing required stock acquisition report) and at that time the Ministry of Finance will announce that the "one other" validation issued during March 1979 was the Chemco subsidiary. In view of unprecedented cooperation on the part of Ministry of Finance we suggest that prior to Chemco announcement late May a visit be paid to Mr. A and Mr. B, Mr. A's immediate supervisor at Foreign Investment Section, to express appreciation and personally inform Ministry of Finance of proposed date of Chemco announcements. Such courtesy visit extremely important for Chemco's continued good relationship with Ministry of Finance. In regard to times of announcement, Ministry of Finance understands it may be made in late May but we believe you can be flexible to some extent. Note, however, that because of peculiar appearance of Ministry of Finance validation announcement in widely circulated *Nihon Keizai Shimbun* (newspaper) some reporters may investigate as to what "one other" is. This possibility should be kept in mind in determining appropriate time of announcements. Best regards Attorneys.

It was only in late 1979, after I had joined American Express and returned to Tokyo to work, that I learned what really happened. One day I ran into the young attorney on the street and thanked him for what he had done to help us. He asked, "Do you know what happened after our meeting at the ministry?" I told him that I knew of nothing unusual. Apparently, a week after our meeting, and after I had returned to New York, the ministry official who had given the approval called the attorney back to the ministry and said it would be impossible to proceed with the application for the leasing company. The attorney dutifully pulled out of his briefcase the legal pad on which both I and the official had written and asked, "Isn't this your handwriting and notation saying OK?" The official acknowledged that it was and said to proceed. The Hong Kong company at the time was inactive and had only $1.42 of capital. What would appear to be a rather junior bureaucrat had made, on his own, a monumental decision in the liberalization process. Our attorneys had been on top of the situation as much as they could be and had seen that I was fully briefed as to all the possibilities. But I was the one that had to do the negotiating, and once I, not an attorney, had been told yes, it was extremely difficult, with a summit on the horizon and the Jim Jones report in the background, for the Ministry of Finance to reverse the decision. Our interests coincided. It was during the same August 1978 liberalization that credit card companies, whether Japanese or foreign, were told that they could have one card that could be used both inside and outside Japan. This started the study that led to American Express in 1979 deciding to issue its own card in Japan in 1980.

Today, many foreign executives feel MITI is easy to deal with if you reason with them. But:

> They can be nasty, but not on their own, when a well-entrenched interest is being threatened by a new entry. This interest will come to MITI and complain, they will play a game together, and take us on.

In that case one must be very careful, because the Japanese businessman has become tougher and much more combative than he was fifteen years ago, when the ministries were the problem. He is prepared and more than willing to do battle with the foreigner.

It is not unusual for a bureaucrat to call a manager in to question him about his corporate plans and what he knows about the competition. The official will also discuss administrative changes under consideration, seek the manager's opinion on those changes, caution him if he might be slightly out of bounds, and help him get back on the field.

In December 1970, the *Nihon Keizai* carried a front-page story that Morgan Guaranty had made arrangements to be the custodian for a number of Japanese banks' American depository receipts. Chemical Bank was very active in this business, and Morgan's general manager made it clear to me that he had pulled off a coup. My head office felt the same way. Three of the major banks had not gone with Morgan. Over the next three weeks I convinced them to use Chemical and was somewhat pleased with myself until I received a phone call to come to the Ministry of Finance to see Mr. Sagami, then Director of the Banking Bureau. Arriving at Mr. Sagami's desk, one of many in the room where the Banking Bureau was located, I was not asked to take a seat but was left standing, while he sat behind his desk.

We were months away from opening our branch, and not all the approvals were in. Mr. Sagami proceeded to ask me three questions, while I stood there shaking. Why had I signed three Japanese banks to ADR arrangements without his permission? I explained that obviously the Ministry of Finance could not object, since Morgan Guaranty had received permission. He bluntly told me to never do anything again without his permission. Second, what else was I contemplating doing? Obviously, nothing under the circumstances, except perhaps committing harakiri. Lastly, what was my competition contemplating doing? I was then left standing there and decided to depart, quickly. As I passed the desk of Deputy Director Toyo Gyohten I heard: "Get the hell out of here, I'll take care of him." He knew me well and knew that I had not intentionally rocked the boat. If I had not heard those words, I am not sure what I would have done. Though the atmosphere can be much more cordial today, at some ministries even now the above scenario is very possible, especially when trying to break new ground.

A former senior U.S. government official's experience in Japan summarizes today's situation:

The Japanese government really does not want to see individual foreign companies unless there is some very specific business, and then you get very low-level treatment. MITI can be very combative, very contentious, pretty haughty. They do not make you feel very comfortable. If you have a specific complaint, they want to deal with it on a generic basis and not on just your specific complaint. They might send you to the Office of the Trade Ombudsman or some such damn thing. The Trade Ombudsman is a waste of time. When that is suggested, best to say, "I have a business to run, and I need an answer."

If you have knowledge, though, officials want to talk to you. They have learned they can learn. They respect you if you have done your homework, if you know the issues and have them all laid out, if you have studied the Japanese position, and if you know how to respond several issues down the line.

The Japanese are very well prepared, far more prepared than we are. They are prepared to hit the ball back and to hit it hard. Then they crouch, waiting for it to come back. If it doesn't come back, they are really disappointed. They really want to get in and negotiate. They will feint and try to make it go away. If this does not work, they will fall back on their next defense. They appreciate a good game, and they are disappointed when they don't get it. American head offices don't want the bumps, but they have to have some. Come in and fight the good battle. A lot of CEOs push it away. They fear Japan and prefer to ignore. It takes so much time and money—many more people and much more management time than they anticipated. This is a war, and we can't go on fighting a defensive war all the time. It is an analogy I don't like, but that is the way it is. In football if you are always out there with your defensive team, you are not going to score many touchdowns. It is amazing that our aggressive society does not seem very aggressive in Japan. Japanese are persistent; Americans just pushy. The Japanese tell you what they are going to do and generally they will do at least that. They are not overly concerned about how they will get there. They just get there. They can be simply monomaniacs. They grab hold of something and never stop. They start with a better education and then they are persistent. The Japanese look for persistence in their personnel and Americans look for pushers. In Japan, the pushers will generally bomb out, both inside the company with their fellow employees and outside with customers.

Home-Country Embassy

Another early call when arriving in Japan is on the home-country embassy and chamber of commerce. Various nationalities use their respective embassies and home-country governments differently from others. Rather than singling out any one country, there are approaches that make sense for all. First, the foreign company is an alien in an alien country, and it is good for the embassy to know what the company is doing and plans to do in Japan. Many embassies have extensive economic sections staffed with both generalists and specialists, from agriculture to pharmaceuticals. Many also are underutilized by the business community and would be delighted to have the opportunity to demonstrate their expertise by helping out.

Second, if embassy staff know what a company is about and it does have trouble with one of the Japanese ministries, they can be in a better position to make representation on its behalf in a timely and effective manner. Japanese bureaucrats are prone to listen to foreign bureaucrats because someday they will need assistance. Big brother to big brother permits bashing, but bashing is not expected or accepted from private parties. The British on scotch and the Swiss on financial access have been particularly effective. The scotch story is explained in chapter 11. The Swiss financial authorities simply told the Ministry of Finance twice, when the Swiss banks originally wished to be licensed in Japan in the early 1970s and again in the mid-1980s when they wanted trust bank licenses, that any Swiss bank that applied should be accepted or the Japanese banks in Switzerland should pack their bags and go home. This was a firm message that the Ministry of Finance reluctantly understood, and licenses were issued when applied for. One questions why other governments have not followed the same procedure on a multitude of occasions.

The turnover at the American Embassy in senior economic and commerce staff has unfortunately been as high recently as at American corporations. Often the embassy staff has used embassy exposure to find jobs in American business, which has its own benefits but does not help the American businessman seeking help at his embassy.

I have been disappointed at the amount of authority in the American Embassy or their willingness to volunteer to help us out in difficult situations. They don't want to get involved with the Ministry of Health and Welfare. They will make introductions and set up appointments with people we have not met, but when it comes to a difficult situation, they don't want to get wrapped up in it with any specific company. That has been disappointing, but maybe I expect too much assistance.

A very senior Japanese general manager of a foreign company commented:

I never go to the American Embassy to ask for any business help, only to shake hands. If the embassy commercial attaché telephones a MITI official, the next thing that happens is that the MITI official gets mad at me and I would not be able to do any business with them [note the "doing business with them"]. In fact, I help MITI by talking to the embassy about what the government wants to tell them, and I tell the MITI people what Washington wants them to know. I keep them both well posted so they can talk to each other themselves.

It takes a very experienced individual with an enormous reservoir of trust on both sides to perform this role. Clearly, the American Embassy is not going to sell a company's product or service for it, though some other embassies might.

Home-Country Chamber of Commerce

The various foreign chambers of commerce have shown enormous growth over the past twenty years. Every country, and even the EC, has one, and they are in many ways businesses themselves. Some, such as the West Germans, have professional staff supported by their government. The American Chamber of Commerce in Japan (ACCJ) has an excellent administrative staff, but all its officers are elected by the membership. There is no question that, like its sister-country organizations in Japan, it has provided a forum for discussion and assistance to many businesses over the years. The committees of the American Chamber have been particularly noteworthy in their accomplishments, whether it be in marketing, personnel, pharmaceuticals, or finance. On the other hand, many Americans find the Chamber to be a comfortable womb, failing to realize that it is only a forum for discussion, a starting place, if you will, in learning from others' experiences and in bringing together views or wishes for submission to either the American government or the Japanese government. One is careful to evaluate realistically how knowledgeable particular individuals are, and not to get locked into one viewpoint. One must be very discerning of those who hide behind the Chamber so that no one disagrees with them when they speak under its umbrella. There are also those who are more interested in collecting imperial awards at home or from the Japanese government than running a business. The chambers cannot do business for a company and are no substitute for the general manager and his employees getting on with what they are in Japan to do. If one has a business to run in Japan, there will not be much time left over for a chamber's activities, beyond the occasional breakfast or luncheon meeting. The American Chamber's publications can be particularly helpful, however, in familiarizing oneself with other individual and company experiences.

Probably the most useful activities sponsored by the ACCJ over the years have been the briefing breakfasts for corporate and government visitors from the United States. These are hosted by the visitor in his hotel from 7:30 A.M. to 9:00 A.M. sharp, with about six attendees who brief the visitor on his interests. They are generally candid, off-the-record, and extremely informative for all of the participants, particularly if the visitor shares some of his experiences when he returns home.

Home-Country Legislators

The ACCJ has taken upon itself an educational role for legislators and bureaucrats in Washington, D.C. These are known as door-knocks, now mini and maxi. There is clearly a danger here as to whether or not the representations made by the individual partic-ipants are representative of a company's interests. They should be watched carefully. One Senate aide, who spent many years in Tokyo, remarked that now that he is on the Washington side, he realizes how marginal the door-knock efforts are.

Perhaps one of the reasons the ACCJ has felt it necessary to do door-knocks in Washington is the miserable job done by U.S. corporations in keeping their legislators and American bureau-crats informed about what they are doing in Japan and how their government could be of assistance to corporate America. Despite recent exceptions in semiconductors and tobacco and to a lesser extent finance, on the whole the record is blemished. More often than not, instead of a concerted program of using the embassy in Tokyo, the Executive, and the Congress in a coordinated fashion, it is one-on-one when the chips are down. If a company has a Washington office, the Japan general manager should visit it on one of his trips to the United States. If there are any crucial issues, the Washington staff also should probably visit Tokyo, so that both sides, as well as the responsible people in head office, are fully familiar with the issues. If Japanese competitors are conduct-ing lobbying activity in Washington or any other American juris-dictions, the Japan general manager needs to be kept fully informed. The Japanese have used lobbyists and state and local officials in the United States to their advantage in a way not even conceived of by American or European businessmen in Japan. Perhaps Japanese officials are smart enough not to let foreigners use them in a similar way.

Japanese Legislators

Nevertheless, the Japan general manager should carefully culti-vate not only Japanese national and local officials but legislators who might have a say in his company's operations in Japan. This should be done after he is settled in, through proper introduction. Those introducers are cultivated first because they will determine whom he meets. One must be very careful not to use the equivalent of paid lobbyists for introductions since it demeans one generally in the eyes of those to whom one is being introduced. The recent Recruit scandal and the following advice from the Japanese general manager of a foreign company are reminders of how careful one must be in dealing with Japanese legislators.

> I don't care if I ever have any relationships with Diet members, because they are not going to be very effective unless you want to pull some dirty political trick. I would not want to have any relationships with Diet members because they are *always* asking for money. I think there are some clean Diet members, but most of them are corrupt. That does not happen with high-level civil servants. They are very clean. You need not worry. MITI officials are generally smarter than Diet members, so I think they know how to handle the Diet members. We therefore do not need to be too concerned with the Diet members on the political level to run our businesses. I am more concerned with MITI officials as to whether they are knowledgeable or do something unwise out of sheer ignorance since they are rotated in their jobs so often. Each one stays two years at most in a job and some only one year, but they are by training quick learners.

An American general manager noted:

> Many American companies did not realize until fifteen years ago the importance of having their own staff in Washington to gather intelligence. It is amazing that virtually none appreciates the importance of doing the same intelligence gathering in Tokyo. Unfortunately, it probably will be another fifteen years before anything is done by the head offices of American companies. No wonder they don't understand why the balance of payments issue grows year after year.

Think Tanks

A recent phenomenon in Japan has been the participation of resident foreign businessmen in governmental and semigovernmental or privately sponsored think groups, on subjects as broad as the future internationalization of Japan or as specific as the monitoring of industrial liberalization in Japan. Some people participate on every committee of this type to which they are invited. A wiser view is to look carefully at who is participating from both the foreign and Japanese sides and then try to discern why they are participating. If the quality of participants and their motivations are constructive and productive for the business, then participate by all means. If one is being used to lend respectability to an endeavor that does not deserve it—in short, being used for someone else's needs—then one should not participate. Serious investigation should answer the question early on.

In all of the above, the emphasis is on participating in the Japanese and foreign community to further the interests of one's business in Japan. As in all other areas of a business, capable staff must be developed to handle intelligence gathering, for the general manager cannot do it on his own. Good staff providing good intelligence will make the general manager's efforts with the Japanese government far more effective than if he is flying by the seat of his pants, as most are. It takes years to develop these relationships. They are both corporate and individual, and tremendous effort and time are required. Participate carefully and selectively, building a good knowledge base, and then actively.

6

Manufacturing; Office and Plant Location

MOST JAPANESE COMPANIES today maintain their head office or at least their international headquarters in Tokyo. More likely than not, the people a foreign general manager will interact with will be in a Japanese company's Tokyo office, if for language reasons alone. Thus, foreign companies usually locate their principal offices in Tokyo or the Osaka/Kobe area.

Real estate in Tokyo is notoriously expensive, and it is no bargain in Osaka/Kobe. Today it is basically impossible to receive permission to build a manufacturing facility in the Tokyo metropolitan area. Manufacturing sites are also difficult and expensive to obtain within a seventy-five kilometer radius of the city. Tokyo offices are therefore service oriented: sales, marketing, and finance.

Historically, foreign corporate offices in Tokyo were located in the Marunouchi central district. It was felt for prestige reasons that one had to be there. With the influx of Japanese and foreign offices and the spectacular growth of the Japanese economy, these limited sites have all been taken, and those that come on the market are outrageously expensive. This has caused many foreign companies to look elsewhere in Tokyo for real estate, most notably American Express's new seventeen-story tower in Ogikubo, some forty minutes by train from downtown Tokyo. Even some of the foreign securities houses like Salomon Brothers and Shearson Lehman Hutton Inc. have moved from the center of town to get the space they need. A prestigious address in Marunouchi is no longer a necessity; it is far more important for a company to obtain adequate space in a location convenient to transportation for employees. Since employees usually commute between one and two hours each way, it is wise to settle on a general geographical area that the company will remain in permanently, so as not to inconvenience them with an office relocation and cause them to leave the company.

Office interiors in Japan can be as simple or fancy as one wishes. An enormous cultural difference should be taken into consideration, however, when the office is being designed. The Japanese use an open-floor plan in their offices. The chairman and president have offices. The managing directors usually have offices near where they sit with their employees. The managing directors rarely sit in their offices, except for meetings, and even then meetings are normally held in conference rooms. The managing directors and/or directors sit at the back of the room, facing those who work for them. Each person is fully aware at all times of what is going on in his or her area of responsibility. Managing directors and directors are usually working employees of the company, the equivalent of executive vice-presidents and senior vice-presidents in the United States. Rarely are there outside directors in a Japanese company. A director can call upon anyone who is in the group under his responsibility to do anything. Partitions or offices and the individual privacy that goes with them are only for the emperor. It is not unusual for a foreigner in his corner office in a gaijin kaisha to be referred to sarcastically by his Japanese employees as "The Emperor." One therefore gives serious consideration to the office form, for it can have a great deal to do with the office's corporate culture and the substantive work accomplished.

An open office forces the foreigners to interact with the Japanese staff and vice versa, and by doing so to have a much better understanding of what is going on around them. Most foreigners are so enmeshed in the office syndrome and the prestige that they perceive goes with it that they will not consider an open office. It would be good for most to bury their pride, get out on the floor, and learn what is happening in their company. Conference rooms can be built for meetings and when privacy is required. With, or particularly without, Japanese-language ability, the place to sit is with the troops. As an aside, this might be worthy of serious consideration at home—one of the easy lessons to learn from Japanese management.

The general manager should routinely get out of his office every day and purposely walk the floors, seeing and being seen. It is all part of his 50 percent allocation of his time to personnel. He is also an example to the other members of management, whether foreign or Japanese, that openness is the norm and not the exception.

"Let's get rid of these walls!" Even the international management came to support it, particularly the younger people, who thought it was a fantastic way to work together. I think it is fantastic also for a manager. He will never have a better chance in life to get people to understand and appreciate the direction he wants them to move than in an open office. He sits on top of a desk and speaks to one individual, but there are fifty people who can hear his thoughts. He creates a whole culture, and his ideas are in forty different proposals the next week. If he praises someone, fifty people also hear it, and the same is true if he criticizes someone. The system is stimulating if used well. It has to be used to one's advantage.

Manufacturing

The first question asked by a potential foreign manufacturer in Japan should be, "Why manufacture in Japan?" Surely it is cheaper to do so at home or, for example, in Taiwan or Korea. Other countries in Asia, though, do not have a gross national product (GNP) of over $3 trillion nor an average annual per capita income of over $20,000. In fact, no other country in the world has that combined financial power except possibly the United States. There are many reasons to manufacture in Japan, but each should be researched thoroughly before a decision is made.

First, there must be a substantial market for the finished product in Japan. The product must also be new to Japan and/or have unique technology and the real potential for ongoing added value to be applied over a sustained period so as to remain in front of the competition. The cost of manufacturing in Japan at current and anticipated exchange rates precludes a company from manufacturing there to export principally to its home market or elsewhere. Any additional sales outside Japan are welcomed but are not a top concern of the management in Japan. If there is a market in Japan, then management there will be fully occupied in exploiting that market. In sum, there must be a market for the product or products in Japan. The life of the products must be long, with potential for extensive add-on improvements.

All of this must be put through the most rigorous research and analysis and be clearly understood in head office, particularly the time frame within which specific sales objectives will be met and pay back and profitability on the investment will occur. When there is a window of opportunity, one makes a move; otherwise someone else will. The realization, though, of whether or not there is a window of opportunity generally requires months of research: analyzing and understanding the competition, determining to what extent the product should or should not be modified to meet the needs of potential industrial or retail consumers, and deciding how the product will be marketed—for example, through wholesale or retail distribution or through new opportunities presented by changes in postal costs and regulations for direct marketing. If the company is going to do it itself, where and how will it hire its sales force, and who is going to manage them? How will the manufacturing plant and sales force interact? Will the sales force be stationed at and work out of the manufacturing plant, or will they be located in an urban sales office? Will the company sell basic lines that virtually can be chosen out of a catalogue, or will each product be custom made to the needs of the consumer? Where are suppliers and customers located?

When the plant is up and running with all the necessary technological input from head office, the product produced will likely be of the highest quality, perhaps better than what the company produces at home, as Anheuser Busch found with Budweiser Beer. A manufacturer of consumer products noted:

> We are doing a damn good job. Ninety-eight percent of our products are manufactured in Japan. The difference between our quality and other countries' quality is people, our operators. According to our outside analysis, everything boils down to the excellent quality of our people.

Many general managers feel that manufacturing quality is much better in Japan than anywhere else. Even in a foreign company, the education level of a blue-collar or clerical work force puts most other countries to shame.

It is much easier to run a manufacturing plant than a service company. People have assigned tasks and stated hours, and the expectations of employees are different than if they are in a white-collar job in Tokyo, London, or New York.

The quality of one's product and manufacturing facility does not mean that anyone will necessarily buy your product. A failure to understand the competition and to know how to compete with them effectively and profitably means you are just going to bleed. Decisions must be made on how the product will be sold and distributed before manufacturing begins. Building a plant is relatively easy once a site is procured. Manufacturing capability even in foreign firms is superb. Selling is an entirely different story.

Research and Development Facilities

Without industrial research and development in Japan, a company will not have a chance to attract the best people from university. Nor will there be a reverse flow of technology or a real dialogue between the home country R&D staff and Japan. Manufacturing and industrial research must go hand in hand to create the dynamics necessary to stay ahead of the competition. Only recently have foreign companies come to appreciate the importance of doing research in Japan. IBM and Hoechst have done it for years and are now joined by the likes of Kodak, DuPont, W. R. Grace, Upjohn, Procter & Gamble, and Dow Chemical, who have made major investments in research facilities.

Plant Location

Every region, every prefecture in Japan is trying to attract business to its locality, much as elsewhere in the world. Locations anywhere are chosen for personnel capabilities and cost; land availability, suitability, and cost; living conditions, including education facilities; technology and research capacity and availability; and supplier and customer locations. There are some meaningful differences to consider, though, when one is trying to determine why it would be attractive to choose a specific locality in Japan versus the considerations in the United States or Europe.

H. A. Samson, the Executive Editor of *The Journal of the American*

Chamber of Commerce in Japan, says in the journal's December 1988 issue (p. 7), devoted to investment in Japan:

Appearances can be deceiving. There are a number of caveats that foreign investment in Japan is subject to. Even regional authorities in Japan are seeking investment only from certain industries (preferably technology laden) and on certain terms. While the situation is far better than in years past, foreign investment in Japan is certainly not greeted with the same enthusiasm that such investment is greeted in most sections in the United States.

Personnel

Again, personnel becomes the major consideration. Who is going to manage the plant, and how important is it for staff in the Tokyo office to interact face-to-face with the plant? One client recently opened a plant in Saitama, seventy-five kilometers west of Tokyo, rather than in Chiba near Narita airport, which would have been much more convenient for foreign technology assistance, because the plant manager they wished to hire lived in Saitama and could also hire workers there.

Most Japanese families, once settled, are very hesitant to move to other locations in Japan because of schooling. Children compete to attend public and private schools. It is difficult to take children out of a good school and enroll them in another good school. As a result, when a man is transferred, he will often go and live in temporary quarters, leaving his wife and children at home. The company often provides special temporary living accommodations and allowances, including monthly travel home. In a Japanese company few men refuse a transfer, for that would be tantamount to stepping off the promotion escalator, a career ender.

For a foreign company, which has a difficult enough time attracting staff, there is little incentive to risk losing good personnel by unpopular domestic transfers. The plant is therefore virtually built around its manager. Moreover, the Tokyo or Osaka staff, particularly sales and development people, should be in constant contact with the plant people, and that means the plant must be in reasonable proximity to the main office.

Even if the local areas welcomed foreign management with more than words, it would be difficult to get foreigners to live in

the countryside unless they were linguistically capable and prepared for their children to be educated in Japanese schools. There
are no facilities outside the major cities for educating foreign
children, except in Japanese schools. Japanese schools are excellent, but reading and writing Japanese, especially when the parents cannot, is not easy for any child. When I asked at a
MITI-sponsored seminar on the then nineteen MITI-approved technopolises whether the regions expect foreigners to work in the
plants built there, the answer was no. Foreign management could
live in the Tokyo/Osaka belt and commute out to the technopolises, which were all established in outlying areas in order to
provide employment for local residents so they would not leave
their parents for the city. They were expected also to attract those
who had left home for urban areas—the "U-turn phenomenon."

National and local authorities imply that there are local Japanese available to run the plants, and to introduce and improve on
the foreign technology. This is impractical, for if one is bringing
new-to-Japan technology—the only way for a foreign manufacturing company to compete in the Japanese marketplace—then
certainly expertise has to come with the technology, both mana-
gerial and technical, if only for corporate communications. In sum,
the regional authorities are soliciting a company's technology and
money but not necessarily its foreign staff.

The labor cost of Japanese employees is fairly uniform throughout Japan, so there is little to be saved in going out to the rural
areas, as for instance going to Wales or eastern Kentucky. At most
there could be a 20 percent savings. Staff transferred from the
main office must be paid allowances for relocation or living
separately from their families (similar to overseas allowances for
expatriate staff), which will usually offset any savings in cost for
local hires.

There has been a great deal of talk in the 1980s about the U-turn
phenomenon, especially in the foreign press. This is often the case
with individuals who return to a family business, usually as a
result of family pressure, but it rarely applies when working for
a foreign company, despite the desire of government officials for
it to be so. The U-turn also rarely applies to Japanese companies
in the technopolises since the local staff hired are usually laborers
under twenty. The same should be true with foreign companies,

since they, like the Japanese companies, have to bring most of the management from elsewhere.

It is generally not difficult to find capable technical high school graduates to work as plant laborers: it requires cultivating the local establishment and high school. Foreign-language ability is not readily available, but it is unlikely that it will be needed at the laborer level. For a foreign firm to recruit specialists, even in such regional metropolitan areas as Sapporo in Hokkaido or Nagoya in central Honshu, remains extremely difficult. One must be careful not to end up with a collection of marooned castaways. On the other hand, Japan has clear regional attributes, and a company needs people who know their way around the local landscape. Without them, it is virtually impossible to be successful in areas outside Tokyo, even in Osaka and Kobe. Once again, the problem of personnel for foreign firms raises its multifaceted head. The solutions are difficult at best.

Land

Land is considerably cheaper in rural areas. Because landholdings are small throughout the country, and because of the resulting difficulty of buying out each parcel of land, foreign companies are realistically restricted to purchasing land from private or public industrial parks, or land that a prefectural or municipal government has designated as suitable for an industrial location. The government-designated centers were established over fifteen years ago to attract Japanese corporations from the urban areas in a MITI-desired reallocation of national resources. Japanese companies on the whole did not find them attractive. It was not until 1982–83 that regional groups, such as Tohoku and Kyushu, began to seek foreign investors, after failing to attract Japanese investors mainly because of geographic isolation from suppliers and customers and the problems of personnel.

The initial, MITI-directed approaches to foreign governments and customers were extremely naive, with the overtone of see, we do welcome foreigners to Japan. The various regions were not permitted to bid against one another on financing and taxation concessions. The only variation was in the cost of the land or if the locality was prepared to assist in finding and screening workers for the facility. The land at the technopolis sites had to be purchased and the plant itself built. Neither the land nor the building could be leased. Some changes have been considered in this area recently. It is also possible to buy land from private owners but rarely possible to lease land and buildings privately. Few buildings are built on land as expensive as that in Japan for speculative sale or leasing; plant facilities are usually built to specifications.

MITI, despite all its claims, really cannot do any more to assist a site seeker than provide a list of sites and call the local authorities for an appointment. The MITI employees are generalists with little knowledge of real estate. Their heralded claim of being able to match needs to sites through a computer program is, as a member of JETRO (a MITI subsidiary), said to me, so much garbage. A company must be prepared to find the site itself, to negotiate its purchase and usage permits, and to build the building. The major construction companies, each of which has an international section to assist foreign clients, can be quite helpful. Their service is generally superb. Just allow enough time and build bridges with the community you are going to work in.

The greatest difficulty is in finding a site to purchase, at whatever the cost, that is convenient to the principal office and its suppliers and customers and where the right staff can be found to manage and staff the plant.

Real estate transactions are not known for their cleanliness in Japan, underinvoicing and kickbacks being common. A medium-size construction and real estate company once insisted I take a 2 percent kickback on a substantial purchase of land, saying this was customary for real estate transactions in Japan. The transaction could not be completed until I took the 2 percent. They could not comprehend that I was there to protect the buyer's interest, which I was being paid to do, and that the deal was off if they insisted on the kickback. They were even more upset when I asked that the 2 percent be deducted from the cost of the land. They finally did, but completion of the transaction was delayed.

Japanese Construction Companies

In Europe and the United States it is customary to ask architectural engineers to submit bids for building an office or plant. In Japan it most definitely is not. All of the major construction companies—

Kajima, Shimizu, Ohbayashi, etc.—bid themselves. To use one of the few architectural engineers that do exist is to up costs as much as 80 percent. The major construction companies have the capacity to bid on a project, to orchestrate approvals for land purchase and building through the authorities, and to work with engineers and staff from head office and in Japan in defining and implementing the construction and completion. Despite evidence that biddings are often rigged, these companies are extremely competitive in bidding to build foreign offices or plants if foreign management stays involved, and they deliver in a timely fashion.

Land-Purchase and Use Approvals

Receiving approval to buy land, even when there are no questions of pollution or possible ecological or health hazards, takes a minimum of six months, and there is no way to speed up the process. The time frames for each stage of the approval are predetermined and charted. Full written responses to detailed questions are required, and the answers cannot be hedged, particularly where environmental issues are concerned. Questions must be answered exactly as requested. Any failure to do so will only evolve into approval delays and possible rejection of an application.

Community Relations

Courtesy calls on governors and mayors are wise. Unlike in the United States, these officials most likely are not going to come to you, though there have been notable exceptions, such as Governor Hiramatsu in Oita Prefecture. Plant managers and the General Affairs personnel of plants in the area should be visited to discuss public and company transportation for employees, local hiring conditions (workdays, hours, holidays), and manpower availability. If a company has a separate sales/service office and plant, the Rules of Employment should be registered in both locations. Many foreigners forget when drawing up their Rules of Employment for one type of facility that they will apply to the other. Unless one is prepared for one heck of a lot of interoffice conflict, everyone works on Saturdays or no one does, the holidays are the same or equivalent, and work shifts are equivalent, as is most everything else.

The Akita Prefecture brochure on their technopolis says: "The Plan is based on a concept integrating industry, academic and daily life to make these vital factors compose an organic community favored with the most advanced technologies of the day." A local government official told me, however, that he did not think any Japanese university from his experience would work with a 100 percent foreign-owned corporation, as they would not wish to share knowledge with a foreign corporation. Japanese universities are only beginning to share their research with foreign universities. The invitation to foreign corporations to establish operations in the technopolises and prefectural-approved industrial parks is really no more than a propaganda charade, saying, "See, we welcome you foreigners to Japan but stay in the *genkan* (entrance-way) and please don't take your shoes off. We'll run the house for you." This realization is far more important to the potential investor than all the comparative analyses of sources of employees, land, electricity, water, and rail and highway access.

The *Wall Street Journal* reported on February 15, 1990, that the present twenty-six areas designated as technology centers have yet to produce a Japanese version of Silicon Valley:

> Started in 1984, Akita New Town technopolis in northern Japan, for example, has attracted only ten firms to its spacious industrial park. Of those, four are manufacturers and six are service-related, including a parcel delivery company. Nearby Akita University, strong in mining and agriculture, doesn't have an engineering department. "That's a bit of a handicap," admits one Akita government official.

Cargill spent several years obtaining permission to build a feed mill in an industrial zone created by Kagoshima Prefecture. The local agricultural cooperative feared competition. Permission was finally obtained in 1986, but only after intervention by Prime Minister Nakasone, who feared worsening trade friction over the application. Cargill's subsidiary, Cargill North Asia Ltd., had to give a written pledge, however, that it had no intention of advancing into the livestock farming business, would not sell grain at unfair prices, would obey Japanese laws and regulations, and would contribute to a stabilized supply of animal feed materials in Japan. This was in 1986, not 1972, when to receive permission for Chemical Bank to open a branch in Tokyo, the chairman of the bank had to use his stationery for a letter, the text of which was given to us by the Ministry of Finance, addressed to the minister of finance. Chemical, among other things, agreed not to ask for another branch in the foreseeable future, not to take retail deposits, and to have a senior Japanese who could speak for the bank, not just the branch, as a whole. This was an extraordinary delegation of authority to a newly hired Japanese employee and obviously meant he and the bank would accept any instructions given him by the ministry. American banks were much stronger competitively in 1972 than today. This type of arrangement severely restricted the growth of foreign banks in Japan while the Japanese banks got their act together and went after the world.[1]

Foreign businesses must realize that as competitors they are just not welcome on Japanese soil. Tolerated, yes, if excluding them is going to cause an international problem for Japanese government or business, but not welcome. This is very different from when the governor of Kentucky or the mayor of Liverpool solicits a Japanese company or any other foreign company to establish an operation in his or her state or city.

Nevertheless, if a manufacturing or R&D facility is needed in Japan because of the potential of the Japanese market, you get on with it. The plant site, particularly if advanced technology is involved and close cooperation between sales and production is required, needs to be as close to the main office in Japan as possible, or everyone needs to work out of the plant. The latter means some foreigners are going to have to learn to live on tatami mats.

Foreign firms must address problems we know exist in both rural and urban outlying areas rather than backing away or, worse, ignoring them. Too many foreign firms naively take the attitude that there does not appear to be any known objection to these areas. We know that this cannot be true, for otherwise these areas would be loaded with Japanese and foreign companies.

---

[1] *Japan Times*, April 9, 1986

7

Corporate Relationships

ENTERING JAPAN as a company or as an individual automatically means that, like anywhere, one must establish relationships with employees, suppliers, customers, and providers of services. Most of these relationships are contractual, whether written or verbal, and the contract has to fit the transaction. The importance of rules in Japan has been discussed, as has the importance of using those rules to protect one's long-term interests. But one cannot run a business on rules alone. It is necessary to go beyond them to establish relationships that will ensure the success of the business in Japan. Contacts take over from where contracts begin.

It is not just how long is your line to head office; it is how long your line is to the decision makers in Japan.

Joint Ventures

Some have chosen joint ventures to further their entry or building strategy. Often these joint ventures were imposed upon the foreign entry by the Japanese government. As one person said, "You cannot imagine how restrictive it was back in 1969. A lot of people forget that." Today that is far less common, but one major investor in Japan said that in the defense sector the Japanese government instructed them on whom to work with and sell to. They work through the government and do not go direct.

Joint ventures have not been known to retain common, long-term, noncompetitive interests, especially when the foreign partner has been relatively inactive in management. If the foreign interests are represented by on-site, head-office management, then the issues are somewhat the same as for a wholly owned subsidiary or branch, except decisions must be shared on someone else's home turf. In any event, the relationships built with the partner and its management will determine a company's success. Japanese companies are as conscious of success and competition as any in the world. Often, though, they measure success at any given time differently than do U.S. or European corporations. Survival and market share will be far more prominent in their thinking than shareholder earnings. Differences in approach are resolved before going into business together and then are constantly evaluated and reevaluated to meet the needs of the partners.

Many joint ventures have been shotgun weddings: neither side got what it wanted. The Japanese wanted a licensing agreement and the foreigner, especially Americans, wanted a wholly owned subsidiary. There was a lack of commonality of interests from the start. Unless the interests and objectives of both sides are quite parallel from the very beginning, there are going to be serious difficulties along the way. Many joint ventures have also suffered with the passage of time and the far-reaching changes in the Japanese economy. Ventures established twenty-five years ago look to be from the horse-and-buggy era, when one considers Japan's ability to market abroad today, the extraordinary improvements in original products, and the amount of capital available to Japan. Many of the foreign partners are selling out to the Japanese side, as the Japanese choose to compete against their partners at home and abroad and as the high value of the yen appeals to the foreign seller. Joint ventures continue to be formed, however, because Japan is so expensive that the foreigners decide they cannot afford to go it alone in capital-intensive industries, particularly when distribution is involved.

When a joint venture is being considered, a company must first ask what it wants from Japan; what are its criteria for success? No matter what the preconceptions are, it must have people in Japan to develop an in-house understanding of that country. A company has to fight its own battles; others cannot or will not. With a 50-50 joint venture, the company will not be running its own business in the broadest management context. The joint venture partner might do very well by one, but a Japanese will have been chosen to be the general. Most important, the company is not developing an asset to build upon in the future. To build a substantial business in Japan one needs predominant control and ownership in order to develop core people who learn marketing, sales, the competition, and so forth. Peripheral aspects of the business, such as distribution, can then be handled as a joint venture. A joint venture in and of itself is generally the first step of a two-step strategy that does not take a second step.

Most foreigners go five years before they understand what is happening with personnel in a joint venture. If one is not alert from the day the joint venture begins, it is probably too late, for it takes at least five years to weed out the incompetents who have been seconded by the Japanese partner. Unfortunately, it appears that almost every foreign company goes through this pain individually. Perhaps the words of those involved in joint ventures will assist those considering this mode of entry or expansion in Japan.

All our joint venture partners are diversifying into the exact same things we are, and they feel they need to move into the United States. They are looking more and more like competitors. We're at a crossroads now with all our joint ventures. We need to take over some and integrate them into our operation. You give technology for a 50 percent share; then they train their people, not yours, further fragmenting and complicating your problems. We now insist on being consulted on all personnel moves in joint ventures and are putting in our own people. When they said it was contrary to the agreement, we said change it.

In a joint venture, Japanese companies want an arms-length arrangement. A foreign partner should never accept this, even if a joint venture is the only viable alternative. In one such distribution case recently, the foreign general manager noted:

The minute the ink was dry on the joint venture agreement, the *kachos* and *buchos* [assistant managers and managers] got on the airplane with me for the United States. A kacho said: "I'm not sure you need your office here at all. Why don't you just go away and we will take care of it." I put this comment on the agenda and the response at home was, "Don't they like you?" It is not a question of being liked. They are just testing us. If someone is well liked here, I would question whether he is getting anything done.

We have our colleagues in Tokyo sit on our joint venture boards. Head-office people can be no more than ornaments. We want truly working boards. We own the shares here in Japan. They are joint ventures of our Japanese incorporated company. We even have joint ventures with German subsidiaries of our parent.

To think from the beginning you can live together with a completely alien organization forever is unwise. If you go in with your eyes open and know it is an interim solution that will last perhaps 20 percent of the time, that is fine for immediate access to the market or technology. Just be sure at the beginning to allow in the future for one side or the other to take over in as nondisruptive a manner as possible or for the joint venture to become stand-alone.

This matter should be confronted up front in any joint venture negotiations and included in all contractual arrangements. Not to do so is unrealistic.

Often a tremendous amount of energy is expended initially in a joint venture, and then interest falls off. The same happens also in wholly owned ventures.

A joint venture has to be a marriage made in heaven, a truly unusual situation where the motivations of the partners are so similar, so honorable and so focused that they are going to manage and see that it works; that people just do not return home saying it is going to work. It won't. You would think people would learn from the past, but we have the same problem today.

There is another view on running joint ventures.

The idea of having a policeman overlooking the joint venture does not work. We like to have the president of the joint venture committed to that venture. We don't want anybody inside. We feel all the personnel should come from the Japanese side. My job as the only expatriate in Asia is to foster a very close relationship between their CEO and our CEO. Our objective is not to control our ventures in Japan. Our objective is to make money in Japan. It is an important distinction. If you try to control anything in Japan as a foreigner, you end up frustrated because you can't control. But you can influence. I have a tremendous amount of power to get things done in Japan, much the same way a Japanese executive my own age has power to get things done. I know people; I have relationships; and I have been working with them a long time. I use that not to force things, because I can't. My position is unique, however, because I have been in Japan a long time and to the Japanese I am the company in Japan. My job is to identify opportunities for the CEO to whom I report. I am here because he needs me here. If it were left up to the corporate divisions, they would decide probably not to have this position in Japan because it dilutes their absolute control over their business.

Pity the poor foreigner who is succeeding him in 1990.

A Japanese general manager, hired from a Japanese company to replace a foreigner in a joint venture, commented:

> I have learned two things. First, the budgeting is very different. The Japanese partner sets a target, a stretch budget. If it is not made because of market conditions, that is understood. When the foreign side sets a budget goal, that goal must be met. The Japanese view is one of vision while the foreign view is one of predetermined reality, which means safety. The foreign view is we will predetermine what share of an existing market we will have and we will grow or decline in proportion with the growth or decline in the overall market. They understand the targeting concept but won't accept it. The Japanese side understands the foreign methodology but will not accept "realistic targets." On both sides you often have understanding without acceptance.
>
> The second difference is in implementation. The Japanese wish to use the plant's capacity to the fullest. If the market is stagnant, you lower your prices, as long as you maintain a marginal profit. The foreign view is to lessen your capacity while maintaining your margin, arriving perhaps at the same overall profit as the Japanese. But in the long run you have not increased your sales. There is stagnation because your capacity is not fully utilized, and you don't have personnel in place when the market turns. As a result, if you follow the Japanese view there will be overall price erosion but perhaps a growth in total world usage. With the Western view, the market will be stabilized without price erosion. One must be fully aware of the importance of whatever action is taken. The pricing element is one of the reasons foreign companies in Japan hinder their growth by not being willing to reduce profit for market share while the Japanese have been flooding their home markets and the world with products. The Western corporations look at their businesses in one-year business cycles while the Japanese look at one year as one year in the life of the product. While the foreign partner in the joint venture is looking for stabilized growth in a market where the product has been produced for forty years, the Japanese are looking to application growth for the product and are constantly looking for new means by which to use the basic product through new development.

This general manager subsequently found that he could not reconcile the differences between the partners. Few, whether Japanese or foreign, could when the basic business philosophies are so different.

Another general manager converted a hundred-year-old joint venture into a wholly owned venture:

> A joint venture in the Japanese context makes a lot of sense, but I think it is even more essential in a joint venture than in a wholly owned operation to have the right kind of people at a high level to bridge the interests and

problems of the partners. It really requires experience and talent.

The joint venture has been reluctant to use research, particularly qualitative. The Japanese feel they know how to do things. This is their country, system, language, culture. They are just not comfortable with our style of research.

Language is a major reason why you are better off with a joint venture. You cannot make a wholly owned venture in this country successful unless you have a very, very special niche. Usually that is based on proprietary technology. More often than not the Japanese and not the foreigner has that today.

In a joint venture you have the same work rules and same computer system as the Japanese parent who has employed the staff in the past or hires them for the joint venture. He leaves his files but not his brain when he goes back to the parent. Nothing is proprietary.

So many companies came to Japan because the Japanese came to them and said, "Come over, you are our counterpart, let's form a venture, bring your technology." That is just not the way. You don't go to the competitor. Go where you have the complementary skills. There are all kinds of possibilities. That is one of the few ways small to medium high-tech companies can play in this market. It makes absolutely no sense to come unless you see yourself having some basis for a sustainable strategic advantage. There is a great risk that you may come in with that but lose it through no fault of your own. A big Japanese company can sink you with price cutting or steal your technology. But there is still an American arrogance. It is more damaging or gets in the way more than it used to because a corresponding Japanese arrogance is also developing. That mutual arrogance is really going to get in the way of a lot that needs to happen. I have never seen the foreigner as isolated as he is today, because the Japanese perceive there is no need today to have interaction.

To be successful, a joint venture requires as much up-front consideration and subsequent effort as does a wholly owned branch or subsidiary.

Global Partnerships

An expression in vogue today in Japan and elsewhere is "global partnership." What this means is far from clear. Everyone who uses the term understands it differently. The possibilities for management confusion are enormous. The term can mean a legal corporate structure such as that formed by Honeywell, Bull, and NEC, or it can mean an informal market sharing. The only way it can make sense for a foreign corporation and a Japanese corporation is if both have decided whom they want to work with on a global basis, if one is the supplier and the other is the buyer of a service or product, and if each has no intention of being in the other's business. Too often foreign companies have gone to Japan and wooed or more likely been wooed by a Japanese competitor, in effect giving up control of their business in Japan and often later outside Japan to their Japanese competitor. There is nothing dishonest or sneaky on the Japanese partner's side. They are just smart, pragmatic businessmen who have done their homework, understand their domestic and global competitors, and want them out of the way as soon as possible, the foreign ones first of all. They will represent the foreigner in the industrial trade association and assure the Japanese community that their partner will not get out of hand. For a foreign company, the only reason to consider a joint venture or partnership that does not call for full participation by all concerned is short-term profitability.

Many foreign companies today do not have the capital, product, service, or intelligence to compete globally. Japan clearly is the largest exporter of capital in the world. The cost of capital to its corporations is also the cheapest in the world. Its products and services rank at or near the top in almost all non–defense-related areas, and its market intelligence is unsurpassed. In short, while the Japanese came to study for thirty years, they are now the teachers with the resources to teach. Now foreigners are going to the Japanese, or should be, much as Japanese came to Americans in the 1960s, with one important difference. Whereas the Japanese came to the Americans systematically in the 1950s, 1960s, and 1970s, studying, learning, and implementing, with results to show in product and knowledge enhancement for every yen spent, Americans and Europeans have generally not been prepared to sacrifice corporate earnings or to sacrifice personally to compete with Japan and its neighbors. Unlike foreign currency borrowings directed by the Japanese government in the 1950s and 1960s, which enhanced Japanese productivity, today the U.S. government is wasting capital in nonproductive, debt-service borrowing from overseas. The learning curve is competitively sloped the wrong way, and the Japanese are not enthusiastic about teaching the foreigner what they have learned.

Potential Japanese partners have completely turned the tables, whether it be in automobiles, facsimile machines, or machine tools. They are going out to the world while Japan remains their citadel. Anyone establishing a global partnership had better know why they want the partnership and why the Japanese party does, for the stakes are enormous today when many of the world's largest corporate entities, with the deepest pockets, are Japanese. In sum, relationship analysis becomes competitive analysis. American insensitivity to corporate history does not bode well for American interests. The same can be said for most European companies in Japan.

Relationship Analysis

Where does the potential Japanese partner fit in the corporate fabric of Japan? Is the Japanese company a member of a particular industrial group? Who owns shares in the company, particularly corporate shareholders, since Japanese corporations can and do own shares in each other? Share ownership has commonly been a means of cementing relationships among Japanese sister companies, buyers, and suppliers. Most important, it has permitted a stable shareholder relationship for management since 60 to 70 percent of Japanese shares on the First Section of the Tokyo Stock Exchange are not traded. Moreover, with Japanese corporate P-E ratios of 45 to 1, not many foreign companies are interested in buying Japanese companies. Management has therefore not had to concern itself with individual shareholders' needs or demands, but focuses on maintaining good relationships with corporate family and bankers. All of this relationship information is available in the Japanese equivalent of the 10K (*Yuka Shoken Hokokusho*) filed with the Ministry of Finance, which is very specific on bank relationships, history of directors, and so forth. One looks closely for any conflicts of interest that a potential partner might have in helping to build either a substantial business in Japan or elsewhere. If a conflict exists, the business will never progress satisfactorily. It cannot be talked or negotiated away if it does not make good business sense. The partnership has to make good business sense for all the partners involved, now and for the foreseeable future. The Japanese concept of the future is considerably longer than the American, but closer to the European. They are quite prepared to wait you out, since they have learned that the foreigner always goes away. They make no effort to assimilate the foreigner or even permit his assimilation. This should also be borne in mind when doing business in South Korea, Taiwan, and China.

Day-to-day relationships with suppliers and customers are easily as important as any larger corporate partnerships. Tying up with a particular industrial group can often mean that you cannot work with the members of other groups, or rather they will not work with you, no matter how much you try. Partners, suppliers, customers, and banks should all be studied to make sure there is not an inherent conflict. Each can either assist or even destroy the other if so desired. If you say the market is one hundred, but someone in the Mitsubishi group is making the product, then everyone in the Mitsubishi group will buy from that company. The market then becomes eighty. If you repeat this exercise with the Sumitomo group and the Mitsui group, then perhaps the market really available to an outside entry is only forty. A Mitsubishi employee drinks only Kirin Beer, at least in public. You will not find him buying a Budweiser in front of his boss, nor a Suntory Beer for that matter.

Pragmatic business and intellectual interests must be identified in relationships for business to be successful. There is very little room for the emotional, unless the relationship is extremely long term. A few are, but again they are not the norm. Foreign corporations should work to see that more are, but with the turnover in personnel and the merger and acquisition activity in American business it is difficult. This is less so with Europeans, who tend to stay longer with their company and also in Japan.

This is not to say that time alone makes for a healthy business relationship. If a particular relationship with a foreigner no longer makes business sense compared to other alternatives, the Japanese will drop it faster than they can say sayonara. One of the bigger myths propagated on foreigners and believed by them is that a long-term relationship cannot be invalidated. This is true at times among Japanese where other obligations come into play, but a foreigner is not Japanese.

Neutrality is often in a foreign company's interest and an

important reason for deciding to have a wholly owned subsidiary or branch. In this way, though the process usually takes longer, a larger customer base, whether industrial or consumer, can be targeted. Both involve having a distribution system, and few foreign companies have the wherewithal to handle distribution on their own. How successfully one distributes a product or service will usually depend on the relationships established with distributors; that is, why the distributors perceive what they are distributing for you to be more important than what they are doing for a competitor or potential competitor. The more one can economically control one's own distribution the better. This is not easy in a country that is the size of California but has 1.6 million retail outlets, excluding eating and drinking establishments. The United States has only 1.4 million, with more than twice the population and twenty-five times the space. Those myriad distributors serve everything from industrial chemicals to agricultural insecticides to mosquito repellent coils (see chapters 11 and 12). Relationships are extremely important if one is to be successful. Without competitor analysis, though, success is precluded from the beginning. A multiplicity of relationships that eventually become instinctive, if not institutionalized, are needed. They must always be mutually beneficial to have life. They are not established through one or two meetings. In short, business is not built on plane schedules.

Acquisition

Why can't foreign companies acquire a Japanese company? Acquisition in Japan is still the acquisition of a failing company. With few exceptions, such as British Oxygen's purchase of Osaka Sanso Kogyo in 1982 and Merck's purchase of Banyu in 1983, foreign companies are in no position to rescue a failing Japanese company. Japan is simply priced out of the market for most foreign investors. Even the companies in bad shape are still high priced because of the inflated value of the Tokyo stock market. The living organism concept of the Japanese company also prevents a foreigner from acting quickly to turn a situation around. Assets cannot be sold off quickly or employees let go without a great deal of rationalization.

Poison-Pen Letters

One last caution on corporate relationships. American (and European) head-office management tends to be much more willing to listen to a Japanese outsider about Japan than to the company's American employees in Japan. The Japanese know and use this trait to try to get around the American company's foreign management in Japan. If their communicant gets burned, another soldier moves forward until they find an ear. If foreigners try to influence Japanese staff in a Japanese company, they are told not to interfere in internal affairs and get nowhere. Nevertheless, the Japanese feel no qualms about carrying negative messages that are in their interest and do so consistently with foreign government and business officials. This is almost always to the detriment of that government or business and its home-country employees in Japan.

Often our head office asks our Japanese distributor for their recommendations. What they don't recognize is that they are getting the Japanese opinion. They don't fully understand the opinion, though they think they understand. They don't know the reason the Japanese said what he did rather than what he might have said. Although the advice might be good advice, it often needs interpretation and puts you in a position of being negative when you contradict what has been said.

One unpleasant aspect of working in Japan that is difficult to explain to a head office is the poison-pen letter. It is not uncommon for Japanese staff members who are upset with a foreign general manager or the company itself to send poison-pen letters to the general manager's boss or even to the chairman of the company. One reason is that the Japanese staff can only take their frustrations out on the general manager and not on a boss eight thousand miles away. It is also a way to undermine the foreign general manager's credibility in head office if he is cleaning up a mess they would prefer not to have exposed, or if the competition has gotten to one of the employees. More than likely, when a head office receives these letters, its general manager is doing what he should be doing. The head office should immediately send the letter back to the general manager. If the writer is not anonymous, the sender should be confronted and dealt with severely, most likely with dismissal, in close coordination with one's attorneys.

If the letter is anonymous, the general manager should file it away and keep his antennae up. If head office chooses to take it seriously and investigate, the general manager should be removed immediately, for he will never again function effectively in Japan. "Unfortunately, poison-pen letters are fairly common. People do not talk about them, because who wants to talk about such an unpleasant experience." They usually arrive about six months after a new general manager takes an assignment.

This has happened to economic ministers in both the American and British embassies and was a major problem for me personally when establishing the American Express Card in Japan. JCB, our partner for years in a joint American Express/JCB Card for use only outside of Japan, was furious when American Express did not agree to let them have the American Express franchise for a Japanese American Express universal card when that became possible in August 1978. In the summer of 1979, American Express, fearing that they could not make it on their own in Japan and receiving this very advice from JCB through indirect channels, offered JCB a half interest in the American Express Japanese operation in return for marketing assistance, but on the condition that American Express would run the company in Japan. JCB turned down the offer unless they could run the company, saying there was too great a financial risk. American Express then offered half the card company in Japan for nothing with no downside risk, but American Express would run the company. Fortunately for American Express, JCB again turned down the offer, but meanwhile it began to do everything possible to interfere with the possibility of a successful launch and to ruin my personal and business reputation at the chairman level at American Express.

To do the card business in Japan, American Express needed the major Japanese banks to agree to direct debit the accounts of their mutual customers once a month since checking accounts are not widely used in Japan. Everyone, from utilities to card companies, runs a direct-debit tape monthly through the banks of their clients. In late December 1979, just one month before the launch advertising was to appear with the names of all the major banks, except one, who would do direct debit for American Express, I learned that JCB had asked their principal shareholder, Sanwa Bank—also the institution from which all their senior management came—to tell the other banks that Sanwa had decided not to work with American Express and to ask them also not to work with us. Several banks came to my office saying they were withdrawing from their agreement with us. Fortunately, our attorneys had advised us to send a registered letter to each bank when they had agreed to work with us, thanking them, and so forth. Early the next morning, after a late-night, knockdown, drag-out confrontation at Sanwa Bank, I called on an official at the Ministry of Finance whom I had known for years and with whom my integrity was unquestioned. After I explained the situation, he suggested I go to the newly established Office of the Trade Ombudsman and file a complaint. I politely told him that I had a business to launch in a month and that if this was not resolved immediately, I was going public and to the Fair Trade Commission, pointing out the collusion among JCB, Sanwa Bank, and several other Japanese banks. He then suggested I let him think it over. The next morning Sanwa Bank called and said they would work with us, and the other banks fell in line. To this day the senior Ministry of Finance official asks jokingly, "How are your friends at Sanwa Bank?"

The story was not over for me personally, however. Over a period of a year I heard rumors and questions about my personal behavior and my reputation in the Japanese business community, in particular with Japan Airlines and the Okura Hotel, the two most important relationships for American Express in Japan. It eventually turned out that JCB was using several disgruntled American Express employees, including one foreigner who had wanted my job in the first place and another who now wanted it, as well as Japanese staff whom I was making toe the line, as communicants to the chairman and my boss. I eventually was confronted with these accusations in the summer of 1980. I figured out their source, told American Express the facts, and asked to be pulled out immediately if they did not have faith in me. Tremendous, inexcusable damage was done, and only because of the support of Louis Gerstner, then head of Travel Related Services at American Express, and several colleagues who told him about working with JCB, was the matter finally resolved. This is the type of credibility issue an outside hire almost always faces. A senior executive who had been assigned from head office would never have his integrity questioned in the way mine was by

American Express (nor would my previous employer have ever questioned it). Sending an outside hire to Japan is done at great risk to the company and the individual. The only satisfaction out of a sick situation came from the dismissal at JCB of the president and executive vice-president, who had failed to gain control of American Express for JCB. The succeeding president did not give up, though, giving anonymous interviews to *Toyo Keizai* magazine and the *Nihon Keizai Shimbun* that said that the American Express Card in Japan had serious financial problems. Although it was totally false, that, of course, is the worst thing one can say about a financial company.

As painful to accept as it is, foreign companies in Japan have to expect personal attacks and that the competition will do anything they can to get rid of them. An expatriate manager in a joint venture, particularly if he is the only foreign executive and tries to implement policies that are opposed by the Japanese partner, is especially vulnerable. This is exactly what happened at the Ogilvy & Mather/Tokyu advertising joint venture. I had warned the chairman of Ogilvy & Mather about this type of personal attack, and six months later it began on the foreign general manager. Ogilvy made the mistake of giving in and transferring a superb employee because of Tokyu's complaints. They should have closed the office then, instead of waiting a few years and doing further damage to their reputation.

Competition comes in many guises in Japan.

8

Finance

ALONG WITH the new-found freedom to fail in Japan comes the freedom to finance a foreign corporate operation in ways never conceived of by the foreign corporate pioneers of the 1950s, 1960s, and 1970s. When I went to Japanese banks in 1979 and early 1980 seeking lines of credit to finance the receivables of the American Express Company, one of the most successful financial institutions in the world, I was able to obtain only one line of credit from a Japanese bank for the equivalent of $4 million. American Express at that time through its banking subsidiary extended extensive credit to Japanese banks, and its treasury department held substantial Japanese bank paper. If it had not been for foreign banks—Morgan Guaranty, Manufacturers Hanover, Continental Illinois, Chemical, Banque Nationale de Paris, and Credit Lyonnaise—it would have been impossible to open our doors in May 1980, because the need to finance card receivables was enormous.

Until 1972 the foreign banks were always illiquid, and therefore the Japanese banks could virtually control which foreign operations would be allowed to enter and to grow. At that time, and even recently, the Bank of Japan required of the banks quarterly submissions on whom they were going to lend to the next quarter. Foreign borrowers were not high on the list of either the Bank of Japan or the principal Japanese city banks. In 1982, prior to a cross-country speaking tour in the United States, I asked a Japanese banker, who had been one of the account officers who extended that original line of credit in 1980, what advice I should give my audiences on starting substantial businesses in Japan. His response was forthright and honest: he could not give any advice since American Express was the only foreign company success he had been associated with. Two other major foreign clients to whom his bank extended credit had their credit withdrawn under pressure from their Japanese competitors and, without funding, had to phase out their operations in Japan.

Fortunately, since the early 1980s, the Japanese banks have been quite liquid and willing to fund foreign companies that take the initiative to seek funding, if this means a global relationship for the bank and company. One of the more ridiculous aspects of foreign banking in Tokyo today—whether American, British, French, or German—is that the foreign bankers are almost all capital markets, money desk, foreign exchange, merchant bankers. Few know what a loan is, and they are darn lazy about seeking them out. One client sarcastically referred to these individuals as a bunch of swap noids and screen jocks. Others refer to them as the American auto dealers of the 1970s: "You have to come to us for the products we want to give you."

As the market became more and more liquid in the 1980s, the Japanese banks became more aggressive in seeking out foreign corporate business. In fact, by 1989 the Japanese were the most global of international bankers. When I was visiting a major German manufacturer's Japan operation, the secretary opened the door of the general manager's office and said, "Here they come!" In walked the Japanese bankers.

> On a micro-basis your Japanese banker will just kill himself to help you. They are not creative, but from a straight banking point of view they are always looking for ways to do things for you. If you can get your Japanese banker to understand what it takes to help you with your business, generally they will do it. You have to insure that they understand you.

Thus a problem of the past, availability of funding, no longer exists, at least for now.

Foreign Banks

It is important to balance off the foreign and Japanese bankers for the company's needs today and in the future. The foreign bankers with whom one has relationships in head office or elsewhere can provide ongoing funds at a reasonable rate and are a benchmark against which to measure the cost of funds. They will be there when they are needed because of the head-office relationship. Their requirements, once agreed to, are easily understood and generally only amended as necessary on an annual basis, since that is about as often as they want to see you.

Japanese Banks

Japanese bankers operate very effectively but differently. To begin with, until the recent history of liquidity, they have been in a position to make demands on clients, or at least constantly to question. They are accustomed to walking in and out of a corporate office at will, talking about the business to any employees they happen to meet. In sum, they make the company's business their business. They can be either very helpful or an aggravation, depending on how they are managed.

Japanese banks come every day, even if they don't have any business, asking questions. U.S. banks come once a year, providing our needs on a yearly basis with yearly terms and conditions. Every day is a nuisance, for I can't let them be alone. Some manager has to be with them. The U.S. way is more businesslike, but I miss them. Once it is done, they don't come in.

The general manager should make it a point to get to know his bankers, particularly the Japanese, as his participation raises the level of attention given by the Japanese banks and sets the tone as to how the relationship will be managed. The financial officers should handle the day-by-day administration of the loans, deposits, and foreign exchange. The percentage of business given to each bank in each of these areas should be administered carefully, as dealings with each Japanese bank will be known to the others. There are no secrets.

It is different. I am used to telling the banks what I want. We were borrowing a billion yen for thirty days when we needed it for only three days every month. They refused to give us an overdraft facility, so I paid them off and went to the foreign banks. Our Japanese banks panicked, and we now have overdraft facilities from them.

The general manager must make clear to all his employees that the only people who can provide financial or other business information on the company are the finance manager and himself, period. Otherwise he will find that information of great value to his competition will be going out the door with his Japanese bankers daily.

At the year-end in-house party there was a banker sitting there. My staff resented that I was upset.

Japanese bankers today are global bankers. The ten largest banks in the world are Japanese, and Japanese banks are the largest national banking group of exporters of capital. In return for service and facilities provided in Japan, they will naturally wish and expect to take care of a portion of the company's global financial needs. They have the capacity and it should be used, for that stimulates them to be even more helpful in Japan. Because of their ratings and the relatively low cost of yen funds, their funding costs are often the lowest in the world. The low cost of yen borrowing has made it an absolute joy to build a growth business in Japan. This has been the case for the past decade, and with the continued high personal savings rate of 15 percent and the liquidity created by the Japanese export machine, there is no anticipation of a change in readily available yen. It does not give a cost advantage over the Japanese competition, but, financially, foreign companies can play today on a level playing field. This is a real incentive to build one's business rapidly. Once the payback begins, it can be substantial in a strong currency. If both foreign and Japanese banks are used properly, one can build a business with little or no input of capital from offshore. Head office should be reminded that it is a yen-based business, and the performance should be measured accordingly, for better or worse to begin with and certainly for the better in the long run if the present yen cost and valuation continues.

Japanese bankers should be used where possible for customer introductions and nationwide service. The Japanese competition thinks, "How can the banks and securities houses help sell my product?" A foreign company should too. It should not choose Sumitomo Bank if its principal competitor is a Sumitomo group company, but if its competitor is a Mitsubishi group company, then no bank could serve it better, for as they say in Japan, "Where Sumitomo Bank walks, no grass grows." It is essential to understand who the competition is before choosing the banks, if the desire is for them to help rather than hinder the operation.

Each category of Japanese banks—the eleven city banks, the three long-term credit banks, the trust banks, the Bank of Tokyo, the regional and mutual savings banks—was formed under different laws and serves different banking functions within Japan and, to a certain extent, outside Japan. Their differences and attributes should be studied and matched against the company's needs and used accordingly. The Industrial Bank of Japan is not used as a retail bank, since as a long-term credit bank their branch network is limited, unlike a Dai-Ichi Kangyo Bank, which in 1989 had the largest number of branches and amount of deposits. Industrial is used for long-term funding, generally two years and beyond, and for research and introductions, for there is no more prominent a bank in Japan or the world. The quality of staff available to assist a company in an Industrial or Mitsubishi or Sumitomo Bank is extraordinary by any global banking standards. Used properly, they can be of immense assistance and can also help keep the wolves at bay. Just don't unknowingly let them graze among the sheep.

Government banks, in particular the Export-Import Bank or the Japan Development Bank, can give a company official blessing if they choose to work with the company. The JDB's blessing for both Japanese and foreign industrial start-ups has been historically very meaningful in attracting subsequent Japanese commercial banking assistance, and the lending rates are generally below commercial rates. Its documentary requirements, though, have often been impractical, if not onerous, and therefore require close scrutiny before proceeding. The official blessing at times is worth the trouble, for it makes it quite difficult for a government agency to hinder one's progress.

Japanese Securities Houses

In Europe and in the United States until recently, the investment bankers and securities houses have carried an aura of professionalism and respect. That has never been the situation in Japan, though few foreigners, ignorant of the society they are living and working in, appreciate this difference. Japanese have viewed securities houses as pawnbrokers, the old three balls, the traders of shares, nothing more. Today, the big four—Nomura, Nikko,

Daiwa, and Yamaichi—are enormous by any global standards. The capitalization of these four is roughly ten times that of the four largest American investment/securities houses, and in this world, including Japan, money talks.

The reputations of the securities houses precluded them historically from attracting the type of university graduates that went, for instance, to the major banks and insurance houses, especially after the four majors almost went under from 1963 to 1965. All but Nomura had to be bailed out by Ministry of Finance management. As a result, their employees have been aggressive peddlers, with few graces by Japanese standards, and that atmosphere continues to permeate their behavior and actions. With their newly acquired wealth and national and global visibility, however, in the 1980s they have begun to attract better graduates, particularly in their research subsidiaries. In dealing with them, whether in listing the parent company's shares on the Tokyo exchange or in raising or managing funds, the general manager must go in with his eyes open and have first-class Japanese and foreign assistance in reviewing any proposals.

The rivalry between the old-line, respected bankers and the nouveau-riche brokers is as intense as any in Japan and is often played out in the halls of the Ministry of Finance. The foreign corporation does not want to be used as a stalking horse by one party or the other at the ministry. If one wishes to be involved in this rivalry for business reasons, then one must be sure to be one's own spokesman for the company. As savvy an institution in Japan as Morgan Guaranty found itself caught at the Ministry of Finance between the Banking and Securities bureaus when the press leaked the story that it was planning a joint venture trust bank with Nomura Securities. There were a lot of red faces and permission was not granted, though it is likely the Japanese who leaked the story felt they could force the issue one way or the other by the leak, either using the foreigner to get an exception because of the trade problems between the United States and Japan, or getting the proposal killed because a securities house was crossing the Japanese Glass-Steagall line into banking. The aggressiveness of the securities houses can be used effectively if managed, but if not, you will soon find them trying to manage you in Japan.

As Japanese financial markets and institutions become more

sophisticated and powerful, foreign corporations are accessing the local equity market and finding ingenious ways to raise funds from local operations for offshore use. Disney, for example, arranged its financing based on the future cash flow from its licensing arrangement with Disneyland Tokyo. Clearly, there will be a growing number of financing opportunities for foreign corporations knowledgeable about and familiar to Japanese financial institutions.

The head office reposits in the general manager the management of both banks and securities houses in Japan, to delegate as he sees fit. The pressures that banks and securities houses can place on a Japanese employee are substantial and must be tempered by senior foreign participation in the relationships, with the company's wisest, most mature Japanese involved, each complementing the other in maintaining and furthering the firm's financial interests. The general manager in turn coordinates with his head office the best way to get the most out of today's important Japanese banks and securities houses, on both a Japanese and a global basis.

9

Accounting, Audit, and Tax Planning

THE IMPORTANCE of and difficulties presented by accounting, audit, and tax planning for the foreign company in Japan cannot be underestimated. As previously mentioned, there are two ways to bring a business to an immediate halt anywhere: serious personnel problems and accounting problems. Regrettably, accounting, audit, and tax planning happen to be the areas where the general manager has the weakest in-house and community support staff in Japan.

Accounting Profession

The public accounting family in Japan is both small and relatively young historically, as is true with many of the professions. There are only eight thousand CPAs in Japan, doing primarily auditing, with few of the additional services provided in the West. Only three hundred accountants a year become what are known as junior CPAs, as only 10 or 11 percent of the candidates pass the examination. About one hundred of those who pass go on to graduate school, leaving only two hundred a year for the entire accounting profession in Japan. Until the 1970s, foreign accounting firms were able to recruit successfully from this limited population because of their international reputations and the opportunities for overseas assignments. Overseas assignments, particularly in the computer area, remain an attraction. With the growth of Japanese accounting firms and the merging of many Western firms into Japanese firms, foreign firms today are having great difficulty in recruiting accounting, audit, and tax people. Western accounting firms, however, do not lose anywhere near the same percentage of employees to their clients as they do in the United States, presumably because there is a great deal more prestige, comfort, and security in working for a foreign accounting firm than for a foreign corporation. A senior partner of a big-six accounting firm cautions:

> After two or three years of employment at an accounting firm, it is very difficult to get an accountant out because they move in lock-step with their peers. The Japanese staff is hesitant to give a critical evaluation, and it is therefore difficult for us to get into our files the documentation that would give us normal cause to review, pass over, or promote annually. The turnover in foreign management also precludes historical memory. Many accountants who could not make it in their Western accounting firms are fobbed off on another accounting firm's client, or they go through an employment agency.

A principal, legitimate reason for an accountant to leave his firm is to return home to work for a family company or to set up shop where he is known locally to handle local accounting and tax needs. With the limited number of CPAs, this can be very lucrative.

Western accounting firms face a serious problem in staffing regional offices, even in cities as large as Osaka and Nagoya. It is difficult to recruit professionals who know the local community and its bureaucratic structure. People sent out from Tokyo are always working to get back. As outsiders, they rarely learn the local infrastructure. Games are also played in all foreign companies, not just in accounting companies, with these assignments. The reason the Japanese staff wants a particular individual to be assigned out of Tokyo is not always transparent. Every effort must be made to find out, or an incompetent may be exiled to run an important office. On the other hand, if a good local person is found, he may encounter resistance from the Japanese staff in Tokyo, who do not like someone building an individual fiefdom. All in all, this is an extremely difficult issue for foreign companies with their extraordinary recruiting problems. Any foreign company that needs accounting, audit, and tax advice on an ongoing, professional basis should review seriously any thought of establishing its principal office outside the Tokyo area.

When hiring or reviewing potential employees for financial accounting, one soon learns that they usually have not had any experience in preparing financial statements and budget forecasts. Generally they have worked on only one particular type of invoice in a specific industry. Moreover, since they have rarely been part of management, they do not understand financial management. When someone is hired from a Japanese company for accounting, he or she should be required to go through the corporate accounting manual and learn it down to a "T." Such employees will simply not be conversant in standard Western accounting procedures; whatever their level, they must be trained by the company in accounting. Financial planning and forecasting should be taught by an expatriate, preferably not an accountant but an actual financial planner with good people skills.

Auditing

The comments of two general managers with extensive management experience in Japan and elsewhere will alert a general manager to the potential for problems in his Japanese operation:

Accounting support is completely worthless in Japan. I seriously question their standards, practices. They are narrow in their approach. Although they see a large number of businesses, they normally only see one facet of that business. When we are trying to get a handle on this or that, can we get an answer? Hell no! The auditors also don't understand the changes occurring in procedures in the United States. They only count your tickets. I also have little faith in my local staff ever blowing the whistle. The staff tends to be timid. Easier to go along, let it go by. The absence of comments is the danger. This is especially true when one's peers or boss goes over prescribed limits, whether in foreign exchange transactions or personal entertainment. I have to stay involved. I say, "Is that right?" and they say, "No, I don't think it is," and then we get the conversation going. I have to be there to provide that kind of stimulation. One cannot tolerate violations of clearly stated company regulations and must make this very clear, especially if the front is put up, "That is the Japanese way."

Don't believe it when you are told all Japanese are honest. There is a presumption by foreigners for whatever reason that there is honesty in this country. You cannot compare countries, but the presumption of honesty here is too highly placed. You need a good accounting system and *very* good audit procedures.

With the difficulty foreign management has in reading Japanese, an internal audit team from head office who knows the business is totally susceptible to internal fraud. An outside auditing firm who does not know the business and is relying upon its Japanese employees—particularly those from an affiliated Japanese company who are not integrated physically into the American or European operation—is likely to let a great deal fall between the cracks. The head office of the branch or subsidiary being audited and the head office of its international accounting firm and their respective Japanese staffs generally work separately instead of together. In the audit firms' Japanese offices, the Japanese and foreign staffs also usually do not look at issues as common problems that have to be worked out together.

To have an effective audit, one has to build common language, background, and knowledge, knowing where the trapdoors are. Few have. A foreign senior audit partner observes: "As to the quality of the auditing of Japanese accounting firms, I think they still have a long ways to go. The level to which they subject management to a healthy skepticism is still questionable." The foreign accounting firms are not immune to this mind fix either since their audit personnel are usually Japanese. Neither local management nor head office ends up with an effective audit for managing.

The Ministry of Finance remains embarrassed by the audit failures at Mitsukoshi Department Store, Heiwa Sogo Bank, Ataka Trading Company, and Osawa Trading Company. As a result, it has put significant pressure on the Japanese Institute of CPAs, which has in turn put some quality control pressure on the profession. But there is a long way to go.

Control

A problem generally encountered is cooking the books to meet some target that has been set, thereby avoiding the loss of someone's face—not necessarily putting money into someone's pockets. A senior auditing partner of a major accounting firm feels that "this could be indicative of two things: the culture or our inability to find other indiscretions. I suspect a little of both."

Companies like American Express Travel have found that embezzlement by a senior manager can be covered for years through the inability of foreigners to read Japanese, combined with their accounting firms not understanding their business. Moreover, as long as they refuse to prosecute the offending parties when caught, they are just telling their employees in the boarding house of no secrets that the cookie jar, refrigerator, and freezer are always open at no cost, and that in effect the head office is one big central bank that will bail out any malfeasance—downright stupid and irresponsible on the part of senior management. The only people just as stupid are those who subsequently hire these fired employees without running thorough background investigations on them prior to employment.

A head office must also be alert to the possibility that the Japanese staff might not blow the whistle on an incompetent or dishonest foreign general manager. The Japanese will only criticize the general manager on a personal basis, not on a business level, because the business level relates to their performance. It is important to have institutional controls in place in Japan that apply to the general manager as well as the staff. A mistake at the general manager level normally terminates a business in Japan because its reputation is ruined.

The general manager needs to be hands-on with the smallest items of financial control to ensure that the business stays under control. Strict rules should be set down from the beginning on what money can be spent individually for what and how. If not, management will not know what is happening and will soon find its staff taking advantage of the company. This is not being negative, just realistic. Certain practices are acceptable in Japan that are not acceptable elsewhere, and vice versa. There is a different set of rules.

One must always remember that the general manager sets the example, and there are no secrets. A general manager who entertains lavishly and uses company assets for personal use will soon find that his employees do the same. If there is reason for major spending to be done on suppliers or customers, then the general manager participates in the entertainment. It has to be meaningful, planned, with a proper location and environment, and explainable to one and all. Don't let the relationship issue get carried away.

Gifts

Gifts for suppliers and customers are given twice a year in Japan, in December and June. The cost of the gift is in direct concurrence with the business relationship. All gifts should be bought and sent by the company, in the company's name and not by individuals, even though the gifts go to individuals. If individuals start giving to individuals, soon the relativeness to the overall corporate relationship is lost, and instead the gift reflects what the giver expects or wishes to receive back from the recipient. All guidelines thus go out the window.

Contributions

Contributions are a real minefield, as noted by a European general manager fluent in Japanese:

> There are a tremendous number of contributions required. Government people call up and ask for money. When Prime Minister Nakasone declared his war on cancer, where were they going to get the ammunition? They went around to every major corporation and told them how much they were supposed to donate. You have to respond, and very often you can negotiate to 60 percent, but there is a floor there somewhere and you had better find out where it is and not go under it. As for retirement parties for ministry officials, where you are required to make a monetary contribution, you go to the party. You have to do what the market requires. If you are really in "The Club," there is no way you can say no to one of these requests. Over the course of the year it is just constant. I get to the point where whenever any Japanese calls me on the phone, I'm asking myself how much it is going to cost.

Europeans are far more candid on the subject than U.S. businessmen. This can be interpreted several ways. Either the U.S. businesses are not doing it, they are not talking about what they do, or their Japanese staff is doing it, known or unknown to the U.S. head office and foreign management.

> The foreign general manager is often excluded by his staff because they don't want you to know or they don't want to be bothered by you.

There can be no question, however, as to what the Japanese companies do.

Chops

A problem that is peculiar to Asia is the use of chops (*hanko*) for signatures. These corporate and personal chops are registered at the office of the local ward in which the company is located and are as binding as a signature in the West. They can be easily copied and are often copied for convenience. Without proper controls over these chops, which means keeping them under lock and key with rigid access controls, a company can soon find itself being obligated to things management knows nothing about. During a recent visit to a major multinational's office in Tokyo, I heard the in-house attorney inform the general manager that a lady clerk of many years' employment was using a copied chop to sign company insurance policies, maintaining she had been doing it for years and what was the problem. The only way to control the appropriate use of chops is to make it public that any misuse is immediate grounds for dismissal, and not to equivocate if such misuse occurs.

Tax

Because a concept of legal tax avoidance has not existed in Japan until recently, and then almost entirely by foreign corporations, insufficient attention has been given to the tax aspects of business. The senior tax partner of a major Western accounting firm in Japan notes that with taxes, no one wants to do anything differently from what is done generally. The tax community refuses to take advantage of loopholes in the tax laws and regulations that would reduce a client's taxes. In the United States one would naturally ask, if we are aware of the situation, why don't we do something?

Tax planning in Japan automatically means confrontation with the Ministry of Finance, which is responsible for all taxation. This demands that the foreign staff become involved, for few Japanese, whether company staff or outside legal and tax advisers, are willing to take on the Ministry of Finance. These same bureaucrats will hound them on their personal taxes or the taxes of their other clients if they become obstreperous. They will do the same to foreigners, but there are times, in the interests of the company, when you have every legal reason to stand up and be counted.

Commodity and stamp taxes can be extremely arbitrary and onerous. If someone does not stand up, it will cost a fortune. In such cases the firm had better have the best possible tax adviser, preferably working together with Japan resident foreign legal counsel. Management will probably have to call in its chips with the bureaucrats it has cultivated at the Ministry of Finance, but not necessarily in the Tax Bureau. This is all aboveboard and appropriate since regulatory guidance, interpretation if you will, is a personal decision of a bureaucrat, unless one is willing and prepared to become involved in lengthy litigation in court.

I have had to call in my chips only twice in twenty years, but the second time it saved my company millions of dollars, when neither my Japanese attorney nor internal Japanese staff were prepared to do battle. I told them I understood their position but that did not stop me from doing what was right and necessary, and I took full responsibility. Foreigners in Japan sacrifice a lot because they are not prepared to go head-to-head when it is appropriate. One must know who his allies are and remember that there is very little in Japan that cannot be discussed or negotiated. If worse comes to worst, one can always sincerely apologize and pay the taxes, if one has been forthright about why he is contesting the taxes with the authorities. Penalties are only monetary and are negotiable.

But again, why does the general manager have to become involved? One general manager said:

> There is a lot of money, real money, to be found there. Most companies handle taxes centrally and the overseas offices are measured on a before-tax basis, leaving no real incentive when you are already extremely busy to get in there and mine your taxes. For the kind of money that can be saved, the local office of your accounting or tax firm should be earning their keep by saying, "Hey look, you guys are insane. You can save X millions by doing this." Unfortunately it is just not there. When we came looking for tax savings, there were people who could answer the questions, but that was it. They were not proactive and certainly not creative. One of the weakest support groups in Japan.

The senior partner of the accounting firm that this general manager went to for advice responded candidly:

> People working on tax matters in accounting firms in Japan tend to be more compliance oriented than client oriented. People have been historically trained to fit into a certain form or shape. It is difficult to get someone who

is instinctively imaginative on taxation or audit. It is very easy to find people who can work at telling you where the white line is in the middle of the road. It is not so easy to find people who can tell you the width of the road. Not all business transactions, proposed or otherwise, fit on the white line. The minority do; the rest don't. They try to fit everything on the white line because that is the safest way; that is the answer everyone knows. The person who is a little different has a long way to go to get up enough steam to work against consensus.

The immediate instinct of staff is to find a compromise up front. Management has to keep probing, pushing. Then, the staff will sometimes say, "Yes, you can do it." The foreign general manager has to keep himself involved. If he does not, he is likely to find that the compromise has occurred and his employees are committed to it. As a result of the realities of doing business in Japan, the general manager quoted above has gone three levels deep with expatriates in the accounting and tax area and has brought in tax management from head office on a regular basis.

Adjust to Japan

We tell our clients when they come here to adjust their minds, because they come from an environment where substance in a way governs the form. Here form governs substance. But you cannot be sloppy. You must be very careful to dot all the "i's" and cross the "t's." Just because you do it another way elsewhere in the world does not mean you can do it the same way here.

American Express made a worldwide promise that an American Express traveler's cheque could be bought in an American Express Travel office with a U.S. dollar bank check. No one told the company that in Japan this can only be done in a bank. When I learned that we were violating the foreign exchange law in Japan and immediately stopped the sales, one of American Express's senior officers threatened to fire me for going against his wishes. He only withdrew his threat when our attorney told him that if the Ministry of Finance had caught us, we would not have received any new permissions anywhere in the company in Japan from the ministry for at least one year. When our actions were subsequently discovered in a ministry audit, we were not punished since we had discontinued the procedure of our own volition.

A company should be especially careful to seek legal and tax advice when changing its corporate legal structure in Japan. There are far too many reminders that corporate politics, whether originating at home or in Japan, if not balanced with good legal and tax planning, can cost a company a great deal in Japan. For example, if a company anticipates losing money for a period of time, it should start with a branch to enable it to write off the losses against the parent's earnings. When profitable, it can consider converting to a subsidiary. Since corporate tax rates in Japan are now considerably higher than in the United States, and dividends in Japan are tax deductible, consider paying the maximum dividend from a subsidiary to the parent.

Titles for foreigners should be reviewed for their tax implications. For example, a director cannot allocate as non-Japan source the compensation paid by a Japanese-incorporated subsidiary for business days spent outside Japan. Also, bonuses (any nonregular compensation) paid by a Japanese-incorporated subsidiary to a director are considered a distribution of profit and are not deductible for Japanese corporate tax purposes. A way around this is to pay bonuses and similar items equally over a twelve-month period as part of base compensation. This, of course, could have an impact on any pension arrangements based on monthly salary. Moreover, even the taxable amount on company contributions toward housing costs, which are astronomical in Japan, is dependent upon an individual's corporate title.

Expatriate Taxes

The foreign general manager and the expatriate staff in Japan often have been ill served in personal income tax preparation, both foreign and Japanese. This has been especially true for U.S. citizens, who are subject to U.S. taxation on their global income and also to Japanese taxes on income earned in Japan for the first five years of an assignment and thereafter on their global income. (This is why many U.S. citizens stay in Japan for less than five years.) Even though they have been assured by their head office that a particular accounting firm will take care of their every need and that the accounting firm, though paid by the company, will represent them as if they were individual clients, as they say in the army, "It just ain't so!" The individuals assigned to handle expatriate tax matters are often spouses of foreigners assigned to Japan and are rarely trained in either Japanese or home-country tax regulations. The client more often than not is paying to educate people who have not advanced beyond the task of entering the information in a computer at the accounting company's head office. The bad advice and gimmicks tried by these people are legend and have caused even long-standing companies in Japan like IBM, Mobil, and Citicorp considerable embarrassment, time, and money with the Japanese authorities. If the tax people in the head office and accounting firm recommend a procedure that does not make sense, one should ask if the Japanese attorneys can review their proposal. This has been known to bury some very unwise proposals. On the positive side, there are a few individual tax accountants, operating either as individuals or as partners in major firms, who have provided legitimately valuable assistance to their clients. One should investigate these individuals in detail to be sure they are professional and ethical. If so, then one might consider using them, if head office will permit, rather than one's normal accounting firm.

Personnel and tax people in corporate head offices need to get together and structure expatriate programs by country. Usually they are not willing to do that, viewing an expatriate as an expatriate. They say, "This is what we do. Whatever the tax consequences, we are sorry. If it's too expensive, pull him out of there." They try to make everybody the same rather than becoming experts in personnel and tax management. There is also an insidious belief that the expatriate is wangling a special benefit for himself. Competent, experienced, international personnel staff, rather than the usual collection of castoffs, would soon dispel that belief. Unfortunately, these kinds of issues can take up an inordinate amount of overseas management's time and can soil other relationships between head office and the field.

The linguistically and culturally illiterate general manager, with limited external professional assistance, is almost naked in Japan in accounting, auditing, and taxation. His only clothes are keeping his guard up and being proactive with his antennae alert at all times, probing anything that cannot be explained by his staff and making it precisely known that any malfeasance or breakdown in controls will be cause for immediate dismissal under the

Rules of Employment, or, if illegal, prosecution.

The general manager has to keep his eyes and ears open to what is going on in his office. He has to check the financial reports himself. He has to look at call reports, having them translated when necessary. This is especially true in a small company. Just because you are foreign, don't let them fence you out. Find a way to get in and see what is going on.

The head office must support the general manager 100 percent, whatever the internal or external reaction, if he is to remain the boss in Japan and if the company is to operate ethically and effectively.

10

Market and Product Research and Development

A FOREIGN COMPANY only should come to Japan with the ability to offer superior products that are price competitive; have distinctive, identifiable characteristics; and are not currently available in the Japanese market. If a company has such products that it wishes to sell in Japan, then it enters the market ready to understand market needs and to offer products or services to meet those needs. To grasp these needs, there is extensive up-front research and then relentless, ongoing research and development.

To be successful in the Japanese market, the second largest market in the world, requires at least the same dedication to research and development that is required in the home market. It also requires the transfer of technology and attributes both into and out of Japan. If this transfer does not occur, inevitably a Japanese competitor will freeze you out or pass you by, first in Japan and then on other fronts, whether at home or in third countries.

Japan must be viewed both as a market in and of itself and as part of a global strategy. A company must have control of its business in Japan to be able to integrate that business worldwide. Japanese companies think globally; they do not have to be in one's business today to be a competitor tomorrow. If there is an identifiable market for a product anywhere, whether for aircraft or beer, they will want to be a player. The only way to compete against them globally is first to compete against them in Japan.

Market Researchers

Although Japan's economy and its population are roughly half the size of the United States's, the total volume of market research conducted in Japan is estimated to be only about one quarter of that of the U.S. market. As a profession, market research ranks quite low on the totem pole.

The quality of research available varies greatly, for a number of reasons. Small companies are often a place to house retirees or peaked-out employees of larger corporations that feel obligated to feed them, even though their expertise is minimal. Furthermore, strong industrial-group consciousness makes it highly unlikely that one large industrial group would go to another group's market research company for research, thus making for increased fragmentation of the market research business. In addition, Japanese see little need for market research because of the attitude that the Japanese are unique, and that all Japanese are the same. The feeling is, "Whatever I think, everybody else thinks."

There is some validity to this line of thought, but the mentality of a sixteen-year-old girl in a 1950s' outfit, dancing on the street in Harajuku on Sunday or in Roppongi on Friday night, is nothing like her mother's or her grandmother's. Today, separate research is required among the teenagers, *shin-jinrui* or yuppies, over-forties, and retirees, and then among subsections within these groups—male and female, for starters. Nevertheless the Japanese perception of their homogeneity has been a negative drag on the development of research in Japan. As one person told me, "Japanese will say, 'You stupid foreigners don't understand Japan, that's why you have to get out and do research.' "

Despite this background, today there are both Japanese and foreign-run market research companies to assist Western companies in market research and product differentiation and development. To use them effectively, a company should have on staff foreign employees with in-depth knowledge of a product's attributes and how that product is marketed and sold elsewhere.

Initial Briefing

The initial briefing given a research firm, such as Nippon Research, ASI, INFOPLAN (market research subsidiary of McCann-

Erickson), or JMRB (the market research affiliate of MRB Companies), is critical. One must assume that they have zero knowledge of the product and should give them a briefing based on one's domestic and international experience. The market research firm will then make a proposal that should, after appropriate modification, be approved. Even if some product or campaign modification is felt to be required for Japan, it is often a good idea as a first cut to test that product or campaign without modification. This enables one to put in sharp perspective the market differences in Japan, and it also helps to quiet the global brand experts in head office. Most important, as much as one should not assume that a product will work in Japan, conversely one should not assume that it will not work. There are no better examples than McDonald's restaurant products, which have been enormously successful in Japan in their basic American format.

As research proceeds, both sides of the coin should be engraved: a competitor analysis must always accompany the quantitative and qualitative analysis. Constructive participation by knowledgeable foreign members of the staff, preferably from both head office and Japan, permits the refining process to occur as the study progresses. The foreigners become exposed to "this is Japan," while the research firm learns the business and prevents the foreigners from jumping to the wrong conclusions. The foreigner and his advisers eventually have to take the research results and lay them on the background of Japan to be able to interpret them meaningfully. No matter what the numbers say, in the last analysis one has to spot what the implications are for the Japan market.

> Often companies come into Japan after their product portfolio has been completed. They are not excited about considering the redesign of their product from the ground up, specifically for Japan. The market might not require a different product, but it is the unwillingness to really consider whether it does or not that forces rigidity on the product design and invites subsequent problems. If from the very beginning companies would remind themselves that in Japan, like everywhere, a product has to be market driven, not product driven, they might shorten the learning process.

At this stage of a consumer product's development, the advertising and public relations firm should be brought aboard. Even if advertising is not required, as in industrial products, the potential of public relations should not be disregarded (see chapter 13). If research and development, advertising, and public relations are not brought together early on, there will be a tremendous duplication of work and communication and a resultant waste of time and effectiveness in marketing. There is a trade-off up front in costs, but proper implementation in the beginning will make this decision more than worthwhile.

Going Native

A recurring mistake often made at this juncture—that is, shortly after the first cut at research—is to decide to go native. "We foreigners," it is said, "will never understand Japan." But who is going to understand Japan for you? There is an extraordinary amount of data available in Japan, but Japanese staff have rarely been trained in how to use it. Qualitative extraction and meaningful interpretation of product research require training in market research, marketing, and selling. Until a company's Japanese staff is as knowledgeable about its product as foreign management is, foreign staff are going to train the Japanese staff. The training must take place in both the home market and Japan. The whole process is very time consuming and, if one is rapidly expanding a business, never ending. It is essential eventually to have foreign and Japanese staff who know what is happening in product and market research and who know how to use the available market facilities.

Just because it is Japan, not everything must be done in the Japanese way. If a company is not bringing to Japan new product or service attributes and marketing skills, it probably has no reason to be there. I am reminded of when the chairman of JCB, Japan's most prestigious indigenous credit card company, told me in 1980 that we would never sell the American Express Gold Card without door-to-door salesmen. The development of direct mail in Japan was still at the stage it was in about 1950 in the United States, but there was no way we could afford door-to-door salesmen. As a result, American Express, which was at the time the largest direct-mail house in the world, took its global expertise and its "take one" expertise and led in the development of both these marketing tools in Japan. Today, American Express has a computerized list of over twenty million names, the envy of any Japanese competitor, and not one card has been sold by door-to-door salesmen. What the chairman of JCB was really saying was, you will never make it in Japan because you don't have the Japanese bankers to sell your card for you door to door. Fortunately, he was blind to what was happening elsewhere in computerization: JCB jobbed out their computer work while we built and adapted our own to our own service and marketing needs. Many Japanese are set in this mental framework for the Japanese market, narrow in their thinking to the point of excluding all considerations that are foreign to them. Nonetheless, the American Express experience was ten years ago, and the Japanese are quick studies, at home and abroad. Just as dangerous as "the Japanese way only" is "the foreign way only" when the product introduction follows what is most often referred to as "The American Way."

Differentiate

The entrenched competition, whether Japanese or foreign, is going to do everything possible to prevent a company from differentiating its product in the Japanese market, particularly if that product is subject to governmental regulatory guidance.

The competition, through the association and its dialogue with the controlling ministry, is constantly trying to restrict our ability to differentiate ourselves. If we are not different, there is no reason for us to be here, so we have to be different. Our competitors have not individually had clear, competitive strategies of their own. Most have acted very much alike. But now they have woken up to the consumer, are brand conscious, and are outspending us on television. This could force us to respond to them, unlike our experience to date.

The 1990s will not be like even the 1980s. Japan today is an awakened consumer market, and few foreign companies are prepared to do battle on the Japan front.

Very few Western businessmen are strategically directed in Japan. They seem to just exist. We hear at home that the Japanese are slow; they procrastinate. If the Japanese want to do something, they do it much faster than we do. When they are not moving very fast, they don't want to make a decision or they need more information. They are very competent; they know where they are going and how to accomplish their fundamental objectives. They will run over you, your company, and any other company in Japan, foreign or domestic. They are extremely aggressive.

Japanese research starts from the point of view that we are all Japanese. We are all the same. I start from the point of view that it used to be all the same, but you are changing rapidly. The myth that everything is homogeneous prescribes the way research is done.

This only reemphasizes how important it is to have cutting-edge foreign staff involved in market research, product differentiation, and target marketing, while at the same time they are training the company's Japanese staff.

As an example of a major change in consumer behavior that has potential ramifications for many consumer businesses in Japan, reflect on the fact that more and more consumers are borrowing to enjoy luxuries befitting their wealth. Although the savings rate remains high, outstanding Japanese consumer debt for purchases of goods and services has increased from about 16 trillion yen ($115 billion) at the end of 1986 to more than 65 trillion yen ($450 billion) by September 1989.[1]

Fulfill or Create a Need

Although much of the market research done in Japan by Japanese in the past focused on what happened rather than on why it happened or what is going to happen, today, market research in that country is becoming as current and as important as anywhere. For foreign companies in Japan it is even more important because they are on the fringe of the market, and a mistake is very costly. To avoid unnecessary costs or even outright failure, products introduced in Japan must meet one requirement no matter what—the needs of the Japanese consumer, industrial or retail. This is a fundamental premise that foreign companies often ignore. There can be no compromise. The product or service must meet the Japanese consumer's requirements. Those needs should be defined through research.

There is no consumer prejudice toward foreign consumer products, especially among young people, if the product is a quality product that fulfills or creates a need. Living well at home is

---

[1]Floyd Norris, "Market Place," *The New York Times*, November 10, 1989.

probably the last foreign luxury yet to be imported, but even that has begun to change. A housewife goes to one of the chic European restaurants in Tokyo, then wants to study the cooking, then wants the ingredients, then the plates and glasses, and then a suitable room to sit in and serve a European meal. The prejudice lies in bureaucratic nationalism and corporate fear of any new competitor, particularly a foreigner who cannot be controlled, whether the product is computers or skis.

The American Express Gold Card created a need or made the people aware of a need. We then had to match the need with the product—for example, Japanese-language service overseas for the international traveler. The promise is the same as English-language service for the American. Although Japanese was more difficult for an American company to implement internationally, it was done because the promise and differentiation from the competition were important. We had to use all the marketing tools available in the Japanese market to convey the availability of this product attribute to Japanese travelers, so that they would become cardmembers. Once they were members, we used monthly billing mailings to communicate other attributes that would encourage their use of the card.

Interviewing

Market research in the initial stages focuses on group discussions or in-depth interviews regarding concepts. Then comes the development of a prototype, followed by target-company or in-home usage tests and finally regional and national expansion. Some 60 to 70 percent of the Japanese consumer and industrial market is along the Tokyo/Osaka axis, and that is where the effort is concentrated. Tokyo and Yokohama together represent the world's largest concentration of affluent consumers, with thirty-six million people or roughly 30 percent of Japan's population. This is just one television or newspaper market. Tokyo is not a test market; it is a lead market.

In contrast to the United States, where telephone interviewing plays a major role in research, in Japan about 90 percent of interviews are personal ones of some form. Because Japanese are not accustomed to talking to strangers on the phone, response rates and quality tend to be poor unless the telephone interview is kept relatively short. Interviewing in the home still makes up the bulk of personal interviewing, since, unlike in the United States, security is not an issue. The use of street or shopping-mall intercept interviewing is increasing, however. Most in-home interviews are conducted with the interviewer standing in the *genkan* (entrance way), where one takes shoes off if one is going inside the house. Standing in the genkan with her shoes on, the interviewer is physically but not psychologically inside the house. If the interview requires the use of many show cards by the interviewer or card sorting by the respondent, problems are inevitable. Often the shoe box is used to place cards on, and sometimes there will be two ladies kneeling on the step leading up from the genkan to the interior of the house; one with shoes on, the other with them off, shuffling show cards.

When doing a theater research session, if five hundred people say they will come, five hundred will come.

Participation

It is essential for the foreign company to actively participate in the research.

When research companies present their summary conclusions, they often do not tie their conclusions to their quantitative results. Participate from the beginning in the framing and reframing of questions. We now design most of the questionnaire. Many research companies job out the research, causing a problem between the analysis of the quantitative and qualitative research because of a lack of communication between the researchers and the interpreters.

Whatever the reasons, there is virtual uniformity among foreign management in their complaints about the research companies' lack of ability to interpret and communicate qualitative research. There is also unanimous agreement that foreign company personnel must actively participate in the research if the results are to be meaningful and if the foreign company's learning curve is to grow at a rate that will permit it to be competitive.

When hiring an "experienced" market researcher from a Japanese company, one should be aware that the experience in a Japanese company might be very different from what is required in a foreign company.

Japanese are loathe to use qualitative market research. Quantitative they will use. They don't like group discussions, the possibility of being proven in black and white that they are wrong. If there is any chance the research will show they should be going in a different direction, they feel very ill at ease. When they do use research, they generally use their own advertising agency, either directly in house or a quasi-in-house organization so the results will have the necessary bias. They justify on costs, since it is one-half the cost of using a Western research firm.

Focus groups can be monitored by closed-circuit television or through a one-way mirror, and it is common to have simultaneous interpreters present to allow foreign staff to get a live feel for the target consumer. At these sessions the marketing head, foreign or Japanese, should be present along with the account officer from the advertising agency. Ideally the interpreters should be briefed in advance so they know the product and are able to translate nuances. This also ensures that after the focus-group session a knowledgeable dialogue can take place among the company, the research firm, and the advertising agency.

Interpretation

A marketer who has experienced all the forms of interviewing in both the United States and Japan observed:

Japan and the United States appear to be extremes in research methods. Perhaps this is the situation in other areas as well. The Japanese are always saying they are unique while the Americans are always thinking that everybody should be and probably wants to be like them. Whereas, in reality the Japanese are not like nor do they desire to be like the Americans at all; they have more of an affinity in historical age and disposition with Europe. But with 1992 approaching, in Europe there is more of a pan-European view, which is beginning to resemble the diversity under one roof of the United States.

There is often, therefore, something very different in the type of research results one receives in the United States and in Japan. Copy point recall scores in advertising research clinics tend to be considerably lower in Japan than in the United States. Japanese commercials often give nonverbal hints while American commercials are talkative and direct, saying this brand is better than that brand. There is little of that in Japan, and until very recently comparative advertising was frowned upon by the authorities.

Japanese advertising is much closer to British and French advertising. There is nothing wrong with having different continuums, but you cannot take one end of a continuum and try to impose it on the other end. That is when problems occur in research responses and in the campaign itself. Whatever the method or methods chosen, the foreign company has to understand and interpret the material gathered in the context of Japan itself. The material is there; the interpretation of that material is what is difficult.

The need to test concepts different from those used both at home and in the Japanese market to date has impressed one consumer marketer:

> All our research is now focused on the negative. Instead of asking people what they like about a product, we are asking what is it you don't like about a product. Through this approach, we are finding new opportunities for product development in Japan.

> You can't interpret research here the same way you can in the United States. Because of the cultural differences, when using similar techniques, the data results can be often misleading compared to how you would interpret the same data in the United States. It takes a lot more to motivate a Japanese consumer to change to your product than it does perhaps in the West. They need a lot of reinforcement and assurance that what they are buying is a good product. The conversion is far more difficult. The U.S. consumer is far more willing to take a gamble to find out about the product. Conversely, I am beginning to think that the Japanese consumer in a research environment is far less willing to tell you they don't like your product. The housewife, for example, appears to indicate far more interest than when she has to put her money down on a day-by-day basis to buy it. We've got some creative that tests terribly but is doing fantastically well and vice versa. We've got a lot to learn in interpreting Japanese interactive research.

Every avenue is explored. There are no low-cost shortcuts to success for a foreign firm that is painstakingly careful in its interpretation of research. If it is not, it will have no idea why its product is succeeding or failing, and what its next step should be.

If a company is in the consumer field, like a Johnson & Johnson, it must come up with a range of products to attract the attention of the distributor, the retailer, and the consumer. Toothbrushes, floss, mouthwash, and toothpaste, for example, are all preventive-care products that the consumer can purchase in the same store without going to a specialist. A stand-alone product will not suffice for long.

Procter & Gamble discovered that Japanese consumers are very company conscious in the products they buy, associating the quality, safety, and reliability of a product with the image of the company itself. To get started in Japan, a foreign company, or any company, for that matter, must direct an important amount of energy and money to the establishment of a positive company image (see chapter 13). To illustrate, P&G recently surveyed an experimental product by testing it against itself, with and without company names. Unidentified, the product broke even against itself, as expected. But when associated with P&G in one leg of the test and with Kao, a major competitor, in the other leg, the product associated with Kao was significantly preferred.

Parenthetically, it is even more difficult to convert an industrial company from one supplier to another in a society that places great emphasis on relationships, on quality control, and, particularly when the supplier is foreign, on timely delivery.

Endorsements

When launching a consumer product and subsequently raising the awareness level, professional endorsements are useful. Determining who endorses a product requires both competitor and target-audience research. A professional endorsement is important for talking both to the trade people (for example, a doctor to a doctor or a hospital about medical products) and to the public.

Doctors require for their endorsement more remuneration than in the United States, including gifts and entertainment. They do not give an endorsement for just a flat fee. There is more to it. Not only with doctors. When you ask someone to do a favor for you in Japan, they expect a lot more than simply a fee. You have to be very careful to explain to head office why it costs so much. How do you control your staff in this situation? We had to terminate several employees for being too generous. Salesmen become overzealous, promising the moon for a doctor's cooperation. The foreign general manager is often excluded because they don't want you to know or they don't want to be bothered by you.

We just pay him off to say what we want him to say. That is how we differentiate our product from Japanese companies who can talk about their long history or heritage.

Extreme caution is obviously required, and the general manager has to be involved.

One of the most successful endorsements of the 1980s was the

"Don't leave home without it" endorsement of the American Express card by Jack Nicklaus in Japan. Although this concept and Jack Nicklaus did not test well on several occasions when I was involved, American Express's management at a later time believed in Jack's popularity and came up with an advertisement that had him saying in Japanese with his very distinct American accent, "Dekakeru toki wa wasurezu ni" (Don't leave home without it). The expression, as Jack pronounced it, has entered the lexicon of Japan. It is today a favorite children's expression, as is "Do you know me?" from an English voice-over on a Nicklaus American advertisement. As American Express's management said, "That is when you know you have made it." Not a bad endorsement for a company that had only a 6 percent aided-awareness level in Tokyo and virtually zero elsewhere when it entered the market in 1980. Most Japanese thought American Express was like Nippon Express—Japan's largest integrated goods transporter. In the United States the "Do you know me?" campaign often used a celebrity, such as an opera singer, who was not familiar to the general public. In Japan, a known, famous celebrity endorsement reassured and reinforced the elderly segment who traveled internationally. The Nicklaus success holds another lesson: Reading qualitative test results is extremely difficult in Japan.

When Unilever relaunched Rama Margarine in Japan in 1978, it used ordinary housewives for the testimonial. Unilever's Japanese advisers said this would not work. Japanese housewives, it was said, would put their hands to their mouths and giggle when the camera was turned on. Unilever tested the concept thoroughly in Japan and found that the housewives' testimonials communicated significantly better than other testimonials. Most important, they created a significantly higher intent to purchase the brand. Market share increased from 12 percent to over 20 percent.[2]

Product Development

Because of the advanced levels of technological development in Japanese companies, the day has passed when foreign companies

---

[2]Roger Brookin, Nippon Unilever Marketing Service Manager, ACCJ Marketing Presentation, June 4, 1986.

can continue to rely solely on products being made available by their head offices. Many foreign companies are not keeping up with the Japanese competition.

We have an ongoing campaign. Take the Japanese seriously. That means developing products in Japan for the Japanese market and even for elsewhere.

Foreign firms have, at times, done adaptive development rather well, but they are not well prepared to develop in house in Japan. Most products have to be in the pipeline at least three years before they come to market in Japan, and even longer when bureaucratic approval is required. For many foreign companies, the day of reckoning is taking place. Kodak, Dow Chemical, Procter & Gamble, and DuPont have all recently made major efforts to develop in-house R&D capability. Almost all of this is applied, not basic, research. They are involved in developing products for the Japanese market or in developing specifications for their headquarters. Principally, it is for the benefit of Japanese manufacturers or consumers. DuPont alone spent $40 million in 1986 for its show-piece research facility and Kodak $80 million for its recently completed research laboratory. It is late in the game, but now is far better than later. Only time will tell if they acted soon enough.

Deep pockets are necessary, but the consequences of not understanding what the competition can develop, of not upping the ante on their home field, and of not having the capacity to transfer knowledge and product to global installations are unthinkable if one wishes to remain globally competitive or even just competitive at home. One can only guess at what the competition for knowledge and information is going to be in the twenty-first century.

Any company that is going to compete in Japan has to be working on a three-to-five-year pipeline. This makes a two-to-three-year expatriate assignment in Japan ridiculous. And unless a company in desperation contemplates going Japanese with its Japan operations, consider the granddaddy of them all, who tried. IBM found after twenty years that it did not have a clue at home as to what was going on in Japan while its market share there was deteriorating rapidly. In desperation it parachuted in over three hundred foreigners to find out. Because of costs, I was told, many foreigners from IBM's headquarters are now gone, and it still doesn't know. The Japan operation must be part of a global strategy, including research and development, and it must involve the active participation of head-office personnel and the transfer of product and knowledge in and out of Japan. Research is essential from day one.

No one in our industry did their research before coming to Japan. The others followed us, thinking we had when we had not. No one knew how to do business in Japan. When they did study the market, they didn't believe it!

Timeliness

Bill Hall again comments on different market practices:

American companies tend to be unbelievably slow in launching a product and in getting their act together between the field and head office. "Will we or won't we? Where is the money? What should we do? What is going to happen to our quarterly earnings, my division's earnings, my bonus, if we invest this money?" Often, by the time approval to go ahead has been received, the Japanese competition has copied the concept, has been in the market for six months calling the brand "Mimbo" instead of "Bimbo," and has preempted the position. It happens time and again in the consumer product area. Absolutely unbelievable! The speed of response is so slow.

A practitioner notes, however:

It is very difficult to get new ideas out of a team of inexperienced people who don't know Japan and people who know Japan but don't know your product. Where do you get the cross-fertilization that creates the new creative ideas? Very, very difficult! You have to constantly push your people because of the speed at which competition copies.

I know how it happened, but I don't know who made it happen. There was one promotional campaign we were very excited about and flew in a team from New York to work on it. We pulled the whole campaign together in March and decided the timing for it should be August. On June 1, one of our competitors launched it. They are very quick to watch what you are doing and to listen. Any idea that they think has been received favorably, they copy immediately.

Research is a serious problem for a small consumer-goods or industrial-products company. It has to sell or not sell largely what it makes. If a product does not sell, it has a big gaping hole in its product line, but it is not going to spend a fortune to retool. The product must be either totally unique or extremely price competitive. Otherwise, don't bother! That is a fact of life in today's environment, and it applies equally to the big and small foreign firms in Japan.

Thus, whether dealing with an industrial or a consumer product, a company must develop a strategy that provides the user with a product with recognizable differences of a superior nature. It cannot be a me-too product. If it is a consumer product, it is difficult to generalize whether to soft sell or shout. This depends on the nature of the product, the stage of the company's and the product's development, and test results. Perhaps at introduction one will want to be careful how one shouts, but, more important, one will want to fulfill all promises. Don't go to market unless you can deliver. Trial and error is a fatal procedure in Japan. Nevertheless, if a company is trying to intervene in the market, it is going to have to find its own way of shouting to attract attention. Unless it can create a need for its product, whether by price, by uniqueness, or both, it is wasting its time.

Your product has to be market driven, but, amazingly, a lot of people don't understand that.

Since there is no native word in Japanese for marketing, Japanese use the word *markettingu*. Until the 1980s there really wasn't a need for the term, since at home they only had to look at market share in a rapidly expanding pie. That pie is still growing substantially in gross terms, but not necessarily at the previous percentage rates. By any standards, though, the Japanese consumer market is booming today, and with deep pockets the Japanese are refining their own research and marketing skills to enhance their competitiveness at home and abroad.

Marketing is simply communicating what your research indicates your clients or potential clients want, whether in Germany, England, or Japan, and thereby convincing that client through marketing, sales, and public relations to buy your product. The only safe harbor in this competitive chaos is the customer franchise. The better one understands that, the better and more successful one will be. Don't ignore what has been learned elsewhere; just filter that knowledge through a Japanese screen.

11

Marketing

FOR THE FOREIGN firm in Japan the marketing process begins with the choice of a marketing director and an advertising agency. They will be responsible for marketing the product. The importance of having as marketing director an employee who knows the company's products intimately has already been discussed. Japan is not the place to begin to educate a marketing director about a product; enough time will be consumed in educating the advertising agency. Both are essential for developing marketing strategy and execution, for integrating these with the sales effort, and for professionally presenting them to head office for approval. They must come up with ideas and concepts that sell in both Japan and head office, an extraordinary accomplishment in and of itself.

Advertising Agencies

Some of the largest advertising agencies in the world are Japanese, and their size comes principally from Japanese domestic business: Dentsu, Hakuhodo, Tokyu, and Dai-ichi Kikaku. There are also foreign joint venture agencies in Japan—McCann-Erickson Hakuhodo, Dentsu Young & Rubicam, and Grey Daiko—and several wholly owned agencies, the most notable being J. Walter Thompson. Others, like Ogilvy & Mather, failed, both as a joint venture and on their own.

The problem with marketing for the foreign company in Japan could not be more succinctly put than by one of the largest foreign users of advertising there:

With advertising in Japan and elsewhere you get what you give. This is, however, where the departure from Western norms is probably the greatest. It is hard to convince agencies in Japan that they should be thinking about how to expand your business in the broadest sense of the word; not just how to get something in print or on television. You must convince them that they are just as much a part of your business as the marketing division of your own firm, because you don't have all the support facilities in house that a Japanese company operating in its own country has. They should be commenting on everything as an adviser, partner. Unfortunately, in the foreign or hybrid agencies, they have the same problems as you in having foreigners who understand Japan and can provide insight and support. I am still not happy with the sense of business-partnership support.

A Japanese general manager of a foreign consumer-product company reflects the view held by many Japanese corporations:

Marketing in Japan is not done as in the West. Marketing is essentially live tests, very pragmatic. Our Japanese resent strategic marketing studies done by a Western management consulting firm. They are purely intellectual. We are very specific, pragmatic in our marketing, putting a marketing section and a sales team together to use their intricate network to sell a consumer product that is heavily dependent on consumer shelf space. We use management consultants only for the big picture, not for implementation.

As discussed in the previous chapter, great care must be taken by the foreign company in its research. Product research must not be confused with product introduction. There is in Japan, as everywhere, a time for research and a time for implementation. Yet research must not stop after introduction of the product; it must be ongoing.

Foreign Advertising Agencies

The principal reason many foreign companies use foreign agencies is that these agencies can communicate with their head offices and foreign marketing directors, who can rarely speak and even more rarely read Japanese. "Foreign clients," I was told, "will pull out if you have a strictly Japanese management team in a foreign advertising agency."

A foreigner often feels that another foreigner can best understand his problems and therefore can interpret Japan better for him than a Japanese can. Whether this is right or wrong, it is the perception. The result, however, is often the disastrous situation of two foreigners who know little about Japan talking to each other, particularly when the foreigner in the agency is linguistically and culturally illiterate and is having trouble communicating with his staff. This is far more common than most foreign agencies would like to admit. The agencies assign rotating expatriates to accounts as senior account officers and leave the grunt work to the permanently assigned Japanese. It is not unusual for a foreign company to have four or five foreign account officers in five years, creating a constant problem of education and reeducation. While Dentsu has been fertile ground for the University of Tokyo's best and brightest, few are found in foreign agencies, which have the same recruiting problems as other foreign businesses. Since foreign-affiliated agencies mainly handle foreign companies in Japan, their growth has been restricted, which in turn has restricted their ability to recruit talented Japanese. The union and personnel problems encountered by foreign-affiliated advertising agencies in Japan are legend.

Nevertheless, often a foreign company can work comfortably only with another foreign company. No matter what the home office of the foreign-affiliated agency promises, appreciate that their Tokyo office is often strapped for personnel and can easily become complacent unless one stays on top of them. This is, of course, true anywhere, but when you are advertising in a language you do not understand at all, the results can be horrendous. Translating everything into English, German, or French from Japanese and back into Japanese in no way gives a real sense of what is being conveyed in Japanese in an advertisement. The littlest things can ruin the effectiveness of a print advertisement that requires a direct response. The address is wrong, or the only phone number listed is a Tokyo number, omitting numbers in Osaka, Fukuoka, and Sapporo. This is an expensive mistake if a company advertises nationally in magazines and newspapers. This is exactly what happened when an ignorantly proud foreign marketing director at American Express did not follow the proper procedures by having his copy checked by someone bilingual.

Foreign advertising agencies have done some superb work or they would not still be in business in Japan. Coca-Cola and Nestlé have received outstanding service from McCann-Erickson Hakuhodo, and Unilever from J. Walter Thompson. They spend enough to force the agencies to put their very best foreign and Japanese personnel on their account. These accounts alone can make a foreign agency in Japan, but they do not necessarily serve another company's needs. Management must stay on top of its agency all the time. Coca-Cola, Nestlé, and Unilever do, and that is one of the principal reasons they are successful in Japan.

Japanese Advertising Agencies

As previously mentioned, marketing as known in the West was a concept new to Japan in the late 1970s and 1980s. Many of the large Japanese agencies were experienced only at buying market share through cornering the market on time and space and obtained foreign clients by making life difficult for the foreign agencies. Sometimes they were brilliantly creative and at other times awkward at best in execution.

Dentsu controls 40–50 percent of the media. It buys up all the prime time at the beginning of the year and then negotiates with companies that want to buy the time. The big people can get on prime time, while the little people have a hard go unless they are prepared to pay a huge premium. In negotiations with me and the then head-office President of American Express Travel Related Services, Louis Gerstner, Dentsu management went so far as to threaten blatantly that if we did not use their firm, they would see that we failed in Japan. They were that confident in their ability to block us out. They had done everything possible to arrange a private meeting with Gerstner on one of his visits to Japan but would not say why they wished to meet with him. Being the savvy businessman he is, he correctly insisted that I attend any meetings he had with them or anyone else. This forced Dentsu management to make their move in front of someone knowledgeable on American Express's business in Japan and also permitted Gerstner not to respond in any way to their comments, which obviously bothered them. Foreign visitors need to be accompanied on every business call by a senior member of the Japan office to avoid being isolated and blind-sided. Any questions about the Japan operation should be referred to the person from the Japan office to avoid misunderstandings. This also gives the Japan office the requisite status to operate in the Japanese marketplace. It is exactly how the

Japanese operate when they visit their overseas installations. Fortunately, we were able to call Dentsu's bluff.

Japanese companies until recently have used non-Japanese agencies overseas to market their products, resulting in a low experience level in Japanese agencies for dealing with foreign companies selling in Japan. This is changing and should be looked at carefully when choosing an agency and its representative. Dentsu, as demonstrated above, has often brutally sold its purchasing clout to foreigners while being extremely inconsistent in its marketing support and execution. Hakuhodo and Dai-ichi Kikaku have gone to extremes to explain to their foreign clients the reason and strategy behind what they are recommending. Tokyu, as shown by its failed relationship with Ogilvy & Mather, has not been particularly adept in working with foreigners.

Most Western companies do not spend the money to get the attention required at major Japanese agencies. A company's importance to the agency is a key element in choosing an agency. Just being foreign does not make you important. This is not the 1950s and 1960s. Full-scale interviews should be done at least twice; the people a company gets the second time will demonstrate the seriousness of the attention it can expect.

Confidentiality

A major concern in using Japanese agencies has been confidentiality. Japanese agencies handle competing products on both a permanent and a case-by-case basis, often being involved in buying space rather than developing the strategy or even the creative aspects of a campaign. Few foreign firms have been willing to risk their marketing strategy and plans becoming known to their competition prior to launch. Some, though, feel that by using two agencies, sufficient competition is created so that a semblance of confidentiality is maintained. They see the threat of changing agencies or providing more competition as the only way to insure proper attention to an account. Whatever tack one takes, the agency or agencies should sign a confidentiality agreement. It cannot be enforced, but it is a statement of principle.

When I arrived, I asked for an agency presentation. What I got was a courtesy call from ten people and a bowl of fruit. The Japanese absolutely do not know how to make a presentation. An agency does nothing but develop graphics and place media. They cannot develop a program for you; absolutely, totally impossible. Our agency does all the work for all of our competitors—all of the American and foreign companies we compete with. There is no proprietary information. We decided to do all our work in house and to use the agency only to place our advertisement.

Everyone Is Involved in Marketing

The research firm, advertising agency, and public relations firm should work together with a company from the beginning in the development of its strategy and product concepts. The general manager in Japan does not have floors of experts to call upon as in head office and must depend on these outside groups working effectively with his staff. Otherwise there is excruciating wastage. It is also important to balance foreign and Japanese input for marketing strategy and implementation.

If you only have foreigners in marketing and not a mixture of foreigners and Japanese, you get two extreme reactions from the foreigners. Either, Japan is very inefficient, loaded with people and distributors who only talk about golf and waste time, or they become so Japanized that with every suggestion from outside, they say, "You can't do that. This is Japan." A healthy tension and a two-in-a-box concept involving foreigners and Japanese bring differing ideas together for consideration rather than up-front acceptance or rejection.

This is usually true in any department within a foreign company in Japan and should be an important consideration in staffing.

You have to have the knowledge and confidence not to let something go out that you are not comfortable with. If someone says, "That is not done in Japan," force him to explain why. Like anywhere, it must be explainable. Otherwise you have pure abdication of judgment.

The opposite is also quite common. If told over and over by an ignorant head office, foreign general manager, or foreign marketing director to do it one way, even a capable Japanese will eventually give in, although he knows it is wrong. There must be someone who will stand up and ask, "What is it you want?" The foreign general manager is really the only one who can do that, but he has to have head office's confidence and has to understand the Japanese psyche and the Japanese situation. To retain good Japanese staff, he must protect them from foreign ignorance, because if the Japanese are exposed to this ignorance, they and the company will soon have serious problems.

A consumer packaging company's general manager close to the changing Japanese consumer environment notes:

> I hear the word arrogance more often than when I was here before, inside and outside. With proper management that is a positive development, because we now listen to good ideas whereas before we didn't. Some of the younger guys say, "Listen to me!" Once you agree to listen and then don't, then you have a double problem. You are not listening and you lied. Creativity is the privilege of youth. You must rely upon them for creativity, but they make mistakes. My job is to prevent their mistakes if possible; but if they make a mistake, I cover. It is my mistake, our mistake. I lead, navigate, but I do not dominate. You must be sympathetic to young people and make every effort to satisfy their needs to grow.

Even with marketing, the general manager must be closely involved with his personnel.

Creative and Strategy

Once the staff is in place and the agency chosen, a general manager will soon discover that in Japan the agency's approach to advertising itself is clearly different from what it would be in the United States, whether the agency is Japanese, foreign, or a hybrid. The agency in the United States is basically strategy driven; in Japan, it is media driven. The greatest difference is in the creativity. In Japan, broadly speaking, strategies are written to fit executions. In the United States, creative is written to meet strategies. The creative people in the United States are accustomed to working to strategies while still exercising their full creative capacity. In Japan, it is more often, "Give me a good creative idea and I will find the money to run it." Contrary to the often-held Western views of Japanese creativity, the creative idea precedes the strategy. The execution is therefore more creative or perhaps "off the wall" in Japan. In America you inject creativity into a marketing strategy while in Japan you inject strategy into a creative idea or concept. Both work in their own environment. An American in Japan usually draws a blank, however, when he says, "Here is our marketing strategy. Now what should the creative strategy be? Don't worry about the execution quite yet." With product brand managers it is probably best to go the U.S. way to maintain sanity, but it puts the creative element at the bottom of the pile. Moreover, it takes incredible creative and an astute account person to sell creative by courier with head office.

The system foreigners generally impose upon themselves is certainly not the most productive. It cuts off the top and the bottom and generally guarantees mediocrity. You will not have the dogs or the exceptions unless you get very, very lucky. A very draining experience. By the time I get to the vice-president of marketing in head office I have lost the creative guy, who stopped talking to me long ago.

In sum, a Japanese company will simply say to its agency, "Give us an ad; no involvement please in planning, pricing, or packaging." This will obviously not work for the foreign company and means the foreign company must be very demanding.

Competitive Profiles

A competitive profile should be done on all competition. This should include financials, people, what they are strategically trying to accomplish, and how they are tactically going about their business. If a general manager understands his competition, he will not let some creative person who does not know his company's product or the competition's product intimidate him. Too many general managers and their marketing staff do not have enough internal information and confidence to interact intelligently with their advertising agency.

They spend a ton of money and end up with a creative that is wrong for their product, is wrong for the media they are using, and does not sell their product. The worst part is they do not know why their product is not selling. If you are in the marketing game, you need a superb marketing director who can keep asking and demanding until you get the right creative.

Product Attributes

Joel Silverstein, General Manager of British American Tobacco, is marketing one of the most competitive products in a market only recently opened to foreigners.

The problem with consumer goods is that you use certain worldwide attributes, but we find you have to alter the attributes dramatically in the Japanese market because people do not think the same. Their whole mind-set is completely different. You cannot find Japanese words for half the attributes that come out of the United States. We did research before I arrived and missed the most important attribute: *kuchiatari* (mouth feel). This I learned when I went to the retail outlets and asked what is the most important attribute. The Japanese researcher confirmed it was very, very important but said he did not tell our people from head office because they did not want to know and it could not be translated. "They would not know what it means."

Often the Japanese working in or for foreign companies are very task oriented, but without the ability to put the task and the message together.

Another's experience:

If you want to do something that really breaks you away from the pack, that's when you get people being cautious, standoffish. I say let's do it. It is such a competitive marketplace. You have to stand out from your competition. You have to be able to risk standing out. I think that the nail that stands out, if you are right and can support what you are doing, gives you tremendous visibility. You are way ahead. You have to be careful. Sneak up on them slowly in a tasteful manner. Japanese are extremely visual people. Shout in good taste.

Adapt, don't adopt. Learn from the Japanese. They have never adopted anything. They have always adapted things from the outside. I have never seen a situation where technology can be successfully seconded from the United States, particularly with consumer products, if you take Americans in America and develop that product for the Japanese. Not only is hair and taste different, it just cannot work. You don't get the commitment. You don't get the quality of people required. You don't get the champion for the product. It takes forever to get the product to market.

With consumer products, advertising is a major expense, next to personnel and overhead. Because of the expense, the general manager must be personally involved, for to operate in the Japanese consumer market you have to spend a lot and be quick about it. In many cases it is time you are fighting against. Again, the Japan office must report to a high level in the head office, and that keeps everything at a boiling point, with resultant staff aggravation. "There are also plenty of *hankos* (signatures) required in the United States."

One is constantly reminded of how competitively tough the Japanese market is for consumer products. The name most often heard in this regard on the Japanese side is Kao, and the name on the foreign side in the same product category is Procter & Gamble.

Kao is tough, is innovative, and has tremendous liquidity, putting its break-even point much lower than P&G, which was swimming in the red for many years until 1988 in Japan. Until that time P&G had not been able, even with numerous products and heavy expenditure, to demonstrate to the Japanese consumer that its technology was any better than, for example, Kao or Lion.

Coca-Cola

On the other hand, Coca-Cola has been a tremendous success story for many years, taking more profit out of Japan in 1987 and 1988 than in the United States. Coca-Cola in 1989 had approximately 40 percent of the total soft drink and juice market, including 84 percent of the cola market. Many of its products were also developed in Japan solely for the Japanese market, including a range of coffee drinks under the name Georgia and a vitamin C health drink. Georgia is second only to Coca-Cola itself in Japan. It comes only in cans and is the number-one canned coffee drink. Georgia is also supported by a unique piece of creative advertising that plays on *Gone with the Wind*. Japan is one of the few countries where Coca-Cola's local management can determine its own strategies and themes and produce its own advertising. New Coke was never introduced. There is a far wider range of Coca-Cola products in Japan than elsewhere, and more of a lock on dispensing machines and shelf space. Vending machines are extremely important in Japan, which has the highest number per capita in the world. Coca-Cola developed the talking vending machine in Japan. It did not care that vending was not very important in the United States.

Pepsi has been a disaster in Japan, with little market share. Coke has the market and the image. It was first, and it chose the right partners for distribution. Why did Pepsi fail? It had lousy management, with no consistent marketing plan or execution. Unless a sustainable record can be created for a product, through price or uniqueness, it will eventually fail. Moreover, product reputation must be maintained. Even Coke experienced trouble when there was a false health scare with Fanta.

Fanta Flavors in the early 1970s were attacked because they had artificial color. Competitors used this to demean the product on television and in other media even though the coloring was quite safe and was used in many other parts of the world. The company replaced the artificial coloring with natural coloring, but the impact on product sales was severe for about five years. The brand subsequently began to grow again. Ironically, grape, which was the primary artificial-coloring target, is now the fastest-growing flavor, and Fanta is currently the fastest-growing flavor line of carbonated drinks in Japan.

In Japan a few products usually dominate in any given category. There is an oligarchic structure. This is especially true in the food categories, such as cola, curry, coffee, and mayonnaise. The only response to such a pressure-cooker environment is to launch new products, to rectify through novelty. Four thousand new products are launched in the food industry every year. Only 10 percent are still on the shelf a year later. Thirty percent of the packaging for existing products changes every year. A company can therefore only grow through imagination and by providing more service to the customer.

Nestlé

Nestlé developed a curry booster to fulfill a market need. Curry on rice to the Japanese housewife is like hot dogs and hamburgers on buns to the American housewife. It is an easy family meal. Japanese parents often prefer a stronger, spicier curry than do the children, much as American parents prefer stronger mustard than their children. American mothers solve the problem by having several types of mustard on the table for the hot dogs and hamburgers; the Japanese mother, however, does not want to make two batches of curry, especially when the cooking area is quite small. Thus, there was a need for the curry booster for mixing into the adult's portion.[1]

Copying

If an item is a hit in the marketplace, you can guarantee it will be copied, faster than anyone can possibly imagine. It is common practice and does not appear to be an ethical problem in Japan.

---

[1] Allan Bernard, Executive Director, Marketing, Nestlé Japan, ACCJ Marketing Presentation, November 26, 1986.

The Japanese do not want to be copied themselves, however. There are strict rules about copying licensed products. Snoopy used the legal mechanism, and this made the copiers wary of licensed products. A local railroad once unabashedly ran a train called the American Express, and American Express's television advertising has been copied almost completely. On the first there was recourse, while there has been none on the second. Foreign companies should not be timid in exploiting the local legal resources, especially when merely the threat of resorting to the courts will accomplish what they want if they have prepared properly.

Image Positioning—American Express

The Japanese compartmentalize a product's image in their minds; therefore, it cannot be changed overnight. It is difficult to lower an image—for example, American Express's mass marketing of the Green Card, even with "take ones" in taxis, after leading with the prestigious Gold Card. When the company used Jack Nicklaus to market the Green Card, the public, because of Jack's prestigious image, thought he was marketing the Gold Card. Jack helped the Gold Card but did not enhance the awareness of the Green Card at all. Young people in Japan normally do not overstep their bounds by being pretentious and purchasing what they feel belongs in their boss's domain. Young company employees will not pull out a Gold Card in front of a senior executive. They know they have to wait a few years. It was not until American Express did some extremely daring new-generation advertising, even by New York standards, that it was able to position the Green Card down market from the Gold. One advertisement has the Green Card in a young, new-generation man's mouth while another has a young man shopping with his wife. You see him clearly impatient but tolerating her shopping because he apparently loves his wife so much. This is not a role one generally associates with older generations of Japanese men. This campaign was extremely successful in repositioning the Green Card and generated an enormous amount of press coverage on the role of the new generation in Japanese society. Some of the actors became virtual cult heroes.

The Japanese also feel that by wearing or using the right thing they cannot be faulted, which is what every Japanese worries about. One will not find the tieless Japanese executive in first class on the airplane, unlike the American executive in his jeans or golf trousers. Comfort, like many things, has a very different meaning.

Service

The Japanese expect a great deal of service with almost every product, at the time of sale and afterward. Consumer marketing and sales is labor intensive and service oriented. There are 1.6 million retail merchandise outlets scattered throughout the nation. Witness the extraordinary number of mom-and-pop shops with some 7 million owners and employees. Mom-and-pop shops represent 58 percent of all retail outlets but only 13 percent of sales. Between these mom-and-pop shops and the large retailers, who with just 1 percent of retail establishments and with thirty or more employees have 28 percent of sales, are many small retailers who account for 59 percent of all retail sales.[2] In fact, in the mid-1980s stores with four or fewer employees still accounted for 56 percent of retail sales in Japan, compared with 3 percent in the United States and 5 percent in Western Europe. Because of limited shelf space, all except the largest retailers are served by a myriad of wholesalers. Manufacturing has to be very efficient and cost effective considering the high land, construction, distribution, and wage costs. What makes products so expensive is the marketing, sales, and service cost. But to circumvent the many intermediate costs might be even more expensive. All the clutter makes it more difficult to understand, but a company most likely will have to sell through it.

Creative vs. Shelf Space

Creative with limited shelf space can make a difference with consumer products, but with the costs of advertising in Japan it is expensive. If shelf space is limited, one must create a pull through quantitative, not qualitative, media.

---

[2]*The Seattle Times*, February 13, 1989, from Ronald E. Yates, *The Chicago Tribune*.

If you pitch the ball without a catcher—shelf space—then the consumer cannot make a choice.

Foreigners often give too much attention to quality rather than quantity. Moreover, if we assume that communication takes place through both distribution and media, then most do not spend enough on distribution. Many foreign consumer-product companies put advertising on a pedestal, feeling that to spend money on the distribution channel is a recognition they are not good marketers. You have to spend on both to have push and pull.

Clutter is unbelievable in all the media and a mammoth headache on television and even in retail outlets. There is a feeling in the retail trade that the retailer should offer his consumer every possible choice, and by doing so he says to the consumer there really is no difference.

Television says almost the same because most advertisements are fifteen seconds as opposed to, for example, thirty seconds in the United States. Watching television is like being tested yourself. There is, of course, program sponsorship, but on all sides and in between, tremendous clutter. As a result, there is much unexpected execution in Japan. Many advertisements are irrelevant in order to gain attention and popularity, to be applauded for creativity. There is also, therefore, a great emphasis on style and class.

With the size of the market and the clutter, it is extremely important to stay in the launch phase far longer than one would in other markets. Western marketing people will be working on their postlaunch campaign before they launch. If the launch campaign is successful, one should stay with it a long, long time. This will build far more awareness than moving from campaign to campaign unless it bombed in the first place. For the American Express Gold Card we had an extremely successful print, direct-response launch campaign with applications for the first four months far exceeding our wildest expectations. We then went into our postlaunch campaign and applications plummeted. In one week we returned to our original campaign and were back on track. The Japanese market is enormous in size and concentrated geographically, and it must be dealt with accordingly. Moreover, any campaign benefits from the fact that income distribution is extremely even nationally in any given job and age range. Although per capita income is higher than in the United States, over

90 percent of Japanese consider themselves middle class.

Some, like Tom Thompson, President of Bristol-Myers Lion, feel the distribution system is not the handicap people say it is:

Tough, yes, but getting the product to the shelf is not that difficult. The difficulty is getting the consumer to pick that product up. The successful companies, except where regulations prohibited them, are those that had products that were needed, that had some uniqueness, and that fulfilled a need that was not met in Japan. Often modification and development took place in Japan.

How do you create a need that permits you to sell through the clutter? Go to a glass bottle, then a can, and then a plastic bottle as Coca-Cola did. Coca-Cola made drinking out of a bottle in public the thing for young people to do, when eating in public was considered socially taboo. Now they are meeting the needs of the housewife with the light, easy-to-carry-home plastic bottle. Microwaves and frozen products create a need. One must look at the Japanese consumer, the Japanese lifestyle.

During the 1980s, two very different foreign products were introduced with great success in Japan. Each also reflected a very different stage in the life cycle of their industry. One, Ore-Ida frozen potato products, was introduced in 1984 at the beginning of the life cycle for frozen food and frozen potato products. The other, Timotei shampoo by Unilever, was an introduction in the hair-care market, which has been around a long time.

Ore-Ida

For Ore-Ida, this was its first venture outside of the United States. As in the United States, its initial success piggybacked on that of McDonald's and Kentucky Fried Chicken, which created the habit of eating french fried potatoes. Ore-Ida did a classic product introduction into Japan. It began by having all the decision makers in the company involved from the very beginning. They took two years to do their initial research, prepare their advertising and distribution strategy, and launch. They also had a lot of luck, but they were aware and took advantage of their luck.

McKinsey studied the market and strategy. ASI did the research with extensive in-house testing. In the latter stages of the testing, Ore-Ida learned that electric toaster ovens, which are in 90 percent of Japanese households, were only used for toast and frozen pizza.

Taking this information, they created a whole new eating concept: hash-brown potatoes for breakfast and french fries for lunch and dinner that did not have to be deep-fried like other frozen potato products. Luckily, McDonald's at the same time was beginning heavy promotion in Japan of its breakfast menu, which happened to include hash-brown potatoes similar to Ore-Ida's products.

The size of the portions and the packages of frozen potato products were reduced to conform to Japanese taste, serving sizes, and freezer space. Dai-ichi Kikaku created for Japan only a cartoon-like potato character for television advertising who became known as Mr. Ore-Ida. The Japanese frequently use cuddly, cute animal characters to advertise their products. Live Mr. Ore-Idas were soon in supermarkets, handing out samples and scaring the children. Television, newspapers, and subway and train posters were all used. An outdoor potato festival was held with live country bands and free potato samples. Thirty thousand people showed up for the first event. Kent Gilbert, the leading gaijin television personality in Tokyo, endorsed the product. He just happened to be from Idaho. To capitalize on Gilbert's appeal, they held a sweepstake contest in which he would accompany the winning family on a ten-day trip through Idaho. Over 100,000 Japanese responded. The next year children went for home-stay visits with Ore-Ida's employees. Reporters from the newspapers in which the company advertised were sent to Idaho with the plane fare paid for by the company and other expenses paid for by the Department of Commerce of the State of Idaho. In the first twenty months, there were over two hundred articles on Ore-Ida in the Japanese press. The *Yomiuri* newspaper, with a morning circulation of over nine million, had five articles in one week.

All of the product was imported, with retail prices in 1986 that were 15 to 30 percent above domestic manufacturers. The premium was used to fund a marketing program to build the business. By 1986, two years after launch, Ore-Ida had the number-one market share, a 64 percent awareness level among housewives, and 92 percent among children. That is success in any country.[3]

---

[3]Damon Darlin, *The Wall Street Journal*, May 27, 1987; Alan Brender, *Journal of the American Chamber of Commerce in Japan* (September 1985), pp. 28–31; Larry Blagg, President, Ore-Ida Japan, ACCJ Marketing Presentation, June 4, 1986.

Unilever

Unilever does not sell products worldwide under its name. It believes in the brand and in brand marketing. With Lux toilet soap, Rama Margarine, and Timotei, among other products, it is one of the most successful global consumer marketing companies and one of the premier foreign companies in Japan. Timotei, a hair shampoo product, is a good example of its sophisticated use of marketing and of how a foreign company can make a decision work. Timotei had started in Sweden and had spread through Scandinavia, Europe, and the rest of the world as a natural hair-care product. The original goal of Unilever in Japan was to kidnap the naturalness dimension of hair care and make it "theirs" so nobody could get at them. "Just own it." There are over one hundred shampoo products on the market. Fourteen months after launch, Timotei was the number-one shampoo and was selling at a premium price.

Unilever's Marketing Service Manager in Japan, Roger Broo-kin, commented on this approach to building brand success:

> We build brands in seventy countries around the world. The secret in Japan is very similar to building brands anywhere in the world. It is simply discovering consumers' needs and satisfying those needs, as simple and difficult as that, by adapting to local conditions in all cases. We use a great deal of research in every country where we work. It is very important as foreigners that we do research, because we don't know how people in Japan take a bath or wash their hands or hair or what they eat for breakfast. Most natives anywhere are not happy about spending money to find out how their fellow countrymen do things. Actually, the worst person to ask how Japanese people do things is a Japanese businessman. The Japanese businessman knows less about Japanese housewives than Englishmen know about English housewives, and that is saying something. We try to understand our consumer, to see what our consumer wants. Around the world we have developed the nugget of the brand, the soul of the brand. We then have to discover what are the local flesh and blood, the local clothes that we have to put on the soul to make it appealing to the body in that country and to make it mean what it means in other countries.[4]

Unilever used ASI for its research on Timotei and J. Walter Thompson for its advertising. It took a lot of money, great courage not to go with the launch until they were absolutely sure they had clothed the soul, and superb execution.

---

[4]Roger Brookin, ACCJ Marketing Presentation, June 4, 1986.

Rejoy

But, as Unilever soon learned, no market is more dynamic nor competitive than Japan. In 1988 Procter & Gamble introduced in Japan a new shampoo, Rejoy. At the end of 1989 the product already had 7 percent of the market, while Timotei had slipped from a high of 10 percent to 5.2 percent. Whereas Timotei is image and mood driven, Rejoy is technology driven, although media spending for Rejoy in 1989 was estimated to be $13.6 million.

P&G's testing confirmed that Rejoy is technologically superior for a larger number of people than the other products on the market. Rejoy combines in one shampoo a cleaner and a conditioner. The hair of most Japanese is coarse and harder to manage than that of most Westerners, which is what the technological innovation targets. The technology is patented and is fairly difficult to conceive and make. Thus, unlike Timotei, which attempted to capture the naturalness market, Rejoy's success is based on performance. While Rejoy is premium priced, Unilever has dropped Timotei's price substantially in order to salvage the market. Only time will tell whether naturalness, technology, or some other attribute will be the winner. The market will not stand still for even a Unilever or a Procter & Gamble.

The obvious challenge is to stay in tune with the potential customers' taste. The market changes faster here in a product's life cycle. A fad comes faster, the competition comes quicker, and it dies quicker. What is now important is lifestyle. Affluence is already in place.

Procter & Gamble

It is generally accepted that Procter & Gamble, after a disastrous initial thirteen years in Japan from 1973 until 1986, during which it wrote off an estimated $300 million, has turned the corner with children's and adult diapers and sanitary napkin products that contributed substantially to sales of over $1 billion in 1989.

During this turnaround, P&G learned that a company cannot succeed in Japan if it knows less about doing business there than its Japanese competitors. In knowing the Japanese business environment, P&G found there are four essential marketing principles: First, know your consumer; second, tailor your products to the Japanese market; third, penetrate the multitiered distribution system; and fourth, sell your company as well as your brand.

The homemaker, who is largely responsible for the consumption of P&G's products, is uncompromising in her demand for excellent quality, value, and service. She has grown up in an environment where virtually every company manufactures products to a standard of zero defects, and she has come to expect that quality in every product she buys. She is the paragon of efficiency in the management of her household and rules the roost.

P&G was a one- or two-brand detergent company in Japan at first, and it was fairly easy for the competition to pin it down. It entered Japan armed with market-size statistics. It knew about the equipment women used and the frequency with which they did their tasks, but it did not understand the Japanese consumer as well as it did the American or European consumer, and some costly mistakes were made.

Cheer

One of P&G's early mistakes was on Cheer laundry detergent, its first major entry into Japan. When it introduced Cheer, P&G was having good success in the United States with its Cheer All-Temperature campaign. The advertising promise was that here was one detergent that would get clothes clean in all three washing temperatures normally used in the American laundry: hot, warm, and cold. P&G decided to use that advertising concept in Japan as well. A great American idea, but in Japan it was a big flop. Three-temperature washing simply was not relevant to Japanese habits. Women either washed in tap water, and thus all their washes were cold, or, on occasion, saved the family bath water, since washing takes place outside the tub, and ran it through the washing machine, especially during winter months when the tap water is very cold. Doing their wash in three different temperatures obviously did not apply to Japanese women, and they rejected the advertising. Eventually advertising that promised superior cleaning in cold water for children's clothes worked.

Whisper

Knowing the consumer helped P&G do it right from the beginning with its new Japanese sanitary napkins, called Whisper, the Japanese version of Always. Japanese women are the most fastidious in the world when it comes to personal hygiene. They do twice as many washloads as Americans or Europeans, and they also do more pretreating, soaking, and scrubbing to get the best possible results. They change their babies' diapers twice as often as their American or European counterparts. This habit also carries over to sanitary napkins. The change-frequency rate is double that of the United States. Japanese women also use a tight-fitting menstrual panty, a bit like a girdle, to hold the pad close to the body and help prevent leakage. Tampons are used by only 5 percent of the population. Perhaps this is because of religious taboos on handling products associated with blood, or because tampons are considered an unnatural invasion of the body. All of this suggested, though, the need for an even better napkin. As a result, the patented Always formed-film topsheet over a thin napkin core was tailored in size to fit Japanese women. The unique hydrophobic topsheet substantially improved skin dryness and prevented back-flow and thus leakage. Consumer acceptance was outstanding. In testing, the product was preferred two to one over the then market leader.

Although sanitary napkins are used by a broad base of the female population, P&G's marketing team in Japan decided to concentrate their whole marketing strategy on women in their late teens and twenties. Research showed that this group was more concerned with the problems Whisper solved. They were also less sensitive to price, and Whisper is a premium-priced product. Younger women were also more interested in trying new products than older women.

The Dentsu advertising agency proposed creating a brand character who would be based on a "Miss Whisper" role model and would be woven through all marketing activities, including the package design. To appeal to the women in their targeted group in television advertising, P&G chose a woman photographer who epitomizes the emergence of professional working women in Japan. The first Miss Whisper was a minor celebrity in that a number of years back she had been a Miss Universe candidate, but she had consciously decided she did not want to be in that glamorous world; she wanted to become a serious photographer.

Here was somebody who had left the glitter and glamour to

enter a serious career, someone who appealed to the conscience of the Japanese. When the agency created the Miss Whisper personality, it felt the brand image was the person. She suited the ideal—a newly emerging professional who was serious, who, for example, listened to classical music rather than rock and roll. The agency did not write her script. She became someone whom the Japanese saw as truly genuine. She was not at the other side of the television screen, talking at them and selling and representing the maker. Rather, she was one with the viewers.

The dialogue in the commercial reflects the open and frank way Japanese women talk to one another about sanitary products. The story line is that "using Whisper feels like wearing just-washed underwear." Miss Whisper and her successors touch Japanese women deeply. There is not a Japanese woman who does not know the Whisper advertising. Moreover, P&G built the first Miss Whisper into a personality, including supporting her photographic exhibitions. She went to all the sales meetings, spoke to the trade, and gave her input on the product. At present a concert pianist and a television newscaster are being used. Dentsu identifies the potential candidates. So far, one out of every three hundred reviewed has been used.

P&G admits that the sophistication it created for this campaign was something it just did not fully understand when it entered Japan. Today Whisper is the number-one sanitary napkin in Japan, and the technology developed there is being used globally to provide a better and more competitive product for consumers everywhere. The advertising concept is now being used throughout the Far East.

Pampers

Today, every one of P&G's major products in Japan, like Whisper, is different in some important way from the products the company sells in the United States. Another good example is Pampers disposable diapers. P&G created the disposable-diaper market in Japan, using the American product to do it, but after an initial success it bombed. That product was relatively thick and bulky, designed for mothers who intended to leave the diapers on babies for relatively long periods of time. In Japan, where mothers change their babies' diapers twice as often as mothers in the United States, the consumer wanted a thinner, more compact product, one that was easier to store in limited space and easier to take along on a shopping trip or visit. Moreover, although P&G makes a good Pampers product in the United States, Japanese consumers found flaws in that product at triple the complaint level experienced in the United States. Japanese consumers, as mentioned, expect zero defects in products. P&G's research eventually told them that Japanese women thought of the American Pampers as a noncaring product of lesser performance and quality than competing Japanese products.

Nevertheless, in the absence of Japanese competition, Pampers initially captured about 10 percent of all diaper changes in Japan. This encouraged two Japanese companies, Kao and Unicharm, to seize the opportunity to introduce more absorbent and better fitting thin diapers. They almost drove Pampers out of the market. Their premium-priced products were more compact, and they used super-absorbent polymers. With this new competition, consumer usage of disposable diapers increased from 10 to 30 percent of total diaper changes within two years, but Pampers' share of the total market declined sharply. P&G was paying the price for not having tailored its product to fit Japanese consumer needs, but fortunately, the lesson did not prove to be fatal.

In the words of the brand manager:

> To *survive* and rebuild the business in Japan, Pampers has had to upgrade its product no less than four times in the last thirty-six months. This Pamper is now three times thinner than the original model. It's shaped for better fit and has a waist shield and leg gathers to stop leaks. It has thick guidelines and refastenable tapes for convenience, and it is now the best diaper in Japan. This diaper allowed Pampers to go from a seven share to a twenty-eight share and market leadership in thirty months. That is important because the market in Japan has grown five times in the last five years. Today, 100 percent of Japanese mothers are using disposable diapers.

The special technology P&G developed to compete in Japan is now the product called Ultra Pampers around the world. Its success is another tangible evidence of how you must be technology driven to compete in Japan, and of the worldwide benefit to competing in the fast-moving Japanese market.

The television advertising developed for the introduction of this new Pampers product had to do more than just sell the product: It had to overcome an image problem that resulted from the company having imported Pampers from the United States in its early years. The advertising that dealt with P&G's image problem, while at the same time introducing their new thin Pampers product, featured a new hero, Pampers-chan ("chan" is an honorific attached to all young children's names). Pampers-chan is a talking diaper—a fairy-tale character who talks to the baby and promises that the baby will be kept dry all over, even after a long night's sleep. It was one of the great introductory advertising campaigns of 1985 in Japan, and the campaign continues to be extremely successful.

Attento

P&G not only sells baby diapers in Japan; it also sells adult diapers for incontinent elderly people. The brand is known as Attends in the United States and Attento in Japan.

Incontinence is a worldwide problem, a sad by-product of increased longevity that often confines otherwise mobile elderly people to their homes or beds. Japan has the most rapidly aging population in the world, with the longest lifespan. Adult briefs can help restore social mobility to incontinents, just as diapers and sanitary napkins do for their users. But here again, U.S. products and marketing methods were of little relevance to Japan. In the United States, the vast majority of incontinent elderly are institutionalized and are cared for by professionals. In Japan, where family ties are very strong, sick and bedridden elderly parents are treated at home, not in institutions. As a result, the market for incontinent products, such as adult diapers, is an at-home market with direct-to-consumer advertising and distribution. In Japan, the caretaker is usually the daughter-in-law, and having a bedridden incontinent at home represents a major burden on top of her normal family responsibilities.

Because of the differences, entering this category truly forced P&G to think Japanese. It was selling a product in Japan that benefited two consumers: the caretaker and the user. It therefore developed a product that had features for both, from refastenable tapes to check the diaper and adjust the fit, to a wetness indicator to enable one to see easily if the diaper is wet, to special sizing to fit the anatomy of elderly Japanese, to levels of performance that would insure that incontinent people capable of being mobile could actually get up and do things as a result of using the product.

Advertising was a major challenge. Adult incontinence is a delicate subject to talk about publicly on television. P&G had no experience in doing so in the United States or Europe. A balance had to be struck between communicating the functional advantages of the product and not alienating the viewer. Here again, an understanding of Japanese culture made the difference.

Attento's advertising features a well-known Japanese storyteller as the presenter of the product. Storytellers in Japan are considered to be wise old men who have lots of experience and knowledge about life and who use proverbs and humor to teach about life in Japan. Through the P&G campaign, Attento has become the leading product in its category in Japan.

Camay

P&G has learned that it must always be sensitive to cultural differences in marketing everywhere, but nowhere is it as easy to make a mistake as in Japan. Not all of its advertising campaigns were as successful as Pampers-chan and Miss Whisper.

Camay toilet soap is a high-quality soap for facial and bath use. Both bar and wrapper look about the same around the world. It is sold in virtually every country in which P&G operates, and its broad positioning is basically the same everywhere: an elegant product, feminine in character and fragrance, and good for the skin. The company has used many different advertising campaigns for Camay, but the one that has worked best in most countries is the campaign based on a strategy they call "attractiveness to men."

The concept behind this strategy is that Camay helps a woman to be and feel more feminine, and that is most easily recognized in terms of her attractiveness to the opposite sex. In Great Britain this subtle concept is dealt with through traditional British wit and understatement, while in France the treatment is less subtle with a more overt display of physical affection and, of course, the distinctively French touch of savoir-faire. Japan decided to use the same advertising approach while adapting to the Japanese market. But the advertising was way off base for that market. Why? Because the advertisement showed a Japanese husband in the room while his wife was bathing. In Japanese society it is just plain bad manners for a husband to impose on his wife's privacy while she is bathing. Consumers resented the breach of good manners and the overt chauvinism in the situation.

It was not all bad, however. Women did like the idea of the European character of Camay, and they liked the idea of a beauty soap contributing to overall attractiveness. P&G therefore developed another campaign in which the commercial takes place in a European setting, with a European woman and a Western-style bath. The advertising is still about beautiful women and Camay, and the commercial has been very successful.

There is one major product area in which P&G has been taken to the cleaners by the Japanese competition. This is in the overall detergent category. The market leader is Kao, with detergent share of market for 1989 of 56.3 percent, while Lion had 27.7 percent and P&G 11.7 percent. In March 1987 Kao introduced a concentrated, powder detergent called Attack as a new free-standing brand. The results have been nothing short of phenomenal. Attack alone had 36.5 percent of the total detergent market in December 1989, accounting for 65 percent of Kao's total detergent sales. Attack is premium priced, and the Japanese consumer clearly is willing to pay a premium price for a superior product that is even as outwardly mundane as laundry detergent.

The Wall Street Journal reported in November 1989 that in December P&G would begin testing a super-concentrated detergent in the United States, as a result of lessons learned in Japan, where competitors have had great success with concentrated soapsuds. It also reported that P&G is introducing such a product to preempt a potential Kao initiative in the United States. The world is truly becoming internationalized.

Nescafé

Nestlé's Nescafé Coffee introduced its "City of the World" campaign with McCann-Erickson Hakuhodo in 1967. As we enter the 1990s, the campaign is still going strong. What is being marketed now is not just a product, but a culture that surrounds a product, showing a consistency perhaps no other foreign consumer product has demonstrated in Japan. This cultural image cannot be created in eighteen months. A great deal of determination to stick to a campaign is required to develop a new culture. Nestlé did, and Nescafé today holds 70 percent of the instant coffee market in the fourth largest coffee market in the world.

Pricing

Foreign companies often have felt that the only way to sell in Japan is by creating a prestige image through premium pricing. They have arrived at this conclusion either through their observations of the imagery and pricing of products in the Japanese market similar to theirs, or because their local advisers told them to, or because they wished a quick return on their investment, or because their Japanese partner set the price, or because of a combination of the above.

Suntory, with over 60 percent of the liquor market in Japan, controls the best products from around the world in the alcohol-related drink category—for example, Bacardi, Budweiser, and Perrier. The principal avenue for Suntory to control their growth has been through premium pricing, which keeps them from competing head to head with Suntory in the mainstream market. Budweiser, which is made in Japan by Suntory, is priced at 240 yen a can as opposed to 210 yen for Suntory Beer and the other three Japanese beer products. Suntory's own brand is ranked fourth out of four among the Japanese brewers, with approximately 9 percent of the beer market. The company is certainly not going to let Budweiser, a foreign product, supplant its own brand in the rankings.

With the devaluation of the dollar against the yen, jobbers are now bringing in parallel imports through Japanese trading companies and are selling Budweiser's American-brewed product at a discount to Japanese distributors. One can now buy Budweiser from the United States in Japanese supermarkets at 190 yen a can.

Remy Martin, the top-selling brandy in Japan, developed a new frosty bottle just for the Japanese market and retained premium pricing to compete with parallel imports in cognac, which are

selling at half the price of those imports handled by their designated agents. Remy Martin kept enough of the heritage of the old
bottle for consistency but distinguished the new bottle clearly
from the parallel imports coming in via Hong Kong. Only time
will tell if prestige in a bottle and not in content will command a
premium price. The profit the company had been taking out of
Japan and the potential for its erosion obviously made it worth
the try.

Another interesting development is the difference in approach
taken by the scotch and bourbon industries. The scotch industry
was disturbed by what it perceived to be entry and distribution
barriers to its products. It researched the situation thoroughly and
enlisted the direct assistance of both the European Community's
headquarters in Brussels and Prime Minister Margaret Thatcher.
As a result, it was able to remove these barriers and to sell ordinary
scotch at a lower price range of 2,900 to 3,100 yen, which went
head to head with the already lower-priced market leader, Suntory Old. The foreign competition has since forced Suntory Old
down to 2,350 yen and ordinary scotch to approximately 2,200
yen. White Horse Scotch has recently sold as low as 1,900 yen
through parallel imports.

Meanwhile, even though the dollar was devalued by 50 percent, the price of ordinary bourbon went from 2,600 yen to as high
as 3,900 yen (in dollar terms a swing from approximately $10 to
$31). Today bourbon prices range widely for even the same brand
at different locations. That is hardly a way to take market share
from Suntory or the scotch industry in Japan.

Far too many foreign companies continue to not price competitively, often accepting the old axiom that the Japanese only buy
foreign goods that are priced at the perceived highest quality
level. You have to come in with a product better than what they
are buying, market the product differently, and price it competitively. If a product has a premium price, it had better offer value
at a premium price. It has to fulfill an absolute need.

An article by Damon Darlin in *The Wall Street Journal* of April
6, 1989, notes:

In 1987, Brown & Williamson took a chance. It dropped the price for a
pack of its Kent cigarettes to 220 yen (about $1.67) from 280 yen, lower even
than the 250 yen a pack charged by Japan Tobacco Inc., the country's tobacco

monopoly. The price cut—the first ever for a major imported consumer product here—was such a striking challenge that it made front-page news in some national Japanese newspapers. Kent became one of the fastest-selling cigarettes in Japan. Other foreign tobacco companies followed suit, as did Japan Tobacco. Foreign companies' market share zoomed from less than 3% to more than 12%.

The same article reports that Sadafumi Nishina, Marketing Director for international products at Dentsu, said: "We would never recommend a lower price." It is not surprising that the largest Japanese advertising agency, with principally Japanese clients, would not encourage foreign competition.

In sum, pricing in Japan is extremely important. By using high prices as a marketing mechanism to say that the product is quality, the foreign product's market potential is limited to the very top of the market, whether fountain pens, whiskey, men's suits, beer, or furniture. If a company only wants the premium end of a market, that is fine. The Japanese, though, will buy much more of quality products that are priced competitively and meet a need. If products are not priced competitively, the market will remain extremely limited and soon someone will come in and meet the market need created below this stratosphere. When price and market share are fixed in an association, then a company can only improve its profit on the cost reduction side. This is often the case with industrial products and makes new entry almost impossible in such areas as petroleum and many chemical products. Market share is rarely fixed today in consumer products.

Packaging

Packaging has a long and prestigious history in Japan. The department store wrapping often means more than the gift itself to the receiver. The packaging of a foreign consumer product generally has to undergo significant modification in Japan. It is not just a question of language, though that, of course, must be appropriate for the product. Roger Brookin of Unilever notes:

Japanese packaging is more elaborate and fulfills a wider range of functions than packaging would tend to in the European or North American markets. By the time you have taken your free carrier bag home and taken your margarine out of the free plastic bag they have put it in and then taken it out of the expensive and free cardboard container and then lifted off the free heavy duty lid and taken out the free grease proof liner paper we put on the margarine, you get to the product. You don't do that anywhere else in the world. The margarine product itself is different than elsewhere. The level of quality of margarine in the Japanese market is the best in the world, without any doubt. Ours and the competition's is significantly better than in the United States or Europe.

Media

If a company is introducing a new product, it has to find a way to be as intrusive as it can be through a quality presentation that is loud, that penetrates, and that creates the awareness it desires. The choice of media used depends on the life cycle of the product or service. All of the choices are expensive. Moreover, it is difficult to test a product in a specific region or city because of the small geographic size of the country. There is a great deal of leakage. Testing also tells the competition what is coming.

Newspapers and Television

Most products are introduced in Tokyo. The launch is the test in a city that is the capital of the country in every way—economically, culturally, and politically. As previously mentioned, Tokyo is not just a test market, it is a lead market. It is where all national relationships begin and end. The major newspapers and television networks are national, reaching a population of 123 million, with local news supplementation. The three major newspapers have circulations of between 9 and 14 million copies daily. They are the three largest in the world, with enormous clout in the community. They, along with the *Nihon Keizai Shimbun* and NHK government television, carry the prestige of the *New York Times, Wall Street Journal, London Times,* or BBC. As a result, television rates are far more negotiable than newspaper rates. The newspapers will not even talk with you, so an agency must speak for you. A company can, however, negotiate what it pays the agency, thus forcing it to negotiate a better rate with the newspapers. Although most newspapers are delivered to the home, fliers in the papers are usually limited to real estate and chain supermarkets. There is, though, plenty of room for testing new concepts.

The two government NHK television stations do not accept advertisement. It is therefore impossible to have exposure on programs that often have the highest viewership. If a representative of the company is interviewed on NHK, however, the business receives tremendous endorsement and prestige. The commercial television stations are cluttered with a great deal of advertising but are also very important.

Because of the costs of using television to advertise a product, a company that does is saying it is in Japan to play in the big leagues. But that is not enough to sell its product. As anywhere, it must have a way for consumers to purchase the product. Unless it is through direct response, for example, direct mail or telephone, this usually means shelf space. Television advertising can often assist in obtaining that shelf space because of the company's demonstrated commitment to its product. Because of the clutter and the buying of blocks of time by Dentsu, however, and because television stations rarely will commit to specific advertising times except for program sponsorship, television's pull or push with the retail consumer can be easily dissipated.

In contrast to the United States, virtually all companies devote the last couple of seconds in a television commercial to a visual corporate identification, in this way enhancing corporate identity. Foreign companies like American Express and P&G have found this extremely beneficial not only for product sales but for recruiting personnel.

Magazines

Magazines are national and are sold on the newsstand, particularly at train and subway station kiosks, and rarely through subscription. It is questionable whether with magazines in Japan there is any believability in the audit if one is trying to determine gross rating points and exposure. You really do not know what you are buying. It is difficult to determine how many people are truly looking at it, and in what age groups. Japan has more magazines per capita than any place in the world, which would be positive if one could target specific markets through specific publications with believable data. There is also some concern over how much the agencies receive in kickbacks from the printing houses, especially for new publications, which are constantly coming on the market. Recommended publications should be looked at carefully. In Japan there is a unique way to determine the response rate to newspaper and magazine advertisements. An advertisement requiring a response often has a small corner tab with a publication identifying number on it, which the respondent cuts out and pastes on a self-addressed postcard with his or her return address and mails to the advertiser. The company placing the advertisement then sends out the fulfillment package. Although this method sounds awkward, it works. It allows a company to determine which publications are reaching its target market. It is also much cheaper than an insert.

Subway Posters

An area not often thought of in other markets is subway posters, which are changed as often as weekly. Though expensive, they are also effective. Japanese subways are clean, efficient, and heavily used. Many of the magazines are read there, since that is where they are often bought. Coordinating print and subway advertising can be powerful, much as reinforcing print with television.

Radio

Radio stations are limited in number and have been used infrequently by foreign companies, although Coca-Cola uses radio very effectively for the youth market. For no explainable reason, most advertising agencies appear unwilling to consider radio. They will say that only housewives listen, that Japanese don't listen to their car radios on weekdays since they commute by public transportation, or that teenagers only listen late at night while studying. Segmented properly, all of these appear to be reasons to use radio. In the agricultural sector, radio is dynamite once a company has name recognition, covering a large area cost-effectively with twenty-second spots. Perhaps the reason the agencies refuse to consider radio is the lower income they receive when they buy radio time compared to television time or print space.

Trade Journals

There are trade journals in every industrial field in Japan. These should be studied carefully to assist in understanding the competition and in turn should be used for distinctly advertising a product. These journals are of course in Japanese. Whoever is following them in an organization has to understand the company's strategy, plans, and products if they are going to provide the competitive information needed to function effectively in Japan. This is true in all efforts to understand what is being said in all the media in Japan that comment on a product, market, or the competition. The management of most foreign companies remains totally ignorant about what is happening in the media and does not put in place a system that provides effective and timely information for managing the business. Watching the English-language CNN cable television station or listening to the American Armed Forces Far Eastern Network radio programs will not help one in doing business in Japan with the Japanese.

Direct Marketing

Direct marketing, including direct mail, catalogues, coupons, and telemarketing, has just begun in Japan. These techniques in general have had a bad reputation in the government ministries that oversee their operations and among the general public. The maze of regulatory requirements resulting from split administrative authority and competition among such ministries as Posts and Telecommunications and MITI makes getting permission for innovative marketing, which is second nature in other markets, a painful experience. One has to be careful to deliver what one promises. It is, however, the one way to communicate directly with potential consumers and thereby circumvent the Japanese distribution maze. For foreign companies this is one heck of an incentive to find ways to direct market their products, and such companies have therefore been at the forefront of developing these marketing techniques in Japan. A warning, however. Some of the major international direct-marketing firms have linked up with Japanese advertising agencies. The Japanese placed in these ventures by their agencies have usually had little if any direct-marketing experience and do not have much credibility with the government or in the markets. In turn, the foreigners are far too junior and rotated far too quickly in and out of the ventures. Some outstanding foreigners in foreign consumer-product companies with direct-marketing experience have naturally come and gone during their career development; unfortunately, some other types have acted extremely irresponsibly, if not criminally, thus tainting all foreign endeavors in this critically important field.

Companies as diverse as American Express, AIU Insurance Company, Franklin Mint, and Cyanamid participated actively in the development of direct-mail lists and techniques in the 1980s, getting doctors to buy their Gold Card, insurance, and collectibles, and farmers their pesticide. The postal authorities are also beginning to cooperate as they learn the potential for profit from direct mail since their profits from postal savings are being squeezed through changes in financial and tax regulations.

Premiums

Premiums have been tightly controlled and restricted by the authorities, principally by severely limiting the value of the premium that can be offered. To date if there is an open campaign where anyone can participate without buying the product, there is no restriction on the value of the premium, e.g., a trip to Idaho. If participants must buy the product to participate, then the value of the premium can be no more than ten times the value of the product bought. Foreign companies have appealed to the authorities on numerous occasions for more flexibility in monetary amount and what can be offered. There are now some signs of relaxation and liberalization. The authorities, however, remain very concerned about, if not focused on, the possibilities of what they call unfair competition—that is, the biggies could offer premiums that could not be matched by the mom-and-pop operators. Fraud has been a secondary concern. As a result, the combining of direct mail or direct response with premiums has unfortunately not seen the light of day. Any company contemplating using premiums would be well advised to clear their campaign with the appropriate authorities and association to avoid subsequent embarrassment or legal repercussions. Push as hard as is realistically possible for a favorable decision, even if that opens the market for everyone; to be a market leader is excellent for a company's image as well as its bottom line.

The best hope for success is based on doing everything as thoroughly and intelligently as possible. That applies to every step in bringing a product or service to market. Failures are just too expensive and final. The higher the knowledge, the quicker and better the preventive care and, most important, the more likely one will discover a concept breakthrough that will position the product or service in the most competitive mode possible. You have to be close to your market.

We learned how close you must be to your market when signing up the major Japanese city banks to do direct debit for American Express cardmembers. We promised them that in the initial stages of our business we would not solicit the sixty-odd regional banks. As soon as the application flow began, we learned that our research had failed to show us a very obvious situation. Our original advertising was focused in the Tokyo area. Although many of our potential cardmembers worked in Tokyo, they slept in the immediately adjoining Chiba Prefecture and Yokohama. Since wives control the purse strings in Japan and give their husbands an allowance, the cardmembers' bank accounts were not in Tokyo but in banks near their residences in Chiba or Yokohama. They were most likely in either Chiba Bank or the Bank of Yokohama, and these were the banks they wished to use. Gingerly, without affecting our existing bank relationships and without upsetting these two banks whom we originally ignored, we approached them because it was essential to our business to sign them up. This led to the realization that the business people of Yokohama are proud of being the second largest city in Japan, larger even than Osaka, and they do not like being serviced from Tokyo. The hotels, restaurants, arcades, and stores were much more willing to work with American Express if the salesman worked out of a Yokohama office. As a result, an office in Yokohama was opened early on, at considerable expense but to the overall benefit of our business, though this certainly was not in our original plan.

As in all other aspects of a business, it should by now be apparent that one can succeed in marketing endeavors in Japan only with exceptional product, talent, money, and effort. There is no room for dilettantes.

12

Selling

THERE ARE as many ways to sell in Japan as there are companies and products. The important lesson for the foreign company is that everyone in the organization, from the chairman at home to the telephone operator in Japan, is selling all the time to everyone in the community: the government, bankers, securities houses, suppliers, wholesalers, retailers, and consumers. It is a full-court press, and it is exhausting because the game never ends.

Sales Force

To understand selling in Japan, and to understand its competitive advantages and disadvantages in the Japanese market, the foreign company must first take its competitor analysis to the depths the Japanese do. Research and analysis is ongoing; from the launch onward, sales personnel are an integral part of information gathering. They are the company's eyes and ears with wholesalers, retailers, and consumers. This ongoing competitor relationship analysis is the basis for a marketing strategy and sales program.

Salesmen must have trust and confidence in the company and its products. That is not easy to accomplish. The only way is to go out and sell with them. As previously mentioned, the sales force manager has to direct the sales force, maximizing the usage of their time in a cost-effective manner that sells. A company's salesmen have probably worked only for other foreign companies or did not make it in Japanese companies. They are not well connected, are insecure, and usually go in selling with their heads down. They are perceived as foreign, because one is who one's company is. They also often feel that their fulfillment promises are unreliable, for they are not confident that their foreign company will deliver. Unfortunately, the task of the American company to prove itself to a Japanese customer as a reliable supplier of a quality product over a long period of time remains an issue. After personally observing so many failures in the sales areas, I find it essential that the sales function be led by a mature foreign employee with extensive sales experience in the home market or internationally. He knows the product and can train and sell side-by-side with his sales staff. He should be a quick study of people and the market. If a foreign company cannot afford to have an expatriate sales manager, then this function becomes, after personnel, the most important and time-consuming task for the general manager.

> Sales is our biggest problem, operating a sales force. Sales is often a disaster while production is excellent. The toughest place I have ever seen for selling. This is mainly because the salesmen are not good salesmen. To begin with, the salesmen feel the position of the buyer is much stronger than that of the salesman.

Much of this is a social situation. Because they work for a foreign company, the salesmen are perceived by the Japanese customer to be second rate, and probably they are, or they would be working for a Japanese company. A good salesman is going to lose easily as many as he wins, but an insecure salesman is naturally reluctant to take risks. He is hesitant to increase prices when necessary, for he fears losing business that the company already has and/or that was obtained by someone else.

> You've got to deal constantly with inferiority complexes. You've got to try to make them proud of working for a foreign company. "You didn't go to the best university, but you came into this company. We've trained you, and your skills are far ahead of your peers in a Japanese company, and you are being compensated for those skills." If you don't, you will soon hear, "I'm less able than the guy I have to call upon." That is fatal.

> Our company only works when it is populated with believers. Peer unity is a sales process, and we had better handle it that way. We had better be as serious about recruiting as selling our product.

When recruiting a salesman, ask him to tell you who he is

without referring to the Japanese company's name on his name card. You will learn quickly whether he really wants to sell.

The employees we have pried out of Japanese companies are much better than those hired from other foreign companies. The inferior Japanese, whom you usually find in another foreign company, will not look to another Japanese or foreigner for support. He is insecure.

The sales force, like the rest of a company's employees, wants a corporate womb. They want the camaraderie of their fellow workers. They should therefore be treated like all the other employees. In Japanese companies, sales is just one aspect or stage in the development of an employee for management. They do not have someone out selling the company and its products who is not potential management. The concept of the loner, the American salesman on the road who calls in once a week, is inconceivable to a Japanese salesman. He wants to know everything going on in the office, particularly in his group. Getting him out of the office is not easy. At American Express we once took all the salesmen's desks and telephones away and replaced them with lock-up cabinets and several ladies who took all incoming phone calls. They did not like it, but it certainly got them out of the office where they were not selling anything.

Sales Force Salaries

The salaries of sales personnel should be the same as for all other personnel of the same age, educational background, and experience. They will ask for special consideration since they know that many foreign companies pay salesmen on a commission basis. When they do, ask if they wish to have the opportunity to grow and be a part of management. If they say no, then they should not be out representing the company. Separate financial bonuses for in-house salesmen are destructive to corporate morale. The salesmen may need, however, a special allowance to compensate for not receiving overtime if their job requires selling beyond normal working hours. Everyone in the company should feel included in selling the company to the entire community. Outings, commendations, and a pat on the back for the group are the best ways to maintain healthy corporateness. In Japan it is an asset to have an in-house sales force. They will develop and maintain relationships and give substance to the company in the eyes of the customers in contrast to commission salesmen who are not really a part of the organization.

Training and Control

Control has been mentioned as an accounting issue. It is also a sales issue. The one area where the Japanese run businesses poorly in the Western sense, though not necessarily in the Japanese sense, is effective sales control. Since the sales function in a Japanese company is generally everyone's job, with some more accountable than others, one does not find the same rigid sales measures found in Western companies, where the sales function is delineated and the salesmen are often compensated differently than other employees. Commissions and bonuses require different accountability measuring systems. The real problem occurs when a firm tries to mesh Western and Japanese sales techniques with a sales staff that would be mediocre in learning capacity by any substantive Japanese company's standards.

Foreign-style sales training has not been particularly effective in Japan, where relationship selling predominates. The concept of the salesman as a consultant to the potential customer is new to a Japanese hired from a Japanese company. They are often unable to discuss the benefits that are so decisive in closing the deal.[1] If a company does not have established relationships, then the general manager and the foreign sales force manager must establish them, or invest in sales training. One Japanese general manager of a foreign company would agree with the former approach but not the latter:

> My salesmen do not respond well to training in a classroom or as an exercise. The sales trainers, which we have everywhere else in the world, are a total waste of time and are destructive in Japan. Sales is a thoroughly Japanese phenomenon in Japan. I would put my salesmen up against any Japanese company's salesmen in technical expertise and business capacity.

This manager has extensive overseas experience and has developed a superb sales force. Unfortunately, the foreign general manager who has to build a sales force or take over and likely

---

[1]Robert White, "Why Japanese Managers Are Short on Salesmanship," *The Asian Wall Street Journal*, February 26, 1986.

restructure one has a tough job on his hands. For him, though, the control mechanisms—objectives, performance measurements—can be as important as the sales training or in reality become the training mechanism, as long as they are not used for compensation beyond minor differences. By setting quantifiable goals, targeting key customers and potentials, setting the number of calls a day, and getting out with the salesmen and showing them that sales can be made, gradually the necessary confidence and skills can be developed. In any case, specific, quantified objectives must be given to salesmen, dealers, and franchises. Never talk in generalities.

When a foreign manager goes into the field and meets customers, there are incredible implications, particularly if there are problems. There is nothing like a president/general manager going out and saying, "Gomen nasai." That is the most sincere way of saying, "I'm sorry."

In the United States sales is price, quality, delivery. That is all. In Japan you have to have a relationship that is preferably long term. You cannot just manipulate the three as you can in the United States. If there are already established players, then any new entry, Japanese or foreign, has trouble because the established enjoy a certain security. The customers sometimes give you the opportunity to match the proposals of established competitors. If you cannot match you are in trouble, but at least they let you know. This is particularly true for Japanese companies. Even established foreign companies like IBM have had to employ a strategy to try to stem the tide of market-share erosion to Japanese competitors. This is a sharp departure from what they did before in Japan or anywhere else in the world.

Foreign Staff

The foreign staff in most foreign companies seldom travel out of Tokyo. When they do, it is for a holiday or to take a visitor to Kyoto. It is extremely important for the foreign staff and working visitors to meet suppliers and customers wherever they are, as well as to have the suppliers and customers visit the office or plant in Japan and at home. Sapporo, Nagoya, and Fukuoka are as different from Tokyo as Edinburgh, Birmingham, and Bristol are from London. People should meet people on each other's home turf if relationships are to be fostered and if business is to prosper. It is one more way in which a foreign company endeavors to become an insider. Western Japan alone, with a population of forty-three million, has an economic output of $400 billion per year, which is equal to the GNP of Italy. This cannot be covered by a telephone call from Tokyo in English.

I go out selling two or three times a week. That is the only way I can keep my hands on the pulse of the marketplace, let our customers see us, and ultimately know what is going on out there.

You have to know your customers. I know them much better than my foreign competitors in my field, for their presidents are mainly representational. They don't deal very much with the customers. When I visit a hospital, I visit seven or eight people in one hour, just handing out name cards, running down the corridors, getting people to think we cared enough to send the very best. The Japanese like that. "How is the machine operating? Having any problems? Feel free to let me know directly." You need to get out there directly; you represent the organization.

Head-office visitors become frustrated. They want to sit down and talk business. The Japanese feel it is impolite to get down to detail. They are complimented by the visit. Too many of the head-office visitors want to debate with the customers. You don't argue with a Japanese customer. The customer is right, period! You can appeal to him but you can't argue with him. The German or American mentality is to explain why your machine doesn't have something the customer wants and to convince the customer it is better without it. The Japanese customer doesn't want to hear it. Psychologically it is the wrong approach. You should say, "I am very sorry it doesn't have it; we will look into it; and please, we appreciate your using it anyway." Get him back to the positive side, but still the head-office people want to argue. I warn them, "If I kick you, drop the subject and don't come back to it. If you don't, I'll kick you again." The trouble is, you need these head-office people, and if you kick too hard, they resist you. To be successful you either have a very powerful head who provides an umbrella for you or otherwise you have to walk the tightrope.

When Japanese salesmen lose their focus and forget they are supposed to be selling, they instead spend their time trying to sell you on what they didn't sell. Japanese salesmen in foreign companies become quite expert at this form of selling, especially when relationships have to be developed from scratch. As previously mentioned, few have been trained in the cold call, "feature, advantage, benefit" approach.

Technically qualified sales people are a rarity in the United States. If you identify them here, it is almost impossible to get them. We had a hell of a time. First can you get anybody; then when you have them, what have you got; and if they are any good, can you retain them? We have not been happy with our industrial direct sales. I could not understand why the customers were not reacting in the same way they do in the U.S. and U.K. when given the same kind of information by our salesmen. I finally got angry and sent out one of my expatriates with a Japanese salesman to a potential customer. I gave the expatriate a tape recorder and told him I wanted him quietly to tape the sales call, bring the tape back and have it translated. My expatriate, an American, started off by saying, "We can save you 25 percent of the operating cost with this process." The Japanese translated: "He seems to think that maybe under the right conditions, you can save up to 25 percent of your operating costs." And again the expatriate: "You will also get better product quality." Translated: "It is possible we may improve your product quality." No one knew it was being taped. It went on and on like that. That is when I got so angry I called in the expatriate commercial development man and said, "I want you to go to the two biggest potential customers we have identified, take our people with you, and get the business and then come back and show the Japanese what we have done." We did it, and today we have two sales groups headed by foreigners, who are sales-oriented engineers and who both speak Japanese fluently.

You have to go out and sell with your people, and you have to understand what they are doing. Our technology is really not in the equipment; it is in the know-how of the process. Our people are experts, not salesmen in the traditional sense. Their job is to know the customer's process, to know how to do it in a more modern and better way than the customer can, to convince him to try our way, and then to get a demonstration. Elsewhere, if we get a demo, we have a hit rate of 90 percent. We therefore have built a $2 million demo laboratory. We now bring the customer in, saying, "OK, we won't disturb your process. We'll show you what our process is. We'll take your product and run it through our demo lab and show you a better way to do it."

Service

When selling commercial equipment, one must not only have an excellent product to sell, one must have an excellent sales and service force: service before, during, and after sales. This requires a partnership between the buyer and the seller and is what the Japanese competition does almost instinctively. The product and the purchase are tied together. If a company is a hot prospect, the salesman, the director, the president, one after another, go daily.

You cannot just sell "service." It is a given and fully expected. Having one person in charge of sales and service forces the employees to look upon service as a sales function. A German company in Japan has its first machine sold by the salesman and the second or repeat machine sold by the serviceman. This is not necessarily unique to Japan, but the Japanese sales force in a Japanese company can be relentless in its personal attention. The Japanese company has a sense of hustling the customer with service. For a foreign company to compete, it must be prepared to compete on these terms.

> The only way to sell in Japan is as they sell. They will drive you crazy. In America, it is yes I will see you or no. You get told. In Japan if you get turned down, you go back again. You rarely get turned down for any concrete reasons, and the door is left open. They do it on purpose because they know things change all the time. They never want to shut things down. It is a full-court press all the time. Americans tend to be too polite with the Japanese.

NCR had the manual cash register market in Japan all sewn up. When electronic equipment was being introduced by its Japanese competitors in the 1970s, NCR's service people continued to repair outmoded machines. The Japanese competition came in and sold the new wave that did not need repairs. NCR has never recovered completely this product market in the mom-and-pop shops in a country of mom-and-pops. What a difference if NCR's service-men had been salesmen!

A company's own field force is there to be sure that any new brands or existing brands are adequately ordered, stocked, maintained and merchandised. Japan is far too expensive for trial and error, particularly when a careless mistake or oversight or poor intelligence can knock you out permanently.

Information Gathering

As a successful seller learned, in-house salesmen are a key to information gathering and networking:

> We can't have the same relationships the Japanese have, but we can establish a mutuality of relationships that are institutionalized. We do not sell through agents or trading companies. We insist that we sell direct to the customers. The name helps. We say it is our policy and they accept. It is the only way we can survive. Information is very important in conducting business, and that is the only way we can have access to information. If we go through agents, the value of the information is diluted—70 percent truth and 30 percent twisted to their benefit. Our technology and patents are our

greatest sales tool. We continually look for change and change ourselves accordingly.

One limitation in obtaining information, data, and suggestions from distributors is that the quality could be distorted because of their position. They may not come up with a fair and accurate assessment of the consumer's real demands. Out of their own selfish motivation, they may make a suggestion to the manufacturer. You have to listen while at the same time being very careful in assessing what their real motives might be in asking you to develop another type of product. Is it to put pressure on another company for whom they distribute?

Direct Sales

For direct door-to-door sales it is very difficult to recruit men. Everyone is second or third rate, even if the company has an excellent name. Direct sales is easily tainted by scandal; witness the Toyota Shoji gold scandal in 1985 and the Encyclopaedia Britannica scandal of the 1970s. One scandal by any player can bring everyone else's sales efforts to a halt. Tupperware was hurt severely in 1985. MITI has never respected direct sales as an industry and therefore does not pay much attention until there is a problem. It does not look at products. It looks at everybody together, and that is one reason the public looks at everybody the same way. The Japanese Direct Selling Association is government sponsored while its equivalent in the United States is completely independent. With direct selling and direct marketing, the appropriate government ministry takes the responsibility for protecting the consumer rather than leaving it to private consumer protection advocates. This can make for regulatory nightmares, with one or more ministries or departments within ministries involved. Direct marketing has a better connotation than direct selling, but neither has a very good image.

Distribution

Distribution, "layering" in Japanese parlance, is a nightmare in Japan for foreigners and certainly very hard for them to understand. Mr. Masami Atarashi, a Japanese and President of Johnson & Johnson Japan, says, "I don't begin to comprehend it." He does add that the only way one begins to comprehend distribution is by "management by walking about."

The Japanese company's attitude toward distribution is simple:

shove the product into the system. Distribution is what it is all about in the Japanese mentality. It is horrendous for the outsider, though, whether Japanese or foreign. Unlike the United States, there is a great shortage of space, which translates into limited shelf space and the need for wholesalers. With one retail merchandise establishment for every 76 people in Japan (more than twice the ratio in the United States) and 200,000 wholesalers, the management of distributors is a major sales function in Japan. If a company does not get into the system, it will not sell anything.

Distribution in Japan is like a tightly woven spider's web. According to a study by the ACCJ, almost 48 percent of home electronics in Japan are sold through exclusively affiliated stores, and 99 percent of cars are distributed through exclusive dealerships.

Foreigners often get fed up in a short time, decide on direct selling, get rid of a trade distribution network, and end up making a blunder. When one first decides on product strategy, one must have sufficient confidence in that strategy to see it through with reasoned modifications as market knowledge grows. A foreign company's difficulty in understanding the distribution system is complicated by the fact that any given distributor might handle 250 manufacturers, and the foreign company is only one of those. Any distributor can live without the foreigner unless the foreigner can account for 20 percent of his business. More than likely it is only 2 or 3 percent.

Before a consumer product is launched, the trade people must be contacted and told you are going to spend X millions of yen on advertisement, or they will never consider putting the product on the shelf. If a company is an unknown quantity, it will often have to advertise on television before it ships the product to prove it is bona fide. If it does not and the product is unavailable when the consumer wants to go out and buy it, that is just too bad.

When we went on television for the first time at American Express and were the first card company to have a television campaign, we were not assisted measurably in the acquisition of cardmembers. It helped tremendously, however, in signing up service establishments to accept the American Express card, because to them we were obviously serious about attracting cardmembers, who in turn would want to use their cards in the establishments. Realizing what was happening, we had still shots from the television campaign incorporated in a sales brochure for the service-establishment salesmen. The brochure emphasized that American Express cardmembers are going to be coming to your restaurant, hotel, department store, or boutique and will want to use their American Express card. Please be able to satisfy your and our clients' needs.

The foreigner or any other new kid on the block has to give the distributor something that makes his product a bit more valuable and distinct and therefore more important to the distributor. That something can be knowledge and enjoyment derived from, for example, visiting a foreign head office on an orientation trip. This the Japanese competition cannot offer, though the foreign competition can.

Obtaining distributors is very difficult and slow, but in many ways that is good, because it forces you to establish a relationship before you sign. We just had our first Japanese distributors' meeting in the United States. Certain goals had to be met to participate. We had a plant tour and a day of training. There was excellent input on the kind of products and pricing they would like in Japan. It was something our competition in Japan could not do. The end result was a heightened awareness of the company and a better feeling about us on the part of the distributors. They want to go again.

There is no better way to bond relationships. One German company brings hundreds of distributors each year to an industrial show in Frankfurt while an American company's distributors have formed their own club for an annual trip to furniture shows in different parts of the world. It helps that all these trips are tax deductible for the participants.

All foreign companies, no matter how long they have been in Japan, have a long way to go in the area of wholesale distribution management.

If you want to break the distribution system here on your own, you had better have a chocolate cupcake with no calories that tastes just like a chocolate cupcake, because it is tough.

With distribution, the pull and push must go together. Some salesmen go direct to retailers, others to the wholesalers. Once a year on a national or regional basis we have a trade convention for our key wholesalers throughout the country. We will also have a similar affair when we have a major new product introduction. Proctor & Gamble tried to bypass the wholesalers with their diapers and created a lot of discontent among the wholesalers. "What an inhuman company!" When a superior product from their competitor arrived on the market, the wholesalers were delighted. "Now we can get our revenge." And revenge they got.

P&G has subsequently successfully realigned and strengthened its distribution network.

If half the money spent on silly-assed creative was spent on distribution, I would probably have had more communication with the consumer, which is the end objective, through shelf presence. Often, though, I get my back up because of the demands of the distributor. This distributor wants an extra 2 percent because of the old man's eightieth birthday. The old man should be happy he reached his eightieth birthday without the 2 percent. With media I have a nice cozy feeling, although the consumer might be rejecting totally the creative. Distribution is also hard to communicate to head office at budget time, but you are upping the ante for the competition and becoming a player in Japan. If I get together with my operating counterpart in the U.S., he will say, "Of course I am doing that. I have to." But it will be a cold day in hell before our mutual boss admits that. I have seen some pretty lavish entertainment in the U.S. of A. What is a convention in the U.S.?

The distributors' quality rather than advertising sells our product: their connections in the local community, service, and know-how. The human touch is very important. There is no self-service at gas stations, although ostensibly prohibited for safety reasons. The attendants go door to door during the day in their neighborhoods, visiting all their potential customers: "Look, we are located around the corner, our service is kind, please take our card and use it. There is a discount in appreciation of your loyalty for using the station's card." Television is used as a reinforcement: we do exist; we are an important player; we are confirming your decision to use a particular company.

Richard A. Floyd, formerly in charge of Dakin Japan, notes:

The wholesalers have absolutely no loyalty whatsoever. That goes against a great deal of the pabulum handed out to the foreigner in Japan. The wholesalers are also highly leveraged, and it is difficult to get solid credit information on them.

The credit issue is one of Japan's greatest myths, particularly in the small business and consumer area. Any foreign company that must depend on the credit worthiness of small businesses or the consumer had better realize that in this area Japan is an underdeveloped country, especially on credit information exchange. Credit controls should be in place before business begins and reviewed constantly.

Relationships can also be a hindrance. Often there is a relationship that has built up over ten years, and no one has ever thought to review or change it. One should price *everything* annually: insurance, freight forwarding, warehousing, loans, everything. For a relationship to continue it must be price and service competitive. The word gets around that you are checking. This makes the relationship a little less smooth at times, but is worth the effort. Sometimes in Japan, as elsewhere, relationships are more costly than they are worth. Some companies like Dakin have found it much more cost effective to establish their own warehouse and to sell direct to the retailer.

Richard Floyd also notes: "I see so many American companies get locked into competitors for distribution. It is a common pattern. They are competing against each other. It is crazy. Nowhere else in the world would they do that!" American Express for ten years has permitted JCB to continue to issue the joint JCB/American Express card (to be used overseas only). Meanwhile, JCB has done nothing to assist American Express and to this day has kept it from being a full member of the Card Association. The relationship began over twenty-five years ago, and no one in American Express's head office has ever been willing to evaluate realistically its worth. Many Americans fear change. "American managers are satisfiers, not maximizers."

We are going to have to make a transition from being a reputable supplier of products in the U.S. to being a reputable supplier of products in Japan. You are going to have to have much closer ties to your customers, because the competition is going to be so fierce that you can't have them shopping around. We are also starting to compete with some of our customers.

There are ways, though, to differentiate and enhance one's position through distributors. You do not go to a Japanese beer company to sell beer for you, for you will never displace its market share. If a company feels it needs a partner, then it should choose a Japanese company that makes a complementary, not a competitive, product and has complementary distribution channels. The foreign company can put its own people into the operation and maintain tight management control through management by committee. In effect, it is joint venturing its distribution with active management participation from its own Japanese operation.

One major foreign consumer-product company had worked under the paradigm that the more wholesalers one has for distribution, the better off one is because more people are reached. Moreover, because wholesalers are competitive, the competition in and of itself reduces prices in stores. With only $100 million in business, it was working with approximately 500 primary wholesalers and 2,000–3,000 secondary wholesalers, trying to visit all of them. By spreading its business, it had no leverage whatsoever with its wholesalers and no chance in competing with its major Japanese rivals. Realizing its dilemma, it had "Dear John meetings" with 90 percent of its wholesalers and reduced their number to 70.

You don't tell distributors that they are no longer wanted. You have them discover that it is in their interest that we separately pursue our objectives, which is a very different process than in Western society, where the attitude is, if somebody wins, somebody has to lose. We are not very good at creating a win-win situation in the West. In Japan you have to have that skill if you want to succeed.

This company previously could not get push from its wholesalers since it accounted for only 2–3 percent of each wholesaler's business. After the reduction in the number of its distributors, it accounts for 15–20 percent and even 30 percent of each wholesaler's business. Now that it is so important to each wholesaler, the wholesaler provides the indirect push. There is no interest in increasing the wholesaler's stocks; all the interest is in keeping them as low as possible since it sends a truck to each wholesaler every day. In Japan the company has moved from four- or five-day delivery to within twenty-four hours no matter where the retailer is. It has the highest level of customer service that it has anywhere in the world. Getting that in place was a major activity.

The Western premise is that you become more efficient if you can be flexible and dictate the terms, if you can have four days to fill an order if you wish. The typical Japanese thinks totally in his customer's terms and accepts that twenty-four hours is the maximum that is reasonable, and that responsive systems can be developed. Getting systems organized on computers and obtaining stock-location sites throughout the country are essential. A company must invest in the infrastructure, and very much in the belief that it can be done.

In the agricultural sector you must have a relationship with the distributors long before they sell anything because all agricultural products have to be registered by the government. To obtain registration a great deal of data has to be accumulated in a dossier and presented. All kinds of field efficacy trials, formulation, and toxicology studies must be carried out to obtain the data. This is done in tandem with identified distributors years before you sell anything. The business is so competitive that the distributors are only loyal to you based on the amount of technology you have to sell them.

The bureaucracy is the real stumbling block in the distribution of agricultural products. It is absolutely overwhelming, particularly the geriatrics in the Ministry of Agriculture and the Ministry of Health and Welfare. As in dealing with any ministry in Japan, you have to give 100 percent attention to detail and it takes forever—five to ten years. The dossiers are enormous. They break them apart and study them by committee, and God forbid that a secretary back in your head-office laboratory made a Xerox for the dossier that shows up here as an eighth-generation Xerox and the numbers cannot be read and you get a bureaucrat on a bad day. He is going to say go back and retype all 375 pages. It has happened, as recently as last week. Give them what they ask for, exactly as they ask for it, and save yourself a lot of grief.

Retailers

Others look at the complicated distribution system as an opportunity to find ways to beat their competition who are caught up in that labyrinth. For some, the retailers in Japan are great to work with. They are hungry and like the prestige of working directly with a major foreign company. Credit problems usually do not exist with the retailers as with the wholesalers, because the former are bringing in cash every day. But the retail market is different than elsewhere. In Japan if a product does not sell, the retailer can return it. If they do not like the color, or if it sits on the shelf a day longer than they expected it to, they ship it back. It cannot be considered sold until the manufacturer is paid. If they return it before they pay for it, then basically there is no recourse. If it is a major customer and they have paid but wish to return, then you negotiate for some fresh merchandise. If you say, "no way," then your shelf space will disappear. Often 10 percent is returned. This becomes an accounting nightmare as to when a product is actually sold. Many retailers will give you more shelf space if you put your product on consignment with them. They will keep it longer since they are not carrying the inventory, and the margin is higher since the retailer is not financing. The system makes it virtually impossible for imports managed from offshore to compete in Japan, because only products managed in Japan can carry the return guarantee. What this all means is that one has to drive one's own business in Japan, whatever vehicle or methods one decides to use.

The foreign automobile companies, especially the Germans, have learned recently that it is not where the car comes from but who controls the distribution and pricing. BMW got nowhere in Japan until it bought out its agent Yanase, took direct control of the pricing, and began to run its own marketing operation. Mercedes is now right behind BMW. They are now, with the leader Volkswagen, the major importers of foreign cars, accounting for 34,674; 33,076; and 31,511 units respectively in 1989. Together these three West German car manufacturers accounted for 55 percent of the imported car market. They also have put after-service in place to maintain their quality image.

One simply must control the distribution to control one's destiny. This was Kodak's problem. As long as it let Nagase and Kureha be its agents, it had no control over its competitive position in Japan. Nagase had 100 percent representation of the two motion picture films in the world, Kodak and Fuji. It was the same problem with Yanase as agent for both BMW and Mercedes and many other foreign automobile makers.

Estée Lauder

Estée Lauder in 1977 had only 220 outlets in Japan, half of which were in department stores, while Shiseido, the prestigious Japanese cosmetic company, dominated the market with 25,000 outlets. Estée Lauder, to everyone's surprise in the Japanese market, determined that Shiseido's Achilles' heel was its distribution. Shiseido simply had too many distribution points. Elsewhere in the world Estée Lauder was very successful in department stores. In the United States there are thousands of department stores, but in Japan there are only several hundred. The traffic in these stores is therefore much heavier than in the United States, and service at cosmetic counters had been a serious problem. Counters were poorly located and maintained, and service was almost brutal, if not vampirish. Cosmetics were distributed principally through small retail stores. Estée Lauder decided to focus on only one distribution channel: the department stores. With its limited outlets the company did not have to worry about competing against its own numerous small retail outlets, as Shiseido did. In focusing on department stores, and in dealing with the service issue, Estée Lauder revolutionized the cosmetic business in Japan.

The company proposed to build a department store–only brand, Clinique, establishing an attractive area in a limited number of stores with distinctive white counters, the only place where customers would be able to purchase Clinique products in a given geographical area. The department stores had to share in both the counter and starter-kit promotion costs, which was unheard of, but if a certain agreed sales target was not reached, the store could kick Estée Lauder out after one year.

Clinique was positioned through using foreign concepts (a differentiated counter; a nonfragrant, allergy-tested cosmetic with Western packaging); through tailoring to Japan (using Western image advertising with special English headlines—Japan is the only country where worldwide slogans differ slightly—and all the copy in Japanese, called "educational advertising"); and through placing almost all advertising in magazines (which permitted excellent placement within the magazines because of the size of the buy in each).

Unlike Shiseido, which uses extensive television mood advertising, Estée Lauder does not use television at all for Clinique, which is set apart as the antithesis of other cosmetic lines. Robert Simon, President of Estée Lauder Japan, explains:

> We differentiate ourselves from other cosmetics with our distinctive, prestigious counters and by being anticosmetic. It's a religion! That gives us a leading-edge product. We don't promote ingredients. We promote deliverance, what the product will do for you, rather than how it acts, what ingredients it has. Service is all-important. All our competition has copied our department-store counter concept.

Today Estée Lauder Japan also has Estée Lauder and Aramis counters in department stores and has increased sales from $2 million in 1975 to $300 million in 1988, greatly surpassing Shiseido's department-store cosmetic sales.

> All the other prestigious brands have followed suit in the department stores and have better presentations in Japan because of the competition and

because of us. Chanel's best counters are in Japan. Dior's best counters are in Japan, not in France. France did not give the signal. We gave the signal.

Ore-Ida

Distribution clearly differs from product to product, even within categories of food products, depending on the stages of the product's life cycle. Ore-Ida found it was not particularly difficult to penetrate the distribution system. The frozen food business was relatively new when they began selling their product in 1984, having only begun to develop twenty-five years before. The layers of distribution prevalent in other industries did not exist. Sixty percent of their business is handled directly by primary wholesalers to the retailers, 30 percent through secondary wholesalers and only 10 percent through third-line wholesalers. They set up a distribution system with the guidance of Mitsubishi Shoji after learning how the supermarkets wanted to be supplied. Each wholesaler was handpicked or directly chosen by the chain headquarters themselves. Eleven wholesalers are responsible for all the business in Tokyo. Ore-Ida found it was competing with its own wholesalers who carry other brands and who often have their own brands of frozen potatoes. As long as Ore-Ida continued to advertise and promoted their products as promised, however, the wholesalers continued to distribute their products very well. Moreover, when they entered the market, the frozen food market had been stagnant for three years and their aggressive advertising campaign was praised by retailers and wholesalers alike.

If a distribution arrangement is terminated, it should be done officially, but the distributor should be given an out. "If you don't get a good deal, give us a call." In the United States you cut and they do not come back. In Japan the door is never shut, or never should be, as in a family relationship. Always leave the door open for your daughter to come home in case the new family does not work out.

You must have control of your distribution, pricing, advertising, promotion, and selling. Absent that, what the hell can you do in the consumer field anywhere in the world?

We used not to listen. "You don't need that. This is the way we do it in the States." They beat up on us so badly that we are now listening. We are also finding that our U.S. customers like the same specifications. Listening to our customers is creating a lot of good things.

When all is said and done, even with the finest marketing plan, one cannot forget that in Japan business is principally relationships. The Fair Trade Commission is weak. A company can have the best product, but the Japanese can do all sorts of things to keep it out. Personal relationships and channels are absolutely essential to doing business. The FTC is not going to enforce monopolistic practices unless they are just plain ridiculous. Dan Fenno Henderson, a noted lawyer and academic on Japan, states: "Let there be no mistake: the Japanese bureaucracy has no background of liberalism towards foreigners, foreign business, or foreign products in any situation where foreigners have the competitive edge. Discrimination has been the rule."[2] As one person who has done battle says: "There is a $50 billion market out there. The Japanese play hardball. We are talking big numbers. That is why they put up restrictions. Do you think there would be restrictions if this were a $50 million market?" The only way to get around the restrictions is to forge substantive relationships, knowing exactly why each of those relationships was or was not established. Far too few foreigners know anything about the history of their company in Japan, ignoring both potential allies and pitfalls until it is too late.

To sell in Japan one has to have a product that has unique attributes, is price competitive, and is not blocked out by regulatory barriers, which are often not transparent. For a company to have life in Japan it must become part of the nation's fabric through relationships established in the total community. Relationships, relationships, relationships. Selling is a full-court press!

---

[2]Gary R. Saxonhouse and Kozo Yamamura, eds., *Law and Trade Issues of the Japanese Economy: American and Japanese Perspectives* (Seattle: University of Washington Press, 1987), p. 138.

13

Public Relations

A FOREIGN COMPANY in Japan cannot depend on the Japanese public understanding by accident who it is and what its true intentions are. It must let the public know, and it must be careful at all times not to try to fool anybody, to deliver what it promises, and to convey that what it is about is good for Japan and its citizenry. Along with advertising, public relations is an effective way to convey a corporate message and to sell a product or service.

PR Firms

Public relations as practiced as a profession in the West is a new field in Japan. Although Burson-Marsteller and Hill and Knowlton have had offices there for over twenty years, their staff turnover has been as rampant as that of many of their foreign clients. International Public Relations for many years was the only substantive Japanese public relations firm. Its founder died recently, shortly after selling out to a British interest. The record of these firms in assisting their clients has run the gamut, but more often than not there have been many promises and little consistency. Nevertheless, their brochures hype their ability to stage events, publish internal and external newsletters, obtain press coverage in both the Japanese and foreign media, and even to do what is referred to in the United States as lobbying.

Another alternative is to use the public relations subsidiary of a Japanese advertising agency like Dentsu or Hakuhodo. My personal experience with Dentsu is that it can be superb at arranging presentations and events for a Coca-Cola or American Express, but it has no understanding of creating or using corporate news, whether generated overseas or in Japan. Dentsu once gave me a year-long proposal in which every recommended article to be printed was purchased by Dentsu with the name of the publication, the writer, and the cost stated. This is expensive, not particularly effective, and, since attribution as a paid advertisement is not given, unacceptable to most publicly held foreign corporations.

Two recent changes in the public relations community could have some far-reaching repercussions. In late 1988 Dentsu and Burson-Marsteller announced that they were merging their public relations operations in Japan. If Burson-Marsteller's international experience and Dentsu's obvious clout can be effectively merged and managed, we might be entering a new era of public relations awareness, effectiveness, and respectability in Japan, although neither company has done public relations well on its own in that country. Hill and Knowlton in 1989 merged its Japan operation into a joint venture with Sumitomo Trading Company. One wonders who would now go to Hill and Knowlton with any product or service that is competitive with that of a member of the Sumitomo group.

Integrate

To be effective, public relations must be completely integrated with the advertising and communications process. This has not been the case to date in Japan, for either Japanese companies or most foreign companies; like many things, it has been compartmentalized. It has also not been as respectable and therefore as effective as it should be. Since coordinating public relations with marketing and advertising is generally lip service, such coordination requires a superb insider who understands the relative importance of all sides. There are not many qualified in-house executives, and the results are generally mediocre. Each function often has its own godfather in head office, which further confuses the coordination.

Public relations, therefore, is analogous to the rest of one's business in Japan. You are never sure how much to accept of what your staff and advisers tell you, particularly if you are linguistically and culturally illiterate. The Japanese staff rarely think about public relations, though they are always thinking of corporate relationships. Few foreigners think about public relations since they were not senior enough in prior assignments to be involved, and since generally public relations in head office is directed by in-house public relations staff who work directly with the executive office and an outside agency.

Account Manager

Today in Japan a foreign company should strive to find one very competent individual in a public relations firm to be its public relations account manager. Fluent if not native Japanese-language ability is an absolute prerequisite. One has to be able to have a very personal relationship with this individual. His success, in turn, will depend on his ability to understand the business and his client personally and to establish relationships with the media.

The most difficult part of public relations is thus picking and listening to the right people. The account manager and his staff, once decided upon, are brought into the bowels of the company as active observers and participants in the business. Making them an integral part of the operation and keeping them properly informed about the business will allow them to assist the company to have a substantive public relations program. Consultants have many clients and will never know a business unless management takes the time to see that they do. They should work on all aspects of directing the public relations effort with the singular exception of government relations, which the general manager should handle himself.

Unfortunately, Japanese public relations advisers usually are ineffective with television. Most are former newspapermen with little experience in television or radio. They need to be constantly reminded of the value of television and radio, especially if the company is using these media for advertising. One foreign public relations adviser did not even have a television in his home and was advising me to go on a late evening television program of questionable repute that he had never seen and could not have understood linguistically if he had.

General Manager

One can have superb public relations advice and strategy, but in the last analysis implementation, both inside and outside the company, depends in large part on the personal management style of the general manager. Does he enjoy meeting people and being involved with community relations and the press? Many general managers look upon public relations as something nice to have but not a must have. Should the general manager be the only one to participate in external public relations? More than likely participation should be restricted to a few people, getting their names up front and providing a consistent image. The foreign general manager and his foreign staff will leave sooner or later, so one needs to get senior Japanese established as spokesmen for their areas of responsibility. If you delegate down very far, though, your efforts are not taken very seriously. Never use public relations people, inside or outside the company, to speak for you. Public relations itself just does not have respectability in Japan.

To reiterate, since there is a lack of public relations professionalism and public relations consultants in Japan and a resultant lack of knowledge of what management needs and how each public relations effort would help, successful public relations really only comes from the efforts of the general manager. Moreover, the general manager or his immediate staff are invariably accidentally misquoted. If the misquotations are only minor details, it does not matter, as long as one's original statements were accurate and any promises can be fulfilled. What matters is getting the overall message across. Again, without a seasoned, senior general manager who has the complete understanding and support of the head office, you will receive 2:00 A.M. phone calls from some junior public relations staff member in head office, questioning why you said what you did to the *Wall Street Journal*. You, of course, have not seen the article yet, and even if you have, there is not much you can do about it in the middle of the night. Or even worse, the public relations manager's secretary calls you at home at 4:00 A.M., just after her manager has left his office for the day at

2:00 P.M., and asks for your office phone number so he can call you the next day his time. Thank God they can't read Japanese and understand what you are really saying in your market!

Awareness and Recruiting

How can public relations assist the foreign company in Japan? It should enhance the awareness of the company as a responsible global firm that is selling a service or product in the Japanese market that will benefit some segment of the Japanese populous, corporate or individual. With enhanced awareness of the company, management will be better positioned to recruit staff and sell its product or service in Japan.

In the West, we generally do not think of public relations as a recruiting tool. Many forget that awareness of the company *in Japan* or lack thereof is a critical factor in recruiting there. Awareness generally comes with size, but reinforcement in the media can help even the smallest operations in their recruiting. The corporate profile should be included in the recruiting handbooks published for a fee for university recruiting. Any favorable newspaper or magazine articles should be part of the corporate package given to universities and to potential recruits.

Reporters

Product-related publications are extensive, and it is not hard to find out which magazines, journals, and newspapers publish information on competitors' products or services and might be interested in your company and its products. Arrange to be introduced to and get to know the people who write the articles. The reporters who visit you or whom you visit, depending on the circumstances, have reason to maintain relationships and be fair. They need stories. Since they are far more specialized than in other countries, they depend on company management as principal sources for their expertise. Because of specialization, one's story is rarely a one-off story and should not be treated as such. The story is ongoing. The reporters are also an excellent source of competitive information. Because of their need to specialize, and because of their egos—journalism is one of the most respected professions in Japan—a compliment here, a probe there can lead to a detailed analysis of the competition.

Press Clubs

Reporters are organized around industry-specific functions and in turn often belong to intercompany newspaper and television reporting groups, known as press clubs, particularly when government ministries are involved. In the financial field, for example, both the Bank of Japan and the Ministry of Finance have press clubs. One has a choice of inviting these individuals to a press conference or going to them. If they are invited as a group to a press conference in one's office, it is customary to provide them with transportation. If only one individual is coming for an interview, it is not. Going to a press club at, say, the Bank of Japan is an experience in itself, and any overseas visitor should be warned. The room is drab, a table in the middle, with open cubicles and telephones and girly pin-ups along the walls. Reporters dart back and forth from a conversation (it being hardly possible to make a presentation) to their phones, talking out loud all the time. The only advantage in going to the press club is that they appreciate your coming to them, and Japanese reporters, as mentioned, have egos larger than watermelons. Magazine writers are not members of press clubs and must be covered separately. Reporters and writers should also be invited out for lunch and dinner for informal conversation and to become better acquainted. Like everything in Japan, public relations is not a nine-to-five job.

Visitors

Senior visitors to Japan or individuals with nonconfidential, specialized knowledge should be exposed to the Japanese press if they have a story to tell that would be of interest to the Japanese, whether in a trade journal or a national newspaper. The press is invariably polite and considerate and often interested in the human interest angle, such as the chairman's family or hobbies. Properly placed articles involving head-office personnel will not only assist greatly in enhancing the awareness of the company's global and Japan operations, they will give the general manager

additional points with the local press, who appreciate the opportunity to meet and interview senior foreign businessmen. This is
just one more effective way to sell the company's story.

Competition

Japanese reporters are often afraid to call up a foreign multinational for information and will telephone a Japanese competitor
to ask about it, accept what they are told as fact, and then write
accordingly. With a joint venture they generally only talk to the
Japanese side. If one is not proactive, one will experience inaccu-
rate reporting. This is not to say that Japanese reporters are not
fair. It is simply that if one does not make oneself available to them
and provide reasonable information, they will go to other sources,
often not so friendly, because they need to provide stories for their
publications in their specific industrial segment. The competition
can be extremely unfair in their comments, but one should appreciate that the more successful one's public relations efforts, the
more vitriolic the response from the competition. Head office
must be forewarned and not be gun shy.

Foreign Press

Coordinating one's approach to the foreign press and Japanese
press can be very effective. One can reinforce the other. A substantive article in *The Wall Street Journal, The New York Times, The
Financial Times, The Economist, Business Week, Forbes,* or *Fortune*
will be picked up by the Japanese press and will give a company
credibility with them. This in turn will arouse their interest in the
operation. The quality of the foreign business press has improved
dramatically in recent years, and they are always looking for
success stories among foreign corporations. A favorable article
also makes the head office a little more predisposed to listening
to one's next recommendation. With head office's approval, the
foreign press can also be helpful in publicizing a firm's feelings
on unfair trade practices. The Japanese have to know that when
you say something, you are going to follow through, and there is
often no better way to demonstrate this determination than in the
press. Clyde McAvoy, formerly of Continental Airlines, used the

editorial pages of *The Wall Street Journal* extremely effectively. "They leave me alone because I raise so much hell."

Television

National television requires fluency in Japanese. With local television there is always a need for filler, and a foreigner is like a five-legged elephant. A foreigner who speaks Japanese well and who runs even the smallest foreign corporation receives numerous invitations for radio and television appearances. He or she is the story, awareness of the company is increased, and employees are tremendously proud. George Fields, the Chairman of ASI Market Research (Japan) Inc., has been a frequent television commentator, especially on NHK, since the publication of *From Bonsai to Levi's*. An unexpected result has been excellent, unsolicited, male university applicants for employment in his firm.

Events

Event sponsoring in Japan has been an effective but costly way to promote the products of foreign companies, ranging from Michael Jackson concerts for Pepsi, football for Coca-Cola, and ladies marathons for Avon, to cash contributions to the Japanese Olympic Team for every charge on the card for American Express. This mode of public relations is generally practiced by those with extensive experience in event sponsorship elsewhere. Although it is relatively easy to get public relations coverage of a company and the person being interviewed, it is much more difficult in Japan to receive coverage for a specific product than in the United States. One company that has is Cyanamid.

Cyanamid (Japan) Ltd.

Cyanamid conducted an extremely successful event sponsorship in 1989 for its Combat product. It ran a Combat cockroach contest, which had been done successfully in the United States, though Combat is its only over-the-counter retail product in Japan. The sole distributor is Taisho Pharmaceutical Co., Ltd., which specializes in over-the-counter drugs and controls a strong sales and distribution network. The contest was covered throughout Japan in newspapers and magazines and on television, including a three-and-a-half minute prime-time news segment on NHK.

The nationwide contest was run by Japan Counselors, Inc., a local public relations firm, which established a "Combat Cockroach Contest News Bureau." The public learned about the contest through a preliminary announcement in newspapers and over the radio calling for contestants to telephone for rules and an application. The cover of the application read, "WANTED DEAD, NOT ALIVE: COCKROACHES! ¥100,000." Hats and T-shirts with the application cover or a cockroach imprinted on them were also used as handouts. Participants sent in their cockroach entries, which were judged by size, with prizes ranging from 50,000 to 100,000 yen for the winners. An award ceremony, which also received extensive national news coverage, was held in Tokyo at which the winners received their prizes and leading entomologists commented on cockroach control in Japan. Appropriately, a woman from Okinawa won the grand prize with her entry of a male American cockroach measuring 1.77 inches.

Although the advertisement, which emphasized new American technology for combating cockroaches, and the public relations campaign were highly coordinated, with Taisho responsible for the advertising and Cyanamid for the public relations, Cyanamid estimates that the 160 newspaper, magazine, and television brand commentaries gave them an investment return equivalent to a 25 to 1 spend on advertisement. "The campaign was fun, educational, participatory, and above all successful." After one season, Combat, with 17 percent, had the second largest market share in a very crowded field. As a result, Taisho itself has become a true believer in American-style public relations, which goes beyond the traditional grinding out of press releases.

Because Combat sales are seasonal, orders are placed by retail outlets prior to the warm season. Therefore, on February 1, 1990, Cyanamid and Taisho introduced a campaign to place 7,000 posters and 120,000 application blanks in retail outlets. The application blanks this year are encoded so that the retail outlets that sell to the winners will also receive a cash prize, thereby giving retailers an incentive to push Combat, whose red, yellow, and black packaging shouts from the shelves. There is nothing subtle, it being as loud and descriptive as any packaging in the United States.

In-House Newsletters

With all the personnel issues faced by a foreign company in Japan, one would think that there would be a plethora of in-house newsletters for the employees. In reality there are only a few, but where they are done with professionalism, there appears to be a welcome, positive acceptance. In the long run, inside people will be much more effective with internal communications than outside consultants. Money is best spent on inside training and on the quality of the product. Outside consultants can be used to train employees for about six months. The most important point on inside communications is to have someone responsible who truly believes in the concept and has credibility in the organization. If not, the communications will not be credible, and a superb means to reinforce positive internal communications is lost. The product, of course, is in Japanese and is a wonderful way to communicate what is happening in the company globally as well as locally. The quality of publication will depend in large part on the resources made available within the company, not outside. It is an exceptional way to involve personnel in publicizing their company.

Annual Brochure

If personal matters such as marriages and births are omitted, in-house publications can also be used as a vehicle for publicizing both the parent company and the Japanese operation by sending copies to the industry association, concerned government institutions, banks, suppliers, and customers. Often a newsletter can be supplemented with a Japanese annual brochure, a mini-annual report that includes what the company is doing in Japan as well as elsewhere.

Stock Share Listings

Share listings on the Tokyo Stock Exchange have recently become as much public relations effort as financial, demonstrating a commitment to Japan and attracting the interest of potential customers and employees. The cost of registering also has been greatly reduced recently.

Academics

Japanese academics are the most untapped public relations resource for foreign companies. Japanese academics sit with the
press, business and government on every industry study group
formed by the government. As much as the press, academics act
as the conscience of these committees and can have a different
agenda from that of the government or business. Japanese companies, particularly in scientific areas, have extensive, informal
ties with academics. If the academics' agenda corresponds with
yours, they can assist in putting forth your views and can keep
you informed about the overall agenda. Professors also recommend their students for employment, and there can be no better
recommendation when hiring. All Japanese companies cultivate
these recommendations assiduously. Why is it that U.S. or European corporations have not contributed to academic chairs in
Japan, as the Japanese have at Harvard, M.I.T., and Oxford, to
name just a few? Some say because prestigious Japanese universities would not accept such contributions, whether from Japanese
or foreign corporations. It would be informative to find out, now
that the Ministry of Education appears to have at least officially
withdrawn any objections.

Government

Interacting with the Japanese government bureaucracy has been
discussed at length in chapters 4 and 5. It should be reempha-
sized, however, that this is the task of the general manager and
his designates, not of outside public relations consultants. One
general manager who does use his public relations consultants for
government relations puts a different spin on the subject, as they
say in the United States:

> If we want to get a clear message to the Japanese government, we don't
> mind telling our consultant, because we know it will go right up the funnel
> to the appropriate officials since he works both sides of the street. We know
> we are dealing with a semiprostitute, if there is such a thing. Others feel you
> fight in the press, because it doesn't matter whom you know. My opinion
> on walking the halls of MITI or MOF without a proper political constituency
> behind you is that it is useless. You have to have many Diet members behind

you, but more likely, since you are a foreigner, a strong sense of Congress or Parliament behind you. You also must be a corporation that matters. If you have substance behind you, then you should be up there yourself.

Crisis Management

One last area that is often ignored beyond the confines of the head office and that has tremendous damage potential is crisis management. Most foreign companies' overseas offices give little thought to public relations preparation for an accident, rather depending upon their head office or their joint venture partners. If a crisis occurs, prior public relations preparation can help manage it in the media. It is only common sense, and a foreign entity will need all the help it can muster. One public failure can be fatal.

Small Companies

Many will say their operation in Japan is too small to afford retaining a public relations firm in Japan. Since most of the public relations effort is dependent on the general manager, so what! It is simple to put together a corporate and personal portfolio that includes the company's history at home and in Japan and says what it is doing or hopes to accomplish in Japan. Personal background and photographs can be included, and the whole package sent to the relevant press so they will have it all on file for future reference. A follow-up invitation for a visit to the office, so they can see that the company really does exist in Japan, and a thoughtful discussion on the company and its management will often result in a surprisingly good story—the quality of story that any CEO would be delighted with in head office.

Overseas Press Visits

When press groups or individual press people are planning to visit overseas anywhere near the company's head office, plant, or service center, tours of the facility should be arranged with knowledgeable staff of appropriate rank, from the chairman on down. When they return to Japan they should be invited to the office for a debriefing, especially if they have written a story that involves the company. Good working relationships with some of the best information sources in the field can thereby be established, and at times they will alert one to a problem one never imagined. Public relations anywhere is both proactive and defensive. In an alien environment, both teams should be fielded.

Trade Study Groups

When Japanese trade study groups ask to visit an overseas installation, one should insist that one of the company's own Japanese employees should be a member of the group. Foreign companies have always welcomed these groups without receiving anything in return, because similar industrial study groups are rarely sent to Japan. The Japanese study the foreigner's operation assiduously, write reports, and incorporate this knowledge into their competitive game plan. If a foreign firm's Japanese employee accompanies them, he learns everything they do and builds personal relationships on the golf outings and during evenings out that last a lifetime. Otherwise, the so-called goodwill is just giving away trade secrets.

Cost Effectiveness

As for the cost effectiveness of the effort, reflect on the following: "I knew I had succeeded when I was on NHK for twenty minutes at prime time. That was worth several million dollars if you were buying time." Or, "We measure the cost of what it would have required to pay for equivalent advertising space. Our return is seven to one." Advertising in Japan influences access to public relations opportunities tremendously. But if you don't use public relations, you miss one of the benefits of advertising. Advertising, selling, and public relations, inside and outside the company, all have the same goal of selling the company and its product or services to the Japanese. An astute general manager will participate, orchestrate, and allocate the necessary resources to public relations, which is one of his most cost-effective sales tools.

14

Management Consultants

THE ROLES of consultants or advisers with specific Japanese market expertise for assisting the general manager operating a foreign corporation have been discussed throughout this book. Management consultants, defined here as outside advisers with no particular knowledge of a business but expertise in managing in general, are commonly used in the West to assist corporations in strategic and tactical analysis. Today most of the major firms—A. T. Kearney, Arthur D. Little, Boston Consulting Group, Bain & Company, Booz, Allen & Hamilton, McKinsey & Company, PA International—have offices in Tokyo. Moreover, there are several reputable local firms with major international clients, including James C. Abegglen's Asia Advisory Service, Inc., and C. Tait Ratcliffe's IBI, Inc.

Management consultants either can be hired to do a specific task, which is most common, or can work inside over a period of time, if the expertise and time to work with them are available within the company itself. Consultants tend to provide a snapshot rather than a drama. When the subject is moving as fast as it usually is in Japan, one's expectations have to be clearly defined or the picture will not be in focus.

Often, as elsewhere, the person who knows his business is better able to advise the management consultant than the consultant is able to advise him or her. The value of the management consultant, though, is in being a discreet sounding board for the general manager. In turn, if the management consultant's opinion is respected in head office, his reinforcement of the general manager's views gives credence to what the local operation wishes to undertake. In this way the management consultant brings an important value to the equation of doing business in Japan.

The importance is not so much in what they say, but that they say it. Most *Fortune* 500 companies have their pet consultant, and to have the senior consultant and his staff involved at the beginning of the development of a new strategy and then from time to time thereafter gives the general manager tremendous assistance. The problem is that their professional caliber and knowledge level of Japan are all over the lot. They can be smart people, but their ability to assist often depends on the questions they are asked. They also have the same problems, if you are using one of the multinational consultants, as all foreign companies in Japan: rotating people through, and developing people and a core body of knowledge and experience and understanding. More often than not you are educating their people not only in your business but about Japan. There is no question, though, that in a start-up or major redirecting of a company's energy, they can generate momentum.

If you have an established operation, they often only confirm what you know. But when someone else, who might even know less than I know, quantifies research on a piece of paper, it is helpful with head office.

One well-known foreign consultant commented on this dilemma:

Consulting should have as great a potential for Japanese companies in Japan as it does for indigenous companies in Sweden and Germany. It is not going to happen. Why not? Because I cannot staff up in Japan. It is easy in the United States. I go to the top 10 percent of the class in the very best schools and pay them enough to get them. Then, I go to my client and say I have smarter people than you have and you had better use me. He nods, agrees, and uses me. Try that in Japan. The Japanese corporation hires a youngster, and he doesn't even talk about compensation. He knows the company is a good one, will take care of him, and his future is good. How does a consulting firm manage to capture this cadre of good guys, keep them, wring them dry, and throw them away after a few years? You can't do it in Japan. It is no different than the foreign service sector in general in Japan, which is in trouble because of the difficulty of getting first-class Japanese. No Japanese in his right mind who has any ability at all is going to work for a foreign bank in Japan. The foreign banks don't make any money; they don't promote Japanese; and they don't grow.

The most important question in choosing a consulting firm, besides its credibility in head office, is who the leader is and who is on the team. A company that is new to the head office should be avoided unless management is prepared to come to Japan to meet with and sign off on the consulting team. During the card strategy study and start-up in Japan, American Express had the finest team player in Japan possible from the management consultants involved, combined, unfortunately, with the worst possible leadership in New York, who had enormous political credibility and clout in head office. The American Express team leader in New York and the consulting company partner in New York had absolutely no knowledge of Japan and only an interest in playing to the loudest senior voices in head office. This was the making of a nightmare, especially when I, as the newly hired general manager, was an outsider with no corporate credibility but a great deal of knowledge on what could and should be done in Japan. The consulting company's partner from New York did not venture outside the environs of the Okura Hotel in Tokyo until after the study was completed, presented, and agreed to by senior management, including the chairman. A trip thereafter out of Tokyo with his equally uninformed American Express counterpart startled him, for there was no awareness of American Express and a great deal of competition already in place.

All of this was in their research, but their recommendations had not followed what their research told them, since their constituency was what they thought head office wanted, not what their research in Japan showed them. This was a perfect example of why the general manager should come from within and why he should have full responsibility for any and all recommendations made by consultants. He alone should be responsible for the selling and implementation of all strategic and tactical recommendations. Otherwise, he does not belong in the job.

There are a number of consultants working in Japan who simply do not have the capacity to come up to speed in most industries and are basically trading on long-term residency in Japan or just being Japanese. A review of any proposals, particularly those that are unsolicited, with other advisers—attorneys, accountants, market researchers—will quickly alert one. Once again, be sure to investigate!

The experiences of management consultants, as seen by senior partners of three multinational management consulting firms operating in Japan, should be borne in mind in balancing off expectations when using management consultants in Japan:

All the problems we see as consultants deal with the differences in the foreign ways of managing a company and the Japanese ways of managing a company or being managed. The quality of Japanese you get in a foreign company is so insecure that they want the foreign company to be more structured than a Japanese company. With a desire for a rigid, delineated corporate structure, matrix management is always a problem.

Our major assignments in Japan have much more of an organizational, people dimension than they do a strategic dimension. Sales and distribution studies are much more operational, organizational, people related than I thought our business would be. Personnel is the single biggest challenge. You just have to have guys as good as your Japanese competitors, and no one has figured that out. If I had the key for unlocking that, I could make a fortune and stay here forever.

If you measure success on a scale of what the business ought to be in Japan as a multinational company, then you really are limited to ten or twelve companies. Only a small number are reaching deeply into their pockets and doing it right.

Management consultants, like all other advisers, are costly in Japan, but the general manager needs the best advice and counsel the community can provide. That advice and counsel is worth much more if the general manager is the filter through which all information passes on its way to head office. Needless questions will not be asked, needless answers will not be given, needless confusion will not arise, and above all, the Japan operation will maintain its credibility in Japan, which is the company's marketplace. Too many forget that head offices are there to support. They never buy or sell a thing in Japan.

15

Transition and the Future

THE ECONOMIC, business, and social changes taking place in Japan today are far more substantial than they have ever been before, even considering the enormous changes of the past forty years. The change is Japanese. There is nothing that says that Japan will become like the West, any more than the United States in its period of rapid growth and change became like Europe. Japan will be its own self. An expectation of convergence is not realistic.

The change is not just in economic growth or affluence. Unlike in the postwar era, the people themselves are today well equipped mentally to interact with and react to the rest of the world and along the way to make structural changes in their own attitudes toward life that will have profound effects upon Japan and the world. They are objective, pragmatic, and businesslike in their relationships. They have a good sense of who they are and where they want to go, far more so than many in the West, and they are much more likely to obtain their goals. There is little, if any, of the emotionalism of the past.

The change is marked for a foreign businessman.

We can discuss very, very difficult, complex problems with our joint venture partners. If we had tried twenty years ago, they would have thought we were trying to screw them or Japan. It is a matter of sophistication. There were no accountants twenty-five years ago. When you used to mention an accountant or attorney, the Japanese would shudder. Today we use attorneys and accountants together to help us both.

Have the gaijin kaisha in Japan grown and acquired the equivalent sophistication during the past twenty-five years that will allow them to operate effectively in this rapidly changing, affluent society? One foreign general manager comments: "My driver knows more about what goes on in this company and I know that." That would certainly not be the situation for a Japanese general manager in the United States or Europe. "Most Americans in head office don't see a communications problem. They are only communicating one way." Another foreign general manager of a German subsidiary notes: "I still don't know who my boss is after five years. I know many who think they are my boss, but I am not sure who really is." How many general managers can say: "I don't find bicultural management difficult at all. It is the only way I know to work."

A foreign general manager must ask himself every day, "How would I run the business if it were my own business?" That is the only way that he can sustain the seven-day-a-week involvement required of him in all aspects of the business in an environment as competitive as Japan. Both the head office and the general manager must appreciate fully that the Japanese marketplace is continuously changing. The domestic economy is extraordinarily dynamic, as is Japan's participation in overseas markets. Japan is waiting for nobody!

The general manager, on the other hand, is also a company man.

The general manager should first speak "the company." What is the company; what is the way we conduct our business; what is the spirit of the company; and what am I going to do in it? You must primarily be a company man. This permeates everything we do. With management transition, there are three golden rules: Never speak against your own country, never against your own company even if you know they are a bunch of bastards, and never against a predecessor or successor.

The parent CEO has to ask, "Do I believe in my general manager in Japan? Do I believe in him all the way?" If the CEO does not, then someone new should be put in Japan in whom he does believe: his potential successor. Then his associates and he can advise and support the Japan general manager with as little nonconstructive interference as possible, saying, for example, "We tried that in Canada three years ago and it did not work for these reasons. You should be careful about those things." That is helpful advice. The general manager can then manage his staff and clients with conviction, with no excuses and with no unnecessary explanations. He can concentrate on opportunities rather than explanations to head office. As previously discussed, too many general managers have had staff visit from head office who were looking for trouble. Not knowing a thing about doing business in Japan, they indeed created trouble, personnel or legal. When head-office people ask the competition how the general manager is doing, he is dead, for the competition then knows he will be leaving shortly. We would never ask such a question of our competitors in our home country. Why, except out of ignorance and insecurity, do we ask it in an extremely competitive foreign country?

In the last analysis, the general manager must have the ability to take a strong stand for the betterment of the operation in Japan, as long as that stand does not damage the company's overall corporate strategy. To do this he must be smart, tough, and resilient. If he is weak in any way, his effectiveness will eventually diminish.

For both the head office and the general manager there has to be a mutual sense of vision combined with a singular sense of urgency—a can-do attitude. Many foreigners have been in Japan too long and have closed out their head office from their mind. Perhaps they did so on their original departure because neither they nor their head office perceived Japan to be that important, or perhaps they are no longer in touch with the life cycle of head office, which is changing all the time. Mutual relationships and expectations have to be maintained through a shared sense of vision and urgency that permeates the thinking on Japan throughout the organization.

> The vision of what you want to become requires you to get off your backside and focus the company's activities.

The late Gene Leonard of General Motors Corporation, who was a professional in the best sense of the word and who spent over thirty years of his career overseas in nine countries, found Japan to be the most different market of those countries.

> Western executives hear what you say but don't really listen. They don't take it in and make it have any meaning. There is too much brashness and self-confidence on the part of American management. They can't imagine that non-Americans can know anything like an American, especially how

to run a business. There is a pretty good indication that some of the people around the world are doing mighty nicely and perhaps we had better look at how they are doing it. Too few in American management have spent the necessary time living and traveling overseas to be able to understand what the competition is doing. We can compete, but as a nation we need to understand we are in trouble. We also need to understand that we must get rid of some of our false pride and look realistically at what the Japanese are doing globally.

An issue that is more often resolved for political rather than for business reasons in head office is whether to run the international business through an international division or along product-line responsibilities. The international division gives the general manager of a foreign company in Japan clearer reporting lines while product-line responsibility gives greater technological support. Whichever is chosen, the real question remains, how do you make a company international? The only answer can be through the development and retention of people in the company who have both product and international experience. The Japanese are past masters at this, transferring a managing director in London to be managing director of the Nagoya branch or the managing director of International to be the managing director of General Affairs in preparation for most likely becoming president of the company. This makes the Japanese all the more formidable global competitors. We must face up to the need for international personnel development in all areas in which we compete, from aerospace to finance. Employees need to be overseas for a reasonable amount of time as part of their career development and then back home in meaningful jobs and back overseas again. It really is a two-way street since their experience is required both at home and overseas.

Westerners should reflect seriously on the following observations if they wish to be competitive with the Japanese globally:

Perhaps the most singular mistake made in transition is the end result in head office. Little expertise is maintained in the corporation at a policy-making level. To appreciate the mistake, just consider what the Japanese competition does with their employees who have been assigned overseas. So often also the head-office people are just plain uncomfortable with Japan. It is very deep, partly racial. They just cannot tolerate Japan and want it to go away. They want to look at the numbers but cannot stand the people.

The business environment in Japan is certainly different. It can be construed to be unfair, but let's face it, it is here and everybody is up against the same environment. I just wish more American companies would become more serious about this marketplace. The Japanese are very serious about every marketplace in the world. They are very, very aggressive. American firms make me sick sometimes. If they continue to limit themselves principally to the U.S. market and not look at it as just a base, they will be eaten alive by the Japanese or Germans and perhaps the Koreans. The Japanese have taken advantage of the opportunities in the postwar period, but we have advantages we could exploit. We can go direct in Japan in a way a Japanese company never could, because they are so locked into the distribution system. The foreigner is free of a lot of pressure. With a lot of work you can choose and develop strong bonds, as long as you realize that windows of opportunity shut very quickly.

The United States is falling further and further behind Japan, and that is really worrisome. We do not truly appreciate the differences. We are going to have to pay for this over the next twenty-five years, and that will put us further behind. This is fundamental to doing business in Japan. These are some very sobering thoughts: not only what are we going to do in Japan, but with the Japanese globally, and in some cases against the Japanese. The overall gap is widening. They are also going to continue to overtake us in a great many areas where we still have leadership. We are going to be the victims of our own mismanagement, ever more. That is very serious. I am speaking as an American who does not want it to happen. I am extremely frustrated. It is not that I do not wish the Japanese well; they have worked extremely hard and deserve their successes. But we have thrown it all away. Family, education, drugs, guns, the way we work or don't work—all very fundamental to our society.

Half the general managers in town are dumped here. Problems were sent here; people who were not the best and brightest in the United States. The merchant banks, the securities firms, the investment houses do not have the best people here. Some good people, but the best are in New York or London. Manufacturing companies are disastrous, the American Club crowd with all the trappings—tea and crumpets. I am very disappointed with the quality of the professionals. Even a lot of the technology companies have very marginal players. Often there is a tragic lack of understanding of the market in head office. They are not committing human resources. They continue to be reluctant to send in individuals who are technologically excellent, state of the art. In many American companies the attitude is, if they are sent out here, they are in trouble. They are forgotten. There is no career planning for a place to go back to. If they stay over five years, they have trouble adjusting back into the company because they are no longer known. They are in purgatory. They are traumatized when they go back. There is no incentive to come out here. They are out of the best and brightest category.

The general European standard is at best average, and in terms of the Japanese market, many of them do not stack up. I reckon the reason many foreign companies give up, saying the Japanese market is tough, is simply because the general manager was not good enough.

American companies do not have career internationalists. An overseas assignment of three to five years maximum is a training assignment as much as anything. It helps you go up the ladder of the professional management ranks. If you are overseas more than that, it is out of sight, out of mind. The folks who stay at home get the promotions.

You can insulate yourself in the bureaucracy of head office, but in Japan you are really exposed. You have to stand up and be counted in Japan. A lot of careers have been ruined or lost when priorities changed in headquarters. Many people are not willing to take that risk. They just don't want to be stripped to that extent.

By the time a guy is here three to five years, he has grown so far apart from head office that they are unhappy, they want to get him out and put in a guy with whom they can communicate. Ninety-nine percent of the business is back there. They all understand each other, but they don't understand Japan. The guy here has grown, learned about Japan, but they haven't grown a bit. They outweigh him tremendously, though, so no progress is really made in the sense you would think progress should be made if a company has been here twenty or thirty years. Surely we should know how to work well in Japan, but we go down the same road over and over again. This is the biggest difficulty for the individual here and the saddest part of the assignment. Although he might have done a great job out here, he is often not looked upon as having done a good job because of the communication problems. Most people go back disappointed to a much more confining job after having been a mini-CEO.

After you have been in Japan for a while, you begin to think head office understands what you are saying, and that gets you in trouble. Japan becomes common conversation, but that is all it is. They are just making conversation, but they don't understand. The educational process is never-ending. People and goals change continuously in head offices. Unless Japan has top priority, you are soon out of the loop, no matter what your mandate was at the time of your assignment. The head-office story is a script run over and over again. When you are sent out by head office you both have great expectations. You and they see clearly what has to be done. Everybody agrees you are necessary because things are usually messed up, and that is why they are sending you. You come on a white horse, ready to do battle. But as you get out on the field, the landscape begins to become a bit fuzzy and certainly more complex. The idiot who was running it before begins to look more intelligent, and head office begins to group you in the same way as your predecessor. No general manager in our company ever left better off than when he came.

You have to be persistent so the Japanese know you are not going away.

You have to let them know you are always coming back. They know us. They know we will go away. We will get fired or transferred, and it will be sooner than we ever estimated.

If these attitudes and situations are allowed to exist or to continue, it will be impossible to compete against Japan and its neighbors.

Many will find the following quotation macho or egotistical. It is, if you only define macho as courageous and egotistical as realistic.

I am the only guy here out of 950 who really qualifies as having previously run a business in its entirety. We don't have any role models. It's coming back to us clearly in both our external competitive studies and our internal reviews. I'm looking for older, more experienced foreigners, who have run a business and can see through the b.s. How long should a guy stay in Japan? Long enough to bother everybody and destroy all your capital. We are telling the local people the nonsense is over, here is your responsibility and authority, come in with a plan and come close to it or have a damn good reason why not. This is the best example in the world for having a stand-alone corporate unit and paradoxically the hardest place to have it, because of the ignorance of head offices and the quality of local personnel many of us inherited.

There should be only one general manager in Japan for the company unless there are legal reasons that require physical separation. Everyone, if possible, lives under the same tent. A company's existence in Japan is defined by the size of its operation there. Everything that enhances the size and public awareness of the company assists in its operating more effectively with the government, in recruiting, and in selling. There can be no tolerance of turf fighting among divisions of the same company in Japan. The Japanese competition will eat you alive, inside and outside the company, if they see or smell any disagreement.

As is clear by now, the toughest job of all is when the new foreign general manager, hired from outside with little knowledge of the parent company, arrives and finds that his predecessor has left him with a business and personnel disaster. The outside foreign general manager does not know whom to go to in head office, or anywhere in the company for that matter, for support. And no matter how much he would like to shake up the Japanese staff, he hesitates to grab them for fear of head office's reaction. Even if he could, he doesn't know what he is grabbing. The only thing worse is if the new general manager is an outside Japanese hire. Then nothing will happen. Substantive change is excruciatingly painful in a foreign company with problems in Japan.

Implementing change has been my greatest difficulty. We have done it. The staff has been admirable in their ability to change, but it has had to be force-fed, because everybody of course prefers the status quo. Change is my biggest enemy. It is so much better to hire the people and develop the physical plant and systems right the first time. If we had not changed, we would be bankrupt now. This market is not as difficult as people perceive if done properly from the beginning. I am paid to make change when it is necessary, but I prefer stability. Change is so difficult.

Sudden change is not absolutely damaging to a Japanese organization. In a Japanese organization there are sometimes sudden changes, but the people who are replacing one another are well known to each other. They have grown up together, so it does not rattle the organization. If you carry out sudden change in a foreign organization, it really does damage to your organization.

A problem for foreign companies, especially American, is that change at home is often abrupt, which cannot help but be disruptive in the field. Size and stability are the two things that make any company, foreign or Japanese, respectable in Japan. How people are treated both at home and in Japan does not go unnoticed by Japanese staff and customers. If you do not treat your home-country people fairly, the Japanese know what you will do to them in any kind of crunch. The general manager of a large and successful European company with over three thousand employees in Japan reflects:

We do not dismiss anyone. If they are not performing properly, that is first of all because we employed them. If they are lazy, we expose them to consultation and psychological pressure and they will leave. We often find work for nice, honest, unqualified people. One was moved successfully from branch manager to messenger.

This is pretty alien to U.S. management, but any foreign general manager new to Japan had better give some thought to it as he goes through transition.

Transition and change can also be systemic. When two foreign companies merge their operations globally, it is a shock for the Japanese employees and requires careful explanation and the building of a new corporate family. The same is true when two divisions merge. For a Japanese it is bewildering. Initial meetings between representatives must be based on substance so there can be a dialogue between the groups. After that, it is extraordinarily tedious, hard work, beginning with the rewriting of Rules of Employment if separate legal entities are involved, and the building of a new corporate culture. Suddenly to impose the Rules or culture of the dominant party would be a short route to hell.

As discussed throughout this book, it takes a great deal of sacrifice on many people's part to build a substantial business in Japan. Without head office's unrelenting support, it is impossible to build that business over the minimum ten to fifteen years required to establish a meaningful presence in Japan. The final question has to be, can we compete in Japan and with the Japanese globally the way we run our businesses at home? Those who ask this question will at least be beginning to analyze what Japanese global competition means to their business now and in the future. They should then be willing to take the steps to learn and make the sacrifices necessary to have us all work in a more efficient and better global business environment in which all our citizens will benefit: employer, employee, and consumer. By being in Japan they can also keep their options open and be flexible enough to make any kind of structural change they may have to make as market conditions change globally.

For the general manager who is giving his all, there will be both a tremendous learning experience and personal sacrifice.

What have been my surprises? Firstly, the stubbornness of the people and the length of time it takes to get things done. The agenda they are working against is not necessarily your agenda. Then the truth that bright Japanese don't work for foreigners. That is hard to appreciate until you get here and see what you have and what your Japanese competition has. I have always worked hard and enjoyed my work, but I have never worked harder in my life than here. The positive surprises were the pleasantness of Tokyo as a city, the challenge and the learning I've gone through, the understanding of myself as a general manager and what I should do as a manager, and working in a different culture and learning to compromise without sacrificing our goals.

I am out every night and work every weekend. There is no question in my mind that it is easier to do business in the U.S. than in Japan. It never lets up. It's not that you are going to work it up to this plateau and turn it over to your successor. Any guy that goes out of here and feels he has done 40 to 50 percent of what needs to be accomplished has had a good run of it.

People think coming to Japan is like going to Europe. It's not a hardship post; everything works and is modern and comfortable, but the stress of building a business here tears you apart. I find myself dipping below the line and try to pull myself back. How do you explain a seven-day work-week? Today is a holiday. The only good thing that happened today was that while in the office, my chairman called, saying: "Why are you answering the phone?"

Perhaps it is time that we realized that multinational corporations are just in their infancy. A general manager of a foreign company anywhere is just bumping against the problems the corporation is having. We would all be much more tolerant if we appreciated this, for it can mess up a lot of people's lives if you are not.

A person coming to Japan has to try to understand Japan but should not believe everything he is told. What you need is money and patience. Money because a quick successful start is not easy. It is one of the most competitive markets, if not the most, and to get a foothold you have to invest. You cannot as in Europe calculate how long until I get my money back. The pay-back period is quite a bit longer than elsewhere. If one is willing to make the investment, have patience, wait a bit longer, then one can be successful.

The Silicon Valley people are so of the moment. They call you on the phone: "We've got to get this. How about it!" They have an impatience which is wonderful for developing products and getting them out in the American marketplace. But the high-tech mentality, which is go, go, go, has difficulties in Japan, because Japan is more deliberate and takes more patience than our friends in high-tech exhibit.

One has to have an interest in the country, but one should not strive to be accepted fully in the society, to be absorbed. If they want to be accepted, then like Lafcadio Hearn they will be disappointed. One should be faithful to oneself. The soul should not put on a kimono and run about the streets. We are foreigners. We only have to look in the mirror to see that we stick out in this society. But if we try to be ourselves, to understand, to incorporate and to like the people, we will be all right.

You can, though, never give up who you are, what you are, and who the company is. Go with who you are and what you feel in your gut. You might be wrong, but it is better to be wrong and learn from it than constantly negating who you are. Just remember that as a foreigner you are not a legal part of the society. You are only a visitor.

Japan is like a fascinating mistress, a lover. One day you cannot live without her and the next day you could throw her against the wall. This fascination is always renewed. The continuous conflict, cold and hot bath, can be quite healthy and refreshing.

There is such a large body of knowledge you need to understand. If you were to go through your interview tapes and started listing the issues that people said you need to be sensitive to in business and society in Japan, pretty soon you are looking at a four-year college curriculum and then you have to throw on top of that the pressure to learn Japanese. As a kicker, throw in the turnover in key jobs at head office. So it is much more than four years of courses, and you still have your business to run in the second largest economy in the world that is sophisticated both in culture and business.

One cannot be dogmatic about any of these issues, but one does have to make the maximum effort to select people who are willing to understand what the cultural and business mores of Japan are and are willing to work in Japan rather than fight it. One has to have the horsepower to be courageous enough to cause what needs to happen to happen.

The company never expected me to do what I said I would do. But they let me do it, and in that sense our expectations became very similar.

Let us also hope that those who find any sense in these words will stop from happening in their company what happened to a foreign company with $400 million in sales in Japan. The general manager arrived in Tokyo expecting to be the last foreigner in the company in Japan. After six months he realized that was not the way to go and spent the next four years arguing with head office that there should be five foreigners in Japan. He left a frustrated man. Perhaps the head office did not take his advice because they only looked upon him as the last foreigner, not as a general manager. Unfortunately, his company was no more prepared for succession when he left than when he came five years before, because his successor had not been chosen. This cannot continue if the gaijin kaisha is to be successful against the many odds in Japan.

With the exception of a few companies like Nestlé, Unilever, Coca-Cola, and Hoechst, most foreign companies have not handled transition well in Japan. What should be guided by common sense more often that not is overwhelmed by corporate politics—the building of careers rather than a business—and ignorance. The failure to handle transition effectively should not be surprising since an overseas office of many European and most American corporations is no more than an appendage, unless the company is truly international, as the above four clearly are.

After eight years of working on or with Japan, one general manager appreciates what failure and success mean there:

By and large since the Second World War, Western companies have not been successful in Japan. They come in with a lot of music and the whole band, and three, four, or five years later they have failed and left. There are only a few companies that are successful and have a high profile. There are not twenty with high profiles. No society that I know of values success more than the Japanese. There is an enormous respect for success in whatever form it occurs. It is open respect for success. Everyone's general interest is in business's success. In the West, big business is generally bad. In Japan, big business is fantastic because they have succeeded. There is enormous respect for education. That is why everyone goes out and busts their tail to get in the University of Tokyo. The reputations of Japanese who work for Western companies are 99 percent, even more, related to the companies being unsuccessful. If more Western companies would be genuinely successful, genuinely innovative, and show a better way, then there is no question the Japanese employees in these firms would be appreciated. It is the chicken and the egg. As long as Western companies are not successful and therefore have people who are third and fourth rank, they will in turn select third- and fourth-rank people.

Everybody in our Japanese company has three roles. One is to be a corporate salesman. Everybody sells. The second role is that everyone has to be a corporate P.R. person. Third, everyone is a corporate recruiter. None of these can be separated. Our company lives and dies by finding our successors. We have many more projects that we would like to do but cannot do at this time because we do not have the people available to do them. We try desperately to make all our people in Japan be company people first and then Dutch or German or American or Japanese.

Criteria for the General Manager

Transition, though, is a fact of life, and to be effective, the new general manager must meet as much as possible the following criteria:

- A proven manager of the company (not an outside hire) who has had general manager responsibilities elsewhere and preferably a previous overseas assignment, with personnel, financial, marketing, sales, and control responsibilities.
- A potential president of the parent company.
- Has the confidence and support of the parent CEO, who can

see that head-office staff are constructively supportive while not overtly interfering with the Japan operation once goals are set.

• Most likely over forty years of age and closer to fifty. Therefore experienced and senior enough to open any doors in Japan.

• Knows his company and its products or services and personnel intimately.

• Excellent operational skills and personnel ability, appreciating that 50 percent of his time will be personnel related.

• Capacity to grow in a new and alien environment.

• Competitive and understands competition.

• A can-do attitude.

• Believes in excellence; insists on near perfection.

• Tough internally and if necessary externally. Willing to stand his ground once his goals in conjunction with head office and his staff are set. Can therefore stand alone, much as if he were the founder of a company.

• Controlled patience but can get angry with reason.

• A sense of proportion and humor with intellectual curiosity.

• Caring.

• Physically healthy. The stress demands are extraordinary.

• Socially gracious and sensitive at all levels, whether with other presidents at association meetings or at the weddings of young employees.

• Married with a stable family life. Preferable that his wife has had prior international experience and has a good ear. She might be the only person he can talk to candidly.

• In sum, the wisdom of the founder, the tolerance of a chaplain, the toughness of a field general, and the zeal of a missionary.

No one individual meets all of these criteria. The general manager and his head office, though, had better know where he does not and compensate for those areas through other members of the management team, remembering that in the last analysis the general manager will be involved in all aspects of his business in Japan, seven days a week, if his operation is to have the potential of being successful.

The new general manager should be in place at least six months prior to the departure of his predecessor. During the transition he works with every in-house group, especially personnel, on a monthly rotation basis. In doing so, he becomes involved with every critical staff member and function, does hands-on questioning and requestioning, and then reviews staff and functions candidly with his predecessor.

Once he begins, after three or four months, to have some understanding of where he is, he should be introduced to key suppliers, providers of services, and customers. The three-month delay avoids the "please educate me" questions, which are the predecessor's and staff's job to answer in the beginning. The new general manager will garner much more credibility in the community this way. It is only natural, but foolish, for the new general manager to want to survey his new command immediately. He should learn the terrain first, however, or he will be setting off one mine after another.

During the first twelve months, including the transition period, there should be no vacation, because the hardest aspect of the job is knowing what is going on in one's own shop when one is a functional illiterate. When the general manager is away, the staff will play. Oh how they will play! They will also make decisions in the general manager's absence that will only gradually become apparent and, of course, will be difficult to undo once they have been made.

On the departure of the former general manager a reception should be held, preferably in the company's own office, to say farewell and introduce the new general manager. The reception is a farewell and a welcome, a sign of corporate continuity as well as an introduction, and very importantly an excuse to get existing and potential clients and members of support facilities into the office and show them the company is truly in business in Japan. A hotel reception only introduces personnel and not the business. Hotel receptions are appropriate for the head-office chairman.

Lastly, six months after his departure, the former general manager should return to Japan, even if he no longer has any responsibility for Japan, to answer any questions the new general manager has on why things were done as they were on the previous watch, particularly with personnel. Once the new person is on his own, he will naturally discover that he has many questions about why certain things are the way they are. This return visit permits any changes to be made in an orderly, nondisruptive, knowledgeable fashion. There will always be need for change. Just know the reasoning behind earlier decisions as you move into the future. Internal and external corporate history is extremely important because that is the basis on which relationships are established and built. In meeting the needs for change, personnel commitments should not be taken lightly. One's options should be kept open but a systematic, long-term management development program is essential for both Japanese and foreigners involved with Japan. Subsequent transitions will be the natural outgrowth of both the global and the Japanese business, for transition is really the issue of the institutionalizing of success: how a company makes it a permanent part of itself, not just a fortuitous result of an individual effort.

Perhaps Jim Firestone's words, after ten years of trying, are his response to my original question, "Can a foreign company succeed in Japan in the 1990s?" It will be his generation's task; they could have no better example.

Becoming an insider is crucial to your ability to continue to compete successfully in the marketplace if you truly want to be a leader in your industry rather than simply reacting to the way the industry shapes and develops in Japan. For large corporations, that are accustomed to working in an environment where they can control and influence that environment, when they go to Japan, the frustration level becomes very high when they realize they control very little. Becoming an insider is a process that operates on a continuum. There are certain ennobling things you have to have done or built into your organization, certain understandings of how to do business in Japan, certain levels of commitment that have to have been demonstrated before you can go to the next stage of the process. Shortcuts don't work and can backfire on you and leave a black mark on your record. You then go back to square one and start again.

The crucial level to becoming an insider is the working level in any company: the relationships with the bankers, ministries, suppliers, wholesalers, etc. A foreigner can only act as a time bridge in making the company an insider. He can create the predisposition. Your senior Japanese have to build the relationships over many years as they grow in the business. A mid-career hire cannot do it. Relationships do not transfer with them when they are hired. The personal relationship does transfer, but the influence generally does not. You have to build them together anew. It is quicker, of course, to build these relationships if you are a senior Japanese and already have them elsewhere and if you are working in the same industry. The influence we are talking about, though, is not on a rational basis. It is not picking up the phone and calling a guy and saying these are the facts, give me a yes or no answer. Things don't happen that way. Relationships are only built over time. Your Japanese competitors all have them because they started when they went to school together.

If a foreign company succeeds in the 1990s, it most likely started at the latest in the early 1980s. A company's options for today are largely structured by what happened ten or twenty years ago. Most important, what it does today will also structure what it can do ten or twenty years hence.

Bill Dizer, in my mind the doyen of American corporate businessmen in Japan in the 1980s, has the last word:

> The CEO operating a foreign company in Japan is so pressured that he doesn't have the luxury of the academic analysis and evaluation of what is going on around him. He is so pressured by the requirement to get out and learn and do the business that he takes the experiences as they are happening, probably never realizing until long after the fact that he is part of an evolutionary process. It would be great if he could read academic articles that analyze what Japan is and why it is. There are plenty of books that do that. And then say OK, I know how to operate. But probably the first thing that happens will be either a contradiction to what he has learned or an exception to what he expects the practice to be. The CEO spends so much time just trying to learn and to get a basic background in his business about what is happening, and everything is now. Hopefully, those with long experience can begin to see patterns, can make valid assumptions, and can make forecasts of what might happen.

By now the chairman and the head-office staff and the general manager in Japan of the gaijin kaisha should understand that management in Japan is a group issue. Nevertheless, the general manager is in charge and accountable for absolutely everything that happens in Japan.

To succeed in Japan one needs the best possible management, products or services that meet the needs of the market, and deep pockets, whatever the size of the company. Make the largest investment possible in people, technology, and financial resources for the biggest return, not the smallest investment for the biggest return, in order to support the product or service and to create the staying power to survive. If not, the foreign company will soon be preempted by a local concern.

Know your market, know your competition, know yourself, and above all, don't let the competition psych you out. Although the pace of change in Japan is extraordinary, do not act in haste, or you will repent in leisure.

Appendix

Individuals Interviewed

John M. Abbott, Financial Attaché, United States Embassy, Tokyo, Japan

James C. Abegglen, President, Asia Advisory Services, Inc.

C. Loomos Alexander, President, Castle & Cooke (Japan), Ltd.

Masami Atarashi, President, Johnson & Johnson K.K.

David D. Baskerville, Vice President–Asia, Siecor International Corp.

Thomas L. Blakemore, Partner, Blakemore & Mitsuki

Jerald A. Blumberg, President, DuPont Japan Ltd.

Thomas C. Boersig, President, Essex Nippon K.K.

William H. Brown, Commercial Counselor, U.S. Embassy, Tokyo

Ira Caplan, General Manager, Cyanamid (Japan), Ltd.

Warren D. Chinn, Senior Vice President, Booz, Allen & Hamilton, Inc.

Kazunobu Cho, President, Japan Tupperware Co., Ltd.

John B. Christensen, Partner, Aoki, Christensen & Nomoto

Robert J. Collins, Vice President, American International Assurance Co., Ltd.

Robert O. Davis, Executive Vice President, American Home Assurance Co.

Alfred P. Dienst, President, Hoechst Japan Limited

Steven W. Driscoll, General Manager, Irving Trust Company, Tokyo Branch

Donald D. Ferguson, Regional Managing Director–Far East, Cilco Inc., Japan

Francis-Regis Ferran, President, Pechiney Japan

James A. Firestone, President, Travel Related Services, American Express International, Inc.

Garrett M. Flint, Regional Vice President–Asia, Brunswick International Ltd.

Richard A. Floyd, Director of Marketing and Operations–Pacific Area, R. Dakin & Co.

William E. Franklin, President, Weyerhaeuser Far East, Ltd.

Michael Golding, President, Franklin Mint Co., Ltd.

David Grant, General Manager, Standard Chartered Bank, Japan Branch

Joseph A. Grimes, Jr., Vice President, Honeywell Inc.

Joseph V. Guilfoile, General Manager, Seven-Up International, Inc. Japan Branch

Toyo Gyohten, Vice Minister of Finance for International Affairs, Ministry of Finance

Peter Rainer Haag, Executive Vice President, Printing Machine Trading Co., Ltd.

William P. J. Hall, Senior Vice President, ASI Market Research (Japan), Inc.

Edwin F. Hawxhurst, U.S. Firm's Resident Representative, Arthur Young

Herbert F. Hayde, Chairman, Burroughs Co., Ltd.

Stanley W. Holt, General Manager, Boyden Associates (Japan), Ltd.

Willard A. Hughes, President, Boeing Far East

George P. Hutchinson, Managing Director, Salomon Brothers Inc

Tom Isetorp, Representative Director, Simmons Japan Ltd.

Hideo Ishihara, Managing Director, Industrial Bank of Japan

Durk I. Jager, Executive Vice President, The Procter & Gamble Company, Cincinnati, Ohio

Weldon H. Johnson, President, Coca-Cola (Japan) Co., Ltd.

Andre Jullien, General Manager for Japan, Banque Nationale de Paris

Keith K. Kaneko, General Manager, Manufacturers Hanover Trust Co., Japan Branch

Yoriko Kawaguchi, Director, MITI

Andrew W. Knox, General Manager, Korn/Ferry International—Japan

William H. Kyle, President, Kyle International K.K.

Eugene H. Lee, President, Siemens Medical Systems Ltd.

Henry V. (Gene) Leonard, Jr., General Manager Japan Branch, General Motors Overseas Corporation

Philip F. Longacre, President, Owens-Illinois (Asia), Ltd.

John F. Loughran, Vice Chairman, Morgan Guaranty Limited

Clyde McAvoy, Vice President Far East, Continental Airlines, Inc.

Norman A. MacMaster, President, J. Walter Thompson Co. Japan

Shojiro Makino, President, Grace Japan K.K.

R. Henry Marini, President, Revlon K.K.

John Mason, General Manager, Hong Kong and Shanghai Banking Corp., Japan Branch

Deryck C. Maughan, Chairman and Chief Executive Officer, Salomon Brothers Asia Limited

Yoshihiko Miyauchi, President, Orient Leasing Co., Ltd.

Hugh H. Murai, President, Mead-Toppan Co., Ltd.

Tadashi Ogiso, Managing Director, Asahi Fluoropolymers Co., Ltd.

Alvin Pederson, Partner, Arthur Andersen & Co.

Geoffrey W. Picard, Managing Director, Morgan Stanley International Ltd.

William Rapp, Executive Director, Bank of America Corporate Finance–Japan

Edward W. Rogers, President, Dow Chemical Japan Ltd.

Robert H. Rozek, Vice President International, Brush Wellman, Inc., Cleveland, Ohio

John M. Sandor, General Manager, Philip Morris Asia Inc.

Thomas F. Seymour, Managing Director, Parker Japan K.K.

Ko Shioya, President, Hill and Knowlton Japan Ltd.

Ernest H. Shrenzel, President, Allied Signal Inc. Asia

Victor L. Shrenzel, Director–International Division, Japan Counselors Inc.

Joel Silverstein, General Manager, Brown & Williamson Tobacco Corporation

Robert H. Simon, President, Estée Lauder K.K.

Herbert M. Singleton, General Manager, John Fluke Manufacturing Co., Inc. Japan

D. Scarborough Smith, III, General Manager, Chemical Bank, Japan Branch

Yasuma Sugihara, President, Mobil Sekiyu K.K.

Satoshi Sugita, Vice President-Employees Relations and Communications, General Electric Japan, Ltd.

Eugene C. Sullivan, Director Japan, Monsanto International

John Sutcliffe, Representative Director, PA International Consulting Services Ltd.

William M. Thaler, President, Thyssen Nippon Co., Ltd.

Wesley M. (Tom) Thompson, President, Bristol-Myers Lion Ltd.

Harold M. Todd, President, Nippon Vicks K.K.

Samuel Waldman, Managing Director, BOC Japan Ltd.

Robert M. White, President, ARC International Ltd.

William A. White, President, Ketchum Advertising (Japan) Ltd.

Kendell A. Whitney, Partner, Egon Zehnder International Co., Ltd.

Robert J. Wilk, Managing Director, INFOPLAN

Anthony Willoughby, Partner, Impact K.K.

Osamu Yamada, Managing Director, Mitsubishi Bank

Taneshiro Yamamoto, General Manager, Gillette (Japan) Inc.

H. Dick Yamashita, President, Marcom International, Inc.

Masamoto Yashiro, President, Esso Sekiyu K.K.
William R. Yates, President, Avco Financial Services of Japan, Inc.

To all of the above and the many others who gave me an ear, a very special thanks.

Selected Bibliography

The following list includes some of the useful works published in English in recent years. They are intentionally diverse so as to give readers an introduction to the many faces of Japan.

Abegglen, James C., and George Stalk, Jr. *Kaisha, The Japanese Corporation.* New York: Basic Books, 1985.

American Chamber of Commerce in Japan, Council of the European Business Community, and Booz, Allen & Hamilton, Inc. *Direct Foreign Investment in Japan: The Challenge For Foreign Firms.* Tokyo, 1987.

Anchordoguy, Marie. *Computer Inc. Japan's Challenge to IBM.* Cambridge: Harvard University Press, 1989.

Buruma, Ian. *Behind the Mask.* New York: Pantheon Books, 1984.

Clark, Rodney. *The Japanese Company.* New Haven: Yale University Press, 1979.

Cole, Robert E. *Work, Mobility and Participation.* Berkeley: University of California Press, 1979.

Dalby, Liza. *Geisha.* Berkeley: University of California Press, 1983.

Dore, Ronald. *Taking Japan Seriously.* Stanford: Stanford University Press, 1987.

Fields, George. *From Bonsai to Levi's.* New York: Macmillan, 1983.

Fruin, W. Mark. *Kikkoman: Company, Clan and Community.* Cambridge: Harvard University Press, 1983.

Johnson, Chalmers. *MITI and the Japanese Miracle.* Stanford: Stanford University Press, 1984.

Lebra, Takie Sugiyama. *Japanese Women: Constraint and Fulfillment.* Honolulu: University of Hawaii Press, 1984.

Nakane, Chie. *Japanese Society.* Berkeley: University of California Press, 1970.

Nevins, Thomas J. *Labor Pains and The Gaijin Boss*. Tokyo: The Japan Times, Ltd., 1984.

Prestowitz, Clyde V., Jr. *Trading Places*. New York: Basic Books, 1988.

Reischauer, Edwin O. *The Japanese*. Cambridge: Harvard University Press, 1977.

Rohlen, Thomas P. *For Harmony and Strength: The Japanese White-Collar Organization in Anthropological Perspective*. Berkeley: University of California Press, 1974.

————. *Japan's High Schools*. Berkeley: University of California Press, 1983.

Schlossstein, Steven. *The End of the American Century*. New York: Congdon & Weed, 1989.

————. *Trade War*. New York: Congdon & Weed, 1984.

Smith, Robert J. *Japanese Society*. Cambridge: Cambridge University Press, 1983.

Trevor, Malcolm. *Japan's Reluctant Multinationals*. New York: St. Martin's Press, 1983.

U.S. Department of Education. *Japanese Education Today*. Washington: U.S. Government Printing Office, 1987.

White, Merry. *The Japanese Educational Challenge*. New York: The Free Press, 1987.

————. *The Japanese Overseas: Can They Go Home Again*. New York: Free Press, 1988.

Whiting, Robert. *You Gotta Have Wa*. New York: Macmillan, 1989.

Index